SEEING THE PAST

Stories on the Trail of a Yankee Millwright

SEEING THE PAST

Stories on the Trail of a Yankee Millwright

James T. Powers

HOMEBOUND
PUBLICATIONS
Independent Publisher of Contemplative Titles
STONINGTON, CONNECTICUT

HOMEBOUND PUBLICATIONS
Ensuring the mainstream isn't the only stream.

Copyright © 2016 by James T. Powers
All Rights Reserved
Printed in the United States of America
as well as the United Kingdom and Australia.

First Edition Trade Paperback
Paperback ISBN 978-1-938846-86-1

Front Cover Image © Jimmy Joe
Cover and Interior Designed by Leslie M. Browning

www.homeboundpublications.com

10 9 8 7 6 5 4 3 2 1

Homebound Publications greatly values the natural environment and invests in environmental conservation. Our books are printed on paper with chain of custody certification from the Forest Stewardship Council, Sustainable Forestry Initiative, and the Program for the Endorsement of Forest Certification. In addition, each year Homebound Publications donates 1% of our net profit to a humanitarian or ecological charity.

In Memory of
Rita Pierce Powers (1946-2014)
Whose love of history was only surpassed
by her love of life and family.

CONTENTS

1 ♦ Introduction

7 ♦ Chapter One: Lifting the Veil

19 ♦ Chapter Two: Roduyns Revealed

41 ♦ Chapter Three: The Promise

53 ♦ Chapter Four: "There but for the Grace of God, goes I"

75 ♦ Chapter Five: Myths through Time

91 ♦ Chapter Six: The Athens of Connecticut

105 ♦ Chapter Seven: For Want of Water

123 ♦ Chapter Eight: Silver Sparkings

143 ♦ Chapter Nine: Utopias on the Quinnipiac

165 ♦ Chapter Ten: The Realities of Circumstance

185 ♦ Chapter Eleven: Insuring a Place

End Notes
Bibliography
About the Author
About the Press

INTRODUCTION

Milo sat by the window, watching the cold November rain pummel the pane as the wind blew hard in waves against it. He held his hand an inch from the glass, palm outstretched. The contrast between the cool brought by the breeze through the window differed sharply with the warmth that enveloped the back of his hand, wrapped and cuddled by the air inside. Milo loved his grandfather's mill, the whir of the great stone wheels as they crushed the corn into mealy powder, the smells, the feeling of power and strength the great wheels represented. Though only six, he looked forward to the day the mill would be his, when he too could move the lever that opened the sluice allowing the water to flow and the gears to turn. "Progress", his grandpa Thelus said, "was in the power of the water and those who harnessed it." It was the future, grandpa said, and Milo wanted to be part of it. Some day he mused, he too would be a millwright and this mill and its power would be his.

As he looked through the droplets that formed and ran down the glass, his hand dropped to the window sill and landed on the small steel chisel he had been using to shape a piece of scrap wood he had found on the floor. "Be careful son" he remembered his father say as he handed the sharply pointed tool to him. "Its edge is keen so keep an eye to your work". Even at play, Milo had learned to focus on his task, to concentrate on what was on hand and do his best. But as his hand felt the smooth wooden handle of the chisel, he suddenly lifted it to the window and began to trace out a letter. The sharp edge scratched the surface much faster and easier than he thought it would and he quickly etched the two triangles that formed the letter "M". An "I" came quickly, then an "L" as well. Nervously he realized he was not using the tool for its intended purpose, a rule his father and grandfather always insisted *on. But he was too far along, with one letter to go he would be done. The "O" proved difficult however as he nervously rushed to finish, his father was calling from behind a cabinet which blocked his view. Since the curves of the "O" were not easy to scratch, it soon took the shape of a hurried square. There it was, his name etched into the pane—Milo. It's alright he thought through a pang of guilt, someday this mill will be mine…*

The past is a funny thing. It surrounds us in every way; culturally, physically, emotionally. Yet as modern Americans, we tend to ignore it as if it were some sort of dark family secret so painful, it's best not even to acknowledge its existence. Yet like that secret, the past is always present and never far away. We might ignore it and we can deny it, but it is always with us. It may be buried under concrete, housed in a dusty house museum, or kept alive in the collective memory of a few octogenarian locals, but it is an irrefutable constant—patiently waiting. Because our culture tends to emphasize the now and immediate future, the past seems to have little meaning or use for us and is usually relegated to what it literally is, the past; often forgotten and seldom remembered. So most of us go about our daily routines quite unaware of how our collective history has shaped our lives and that we are all the products of who and what came before us.

The reasons why history plays such a small role in our culture are many and complex and a subject for others to analyze. It is sufficient to say here however, that we often ignore the past to our collective detriment and that its lessons can often help shape our present and future choices. But that requires slowing down and taking the time to recognize what those who came before us have left for us to learn, to acknowledge their motivations, dreams, and traumas; to look at their handiwork and see in it our own, to appreciate that over time we are linked in a chain of thoughts, events, and accomplishments that have helped bring us to where we are today.

The often quoted philosopher George Santayana (1863-1952) wrote:

"Those who cannot remember the past are condemned to repeat it"

Despite Santayana's warning, culturally, our track record as modern

Americans has not been stellar in this regard. We tend to dismiss the past as a quaint story that we collectively hold like the image of the Pilgrims in their black hats. The story is comfortable, unthreatening, and easy to push to the side like an odd and unwanted gift from an old and distant relative whose only remembrance of you was when you were five and not the person you are today.

Less often quoted however, is Santayana's prequel to his more famous statement:

"Progress, far from consisting of change, depends on retentiveness"

Thus the danger; for without a collective retention of life before us, the very progress upon which our society has been built sits within a fragile vacuum that leaves us precariously dangling on the edge without a backup plan wrought of experience. Without retention of the past, we can only understand our present in a disjointed and unconnected way; the present loses its meaning and the future becomes a cloudy continuation of today. How can we know who we are and where we are going if we don't know who we were?

Many of us, of course, were exposed to various history classes and may still occasionally read about history when time permits. But that history tends to be a national one that ignores the history of and connection to where we live. As a result, our society has a very general and collective understanding of American history; a sort of "George Washington was the first president" syndrome. That's fine and is certainly important as those stories bind us as a people and nation. But in general as a culture we are loathe to journey beyond that, certainly on a local level.

As our society has become more suburbanized and mobile during the latter half of the 20th century and the start of the 21st, the distinguishing characteristics that differentiate one community from another have become blurred and buried. The same strip malls and streetscapes greet us on a daily basis. With the homogenized franchising of our culture, we have lost the many unique and distinguishing cultural elements that for generations surrounded our predecessors. They knew who they were; their collective past was an integral part of their lives. The meeting house or church, the village, the family farm, or the city neighborhood all linked them in a chain to those who came before. They knew who they were the children of and understood the meanings of what that entailed. They were rooted in a sense of place. Their sense of progress and the future were built upon and wrapped in an awareness of the past; they had retentiveness.

Today, as we drive along an interstate that connects us from one sprawling overdeveloped landscape to another are we aware of those who once lived there—of the past buried beneath the asphalt? How could we? Those who once farmed the land or walked the dusty trails are long gone. Their memory might live in a name place or street sign, but that's it. To assume we would know more or want to know more is often a curiosity at best. It seems their lives have little meaning or connection to our own. But do they? Sometimes, if we look deeper and are persistent, their shadows can still be seen, wrapped in the mists of time. If we keep looking, we can often see, not their images, but the clues they left behind; road names, buildings, stonewalls, and millponds. These become sign posts, beacons to another time that can point to and light our way to a better understanding of who we are.

What it really comes down to is this; the past is all around us and we are in fact only temporary residents in a specific place that has constantly evolved over time and continues to do so. What exists today is only the latest phase in that continuum. The communities we live in are thus inherently the total sum of the many forces of change, both physical and human, that have taken place. We walk in the footsteps of time through the shadows of the Native peoples who long ago left their impressions alongside those of the first Europeans to arrive and the generations that have followed them. As we go about our daily routines we see the same topological features and vistas; the mountains, rivers, and valleys they saw. Though time and our culture have done much to shape and clutter the view, those from the distant past would recognize it still.

Just like those who came before us, we leave markers of our existence as we go about our lives. Every community has them and some of those created today will survive into the future and undoubtedly be recognized as expressions of our time. These signs will bind those in the future to us and become our link through time and place.

Stories on the Trail of a Yankee Millwright

The past thus surrounds us and points to a deeper understanding of who we are. These shadows of history offer lessons for our time and by seeing them more clearly our lives can become richer and more meaningful. In exploring the life of Milo Todd, I embarked on a journey of discovery that allowed me to examine episodes in our historic past that are now mostly forgotten or at best known to only a few. Yet each episode, some tied directly to Milo and his family while others linked only by time and place, reveal moments that have shaped us as a people. Collectively, they offer a broad sweep of stories across time that we can learn from for ourselves and future generations and through remembrance and retentiveness create a culture that values the past as an essential part of our present and future. That is the premise of this book, which brings us back to Milo.

CHAPTER 1
Lifting the Veil

Milo Apollos Todd lived in a small village called Northford in the Connecticut town of North Branford. Born in 1834, he led a life of grasped opportunities and lost possibilities in his determination to find his place in a rapidly transforming world. This quest led him from one Connecticut town to another as he chased the promise of the industrial revolution that swept across his state and the nation during his lifetime. By examining his life as well as episodes in the histories of the places he and his family lived, it is possible to gleam a better understanding of what happened before us and become connected through time and place with Milo and the world he lived in. Like all of us, Milo and those involved in the moments in time described in the stories made choices and lived with the consequences as the currents of change and the challenges of life enveloped them. Above all, Milo and the others were shaped by the culture, time and place within which they lived and by that of those who had proceeded them. Like us, the past lived in them, through them and around them. The difference was they, including Milo, were aware of it.

I first came across Milo by chance. I had received a phone call from Mr. Gordon Miller, a local historian and enthusiastic promoter of Northford, Connecticut history in 1991. Gordon was looking for help in starting a program involving his town's Totoket Historical Society and the local school system and had recently read in the area newspapers about work I was doing of the same type through archeology in neighboring Guilford. The goal was to explore a former 19th century mill site by conducting an archeological dig teaming members of the society and local high school students. Gordon's enthusiasm for Northford history was contagious and because I loved a good mill site, I was hooked. In no time I was organizing a program that focused on investigating and excavating an abandoned mill site that was the location of a variety of early 19th century enterprises.

Over the next few years, I led various groups of local residents, historical society members, and students in excavating the site named Industrial Site #3 from an earlier survey done by the Totoket Historical Society of early industrial sites in Northford. Overgrown with brush and trees, it was bisected by a small meandering stream haphazardly sprinkled with large cut stones, the remnants of an old dam and foundations. As more information about past activities there were unearthed through both digging and research, it was renamed the Todd-Stevens Site.

Following the end of the first year of excavation, as my wife Rita and daughter Kate were helping me sort through bags of artifacts for analysis, we suddenly had a remarkable personal encounter with Milo Todd. On many digs that center on the remains of a 19th century building, the most abundant artifact uncovered is often broken window glass and the Todd-Stevens Site was no exception. Apparently, whenever a building from that period met its demise, windows were broken and shards scattered everywhere. This made excavation tricky and a bit dangerous so extra caution and proper archeological techniques were a must as the location of each glass piece, along with all other artifacts, were carefully excavated, recorded, and bagged. The site had hundreds.

As we worked our way through twenty bags or so of jagged fragments lying across our kitchen table, each bag representing an area of excavation by depth, we sorted, counted, and recorded the contents. While we were surveying the mix of greenish-blue and clear shards, Kate stopped suddenly and held one up to the light to get a better look. "There's writing on this one" she exclaimed, handing it to Rita for a second opinion.

Stories on the Trail of a Yankee Millwright

Scanning the jagged, greenish piece with her eye for detail, Rita quickly confirmed Kate's suspicion declaring excitedly "I think it says Milo!"

"You're kidding" I replied as she handed me the fragment so I could get a look, holding it up to the light and turning it every which way. Sure enough, there it was, crudely scratched onto the surface the rough letters M – i – l – o. It was as if his voice was reaching out across time and space right there in our kitchen. Milo. What were the chances that out of the hundreds of shards found, many scratched and scarred, this one would come to our notice? Was it chance or fate? What did this message mean? Our minds raced with the possibilities as we excitedly rejoiced in our discovery.

Thus began my relationship with Milo Todd (1834-1907) and as I learned more about the mill site that he and his family worked since the 18th century, my curiosity and interest became more acute. Not only did his mill reveal a variety of early industrial activities; from grist mill to leather production, bone buttons to paper making, then finally silver plating, it also became clear that the site itself was an enigma, never providing enough water power needed to become a true center of production. This it turned out sent Todd on a journey throughout Connecticut in a quest to at first find a better location for his mill operation and ultimately to make it in the new industrial age he desperately sought to be part of. His pilgrimage would take him and me from Northford to the towns of North Haven, Wallingford, and Windsor Locks, then the city of Hartford, and finally, back to Northford. For Milo, it was a journey to find his place in a new world of commerce and industry, chasing the American Dream. For me, it was to see in his life and wanderings, episodes and stories from the past, most little known, that led me to a deeper understanding of how they have shaped and influenced our today.

It is easy to miss what is left of the Todd-Stevens mill site as one drives along Connecticut Route 17 heading south into the sleepy community of Northford from the town of Durham. A busy commuter route to and from the greater New Haven region, the site looks like any other overgrown area of tangled, scrubby brush and motley secondary growth trees found throughout Southern Connecticut. There certainly is nothing that would catch one's eye or even remotely indicate that any type of activity let alone a series of 19th century mill operations ever took place there. But on second glance, there are a few clues. On the southern edge of the site the highway crosses a small stream, the Pistapaug, as it meanders eastward down from the highlands to the west from a pond of the same name to the Farm River. To the immediate north of the site is an 18th century home, standing prominently but time worn, rooted to the land as only a home of that vintage can. Both hint at a much different time.

The property was in the Todd family since the 18th century and came into their possession following the orderly settlement process that took place in most Connecticut communities during that time. Originally allotted to Joseph Bradfield in 1736, through a series of transactions it came into the possession of Stephen Todd of Wallingford in 1747.[1] This began a string of Todd owners that would eventually end with Milo Todd selling it to David Stevens in 1868. But before the history of that period can be addressed, a look at the settlement of Northford, North Branford, and Branford just to the south along the Connecticut shoreline needs to be explored.

Northford as it exists today was originally part of the early Connecticut town of Branford that came into existence in 1644 when settled following the purchase of land from the original inhabitants who were members of the larger Quinnipiac group that inhabited the shoreline of Connecticut from present day Milford east to the mouth of the Connecticut River at Old Saybrook and north to the area around Middletown where their relations, the Wangunks lived. They called the place Totoket. English Puritan settlers from the recently established colony of New Haven (then called Quinnipiac) eight miles to the west, among them Milo's ancestor Christopher Todd, were expanding beyond their original 1638 holdings and the area along the northern shore of Long Island Sound was perfectly located between their growing settlement and the soon to be settled plantation of Guilford (1639) just to the east.

Stories on the Trail of a Yankee Millwright

Montowese knew that these English were different than their look-a-like competitors who had been here before. Unlike the Dutch who had come to trade and cut the forest, these newcomers wanted possession of Mother Earth herself. They are strong willed and tend towards violence when denied what they want Montowese thought as he pondered their proposal to purchase some of the land his people had been given by the Great Spirit. His uncle Momauguin had already done so on the western side of the mouth of the Quinnipiac when these newcomers came in their great ships from across the eastern sea. Now they wanted Totoket as well and promised in return protection from the fierce enemy of his people who came from the setting sun, the Mohawk.

Montowese recalled how he had witnessed the way the English had brutally and relentlessly destroyed the arrogant tormentors of the Quinnipiac, the Pequots a year earlier and watched as they, along with the ambitious Uncas and the Mohegans, had hunted down the survivors in running skirmishes through his people's lands, trapping them as they fled into a swamp near the home of the Paugassetts to the west. As sachem responsible for the remnant few of his band, decimated by the terrifying sicknesses these English and others had brought over the last twenty years, he knew that securing their protection meant giving them what they wanted.

Montowese had sought the council of the elders and other sachems as well as that of the spirits who had always protected and helped his people before he committed himself to the loss of Totoket. In the end, in securing this agreement, his people would keep the ancestral seat of their Grand Sachem at Mioonkhtuck on the eastern shore where the Quinnipiac River met the sea and their hunting grounds that extended inland north from the English settlement that they were calling Quinnipiac and some were beginning to call by the odd name of New Haven. At least now Montowese felt his people would be safe and over time become equal partners with these strange and demanding new neighbors.

According to *The History of North Branford and Northford*, by Dr. Herbert C. Miller, Totoket was occupied in 1638 by a small group of eleven native men and their families, under the leadership of their sachem, Montowese.[2] A treaty and agreement was signed by the leaders of the New Haven Colony and Montowese on December 11, 1638 and in return for the land the Quinnipiacs at Totoket were granted three conditions they had asked for: protection by the English against all hostile attacks by other native groups, a section of land two miles long along the eastern shore of the Quinnipiac River as a home for the group, and the ability to hunt, fish, and trap beaver during the season when appropriate in Totoket.[3] In payment the Totokets, as the English called those residing there, received "eleven coats made up of English trucking cloth and Montowese was given one coat of English cloth made up in the English manner".[4]

Totoket, "at-the-tidal river" in the Algonquian language spoken by the Quinnipiac, was aptly named for the gentle estuary formed by the Branford River as it enters Long Island Sound and it is there that a little known story of discovery and commerce took place in the years prior to English settlement. Interestingly, there has always been an oral tradition in the town, passed down generation after generation, that Branford was the site of an early 17th century Dutch trading post. The location has even been understood over the years to be on the Branford River at a spot still called "the Dutch House Wharf". Today there is even a local marina bearing that name, a testimony to the strength of local tradition. Yet scant mention of the Dutch presence or evidence of it has ever appeared in the history of any early European presence in Connecticut. The Dutch did not fit neatly into the concise history put together by historians in the 19th century who in particular described the heroic English settlement of New England in which the 1620 arrival of the Pilgrims at Plymouth, Massachusetts is sacrosanct.

Yes, there is the story of the Dutch in what is now New York and how they ventured out to trade along the Connecticut River; they called it the Fresh River, following the recorded exploration of Long Island Sound and the river by Adrian Block in 1614. They even feebly established, history states, the House of Hope in what is now Hartford as a trading house with the local natives. This post, was quickly absorbed by the English from Massachusetts establish a settlement of their own where Hartford now sits, to with neighboring Windsor and Wethersfield, to form the Connecticut Colony in 1635. From that point on the Dutch quietly fade away. Or did they?

Though many in Branford may not be aware of the early history of their town or why certain landmarks are named as they are, the Dutch Wharf among them, there are many signs that hint at that lost past. Many residents for example, often travel along a road connecting Main Street and the center of Branford to the shoreline section of town and in particular a peninsula known as Indian Neck never knowing why it carries the exotic name of Montowese Avenue. Why they might ask, does that busy road have that name? Do they ever wonder what or who he might have been? Yet there it is a name that is all that remains of a proud leader and survivor of a people, decimated by disease that had killed 90 to 95% of their number in twenty years, who tried to secure for them a place in a drastically changed world. Having seen the terrible destruction visited upon the Pequots, the most powerful native group in the region in 1637 in a war against the combined forces of the English from the Connecticut and Massachusetts Bay Colonies as well as the Mohegans under their leader Uncas, Montowese certainly understood that it was a matter of survival that led him to parlay with these strange yet powerful newcomers. Should he and his legacy matter?

Equally unknown to most of the current residents of Branford and the Shoreline Region of Connecticut, a revival has been taking place the last fifteen to twenty years among the descendants of those original inhabitants of Totoket and the Shoreline of Connecticut. They have recognized their collective survival and have come together to resurrect their heritage as the *Quinnipiac Council of the Algonquian Confederacy* and are actively reclaiming their rightful place as a people and culture. Their official website states emphatically:

Seeing the Past

"The Quinnipiac have called the Long-Water-Land their wejammoke for over 10,000 years and have survived all manner of natural and human catastrophes. The Ean•sketambawg of Quirri/pe/okke strive to be True RENNAWAWK human beings who live in harmony with our ecosystems. This is the legacy of the Long-Water-Land, Our Heritage and we have reserved this space to demonstrate that WE ARE STILL HERE and our existence is defined in our own traditional terms not the policies, practices, stereotypes and Wapsu-Oriented-History that has distorted our presence to fit the goals, purposes and intentions of Puritan-minded individuals and state-sanctioned agencies who want us to vanish and go away. But we are here to stay and we have always been the reason this Legacy exists".[5]

Theirs is an inspiring legacy of survival and connectedness to place that evokes the very spirit of the land they have always called home. Pushed to the very edge of extinction, the Quinnipiac have struggled back to reestablish themselves as a viable cultural entity and a people who never went away, but survived in the shadows of a dominant society that had overwhelmed them. Today they are proudly reclaiming their heritage and are eager to share it with that dominant culture. According to the *Algonquian Confederacy of the Quinnipiac Tribal Council* website, their goals are:

1. To preserve, protect, enhance, and propagate our Native American, Algonquian-speaking cultural heritage;
2. To revive, restore, and revitalize the language and culture in particular of the Quinnipiac people (originally of Connecticut) and our kindred;
3. To protect and restore Mother Earth, Father Sky and all our relations to their natural balance and to foster respect and harmony in this quest;
4. To teach and share the values, history, culture, language, arts & crafts, of the Quinnipiac and kindred Algonquian peoples, whose

traditions were considered lost until the ACQTC was formed;

5. To research and keep current with indigenous affairs and to promote both unity and harmony in the Native American communities, on and off the reservations;

6. To share our personal pride, ancestral knowledge, and wisdom;

7. To lecture, perform, and teach or otherwise present our culture, values, and ceremonies as an Algonquian ethos and map for living in balance in our world.[6]

For some in the greater Anglo-American culture, their efforts may seem quaint and even indulgently self- serving, but the fact that they even still exist and are seeking to reclaim their rightful place within our modern society is a testimony to the tenacity and power of the human spirit. Plus, their goals are those that we all can embrace. Montowese, I am sure, would be proud.

So, who would know that the people that once called Totoket home for thousands of years either did or still exist, and why is that important? To start with, their experience at the hands of the greater Anglo-American culture beginning with the arrival of English colonists in the late 1630's became the unfortunate template for treatment of most other indigenous people throughout what is now the United States. Although initially addressed through the legal mechanisms and traditions brought to their shores by the English through treaty making, indigenous people like the Totokets were quickly and routinely pushed from the lands they had always called home by the smothering nature of the increasingly dominant culture as it grew in numbers and strength. Through the scourges of disease and assimilation, the surviving members of the Quinnipiac and Totokets seemed to literally vanish though many continued to dwell on the margins of our society. All that was left it seems, for even those who today know of their former existence, are occasional street names, a university called Quinnipiac, and in Northford, a boney ridgeline called Totoket Mountain that separates the village from North Guilford to the east. The Todd-Stevens site lies in its shadow.

Seeing the Past

Thus what of the Quinnipiac's legacy? It is interesting that in today's modern America, many individuals are turning to the traditions of Native Americans in two significant areas; our relationship with the environment and spirituality. Since the 1970's, there has been a growing awareness among Americans that we have done irreparable harm to our environment through the blessings the Industrial Revolution and through the growing impact of Global Warming and Climate Change a radical adjustment in our relationship to the Earth needs to take place. Here, the Quinnipiac Tribal Council says it best:

> "Our people knew the Great Mystery of the Creation in a way and to the depth of understanding that can never be achieved by a people with no remembered roots to the past, no real relationship to the land, and no consuming concern for every life form (animate or inanimate) within the universe".[7]

The Quinnipiac Tribal Council goes on to say:

> "Born through countless millennia of living as an integral part of the total Creation, this connectedness gives a depth of spirituality and an understanding of the meaning and purpose of life that had no equal among those who live only to use and exploit the Creation, the land, the rocks, the atoms, the wildlife, the water, the air, the stars, and even each other for their own selfish ambitions". (Algonquian Confederacy of the Quinnipiac Tribal Council, 2013) In the end, might the legacy of Montowese and his people be a transformation of our own culture?

And what of the Dutch? What brought them to of all places—Branford? It is an enigma looked at from our 21st century world but the Dutch traders who prowled the waters of the New World beginning around the first decade of the 17th century were pragmatic businessmen who would not waste their time and more importantly, capital, on flimsy perchance endeavors. These were hardnosed capitalists in the strictest sense of the word. So why Branford and what evidence actually exists of their presence?

CHAPTER 2
Roduyns Revealed

In 1998 and 1999, I was fortunate to take part in an archeological dig that would change our understanding of early European contact and presence in Southern New England. We located what we understand is a Dutch fort in Branford. I first came across material identifying the presence of a fort built by the Dutch while researching the history of Native Americans in the town of Guilford, Connecticut for a graduate course I was taking at Wesleyan University with Adjunct Professor Dr. John Pfeiffer in 1989. An early president of Yale during the 18th century, the Reverend Ezra Stiles, had drawn a map dated 1760 of a peninsula in Branford called Indian Neck on which he prominently located a four cornered structure labeled "the Dutch Fort". Stiles, a prolific chronicler of Connecticut's history, culture, and features recorded and often drew what he saw as he traveled throughout the state in his journals which can still be seen at Yale University. The fort, located on a narrow section of the neck of the peninsula, commanded both the approach to the mouth of the Branford River and the shallow estuary formed by the river on the other side of the peninsula, almost directly across from the location of the spot known as the Dutch Wharf. I had also found a secondary source written in conjunction with the U.S. Bicentennial in 1976 detailing the history of towns along the Connecticut Shoreline that stated emphatically that the Dutch had established a trading post in the 1620's in Branford.[1] We both noted the fort's presence and discussed what we thought it might mean, adding the fort to our growing knowledge of early 17th century European/Native American interactions. During the ensuing years, we pursued other projects both together and separately but the fort was never far from our thoughts.

Then one unusually warm Saturday morning in February, 1998 with the Stiles map in hand, John and I decided to take a walk along the shore of Indian Neck just to see what we might discover. In Connecticut, most of the shoreline along Long Island Sound is privately owned so the only time one can traverse it is during low tide since the State owns up to the high tide mark. For our expedition, John had printed out a modern copy of a map of the Neck and had overlaid that of Stiles on top of it so we had a good idea where we might look, never really hoping to find the spot due to the level of modern development and substantial erosion of the shoreline over the last two hundred thirty nine years. As we found a place to park, a way to access the beach, and began the obstacle course of seawalls and jetties, our conversation was dominated by hopes while our eyes looked for any possible sign from the past.

In 1614, Adrian Block, sailing for investors from the Dutch East India Company out of The Netherlands, was the first European to officially survey and map what was to become the coast of Connecticut as he worked his way eastward through Long Island Sound. Block was following in the footsteps of Henry Hudson who in 1609 had sailed from Amsterdam on his ship, the *Half Moon*, looking for what was believed to be an all water route to China and the Pacific. Hudson's original plan was to sail north along the coast of Norway and then turn east across what is now the Arctic Ocean. By the time he had reached the northern latitudes of Norway, he made a radical and probably preplanned decision to turn west across the Atlantic instead. Armed with a map from his friend John Smith who had recently returned from Virginia, Hudson's gamble was that he might discover that all water route to Asia by finding a way through or possibly around the still mostly unexplored continent of North America.

After first making landfall in Labrador, Hudson turned south skirting along the coast of Nova Scotia, Maine and then Cape Cod. His goal was to find an estuary and river system large enough to lead through the largely uncharted land mass to the Pacific. Once off Nantucket Island, he moved directly south to the Chesapeake Bay, no doubt utilizing Smith's map, and then as far south as Cape Hatteras where he turned north, skirting the coast and entering and exiting Delaware Bay. Sailing northward along the coast of New Jersey, he entered New York Harbor and the mouth of the river that bears his name, journeying as far up as present day Albany before realizing his quest to find an all water route through the continent was not to be.

As he readied his ship for the return to The Netherlands, Hudson filled the ship's log with glowing accounts of the richness of the land teeming with deer, beaver, and otter who's pelts were highly prized back in Europe. He also wrote of the many Native villages that in particular lined the banks of the river with their cultivated fields of maize. Upon his return, The Dutch East India Company though impressed with his accounts, was bound by the terms of their charter to concentrate on trade with Asia and thus reluctant to capitalize on his discoveries. Individual groups of merchants weren't however and some began sending ships to capitalize on trade with the inhabitants who were eager to barter their furs for European goods. Thus by 1614, though Block was the first to chart the coast of what is now Southern New England, other unknown adventurers and opportunists undoubtedly visited the shores of Long Island Sound prior to and after his arrival.

Historians now understand that as early as the mid to late 14th century European fishermen, most from the Basque region of northern Spain, Portugal, as well as others from Brittany in northwestern France, had been venturing out to fish off the far northeastern shore of North America following its first recorded discovery by the Norse from Iceland and Greenland three centuries earlier. Their goal, to exploit the rich fishing grounds off those shores known as George's Bank. Here the ocean teemed with what had become a European staple, cod, to be salted and dried. Salted cod was a food that could be preserved and then kept over an extended period of time before the invention of refrigeration and thus an important and increasingly necessary commodity just as the population of Europe began to explode. It was inexpensive and it lasted. In order to dry and salt cod, the fishermen had to establish temporary stations on land to process and dry the fish and thus Europeans became seasonal visitors to the shores of Newfoundland, the farthest east part of North America.

In order to salt and then store the cod for shipment back to Europe, the fisherman needed two important items, salt and oak. Many of the fishermen would carry salt in the holds of their vessels when they left their home ports; the shores of western France, Portugal, and northern Spain are still important salt producing regions. Beginning in the early 1500's they could also procure salt in the Caribbean Sea region as well which was often the first stop for larger vessels sailing from Europe due to the prevailing winds and latitude. From there they would ride the Gulf Stream north along the east coast of North America from Florida to Nova Scotia and then on to Newfoundland. Once there, the salt would be used to dry and preserve the fish for shipment back to Europe.

But there was that other necessary item needed in the process—oak. Why oak? Since the Middle Ages, Western and Northern Europeans had relied on wooden storage containers in order to ship and store a great variety of food items, from wine to salted beef. Wooden or ceramic containers were the only practical options in a pre-plastic world. Thus wooden barrel making was a necessity for any volume of produce or material to be stored or shipped. For the salt cod fishery, the containers of choice were wooden barrels of all sizes. The sides of wooden barrels are made of individual pieces called staves which are arranged around a circular wooden bottom and top, then pulled together by a skilled craftsman called a cooper into a barrel which is secured with wooden rings. These containers, when built correctly, are air and water tight. Because each stave is shaped slightly concave, when fit together the pressure of each tightened by the rings on the bottom, top, and middle creates a tight seal between each stave. The result is a round, sturdy, and heavy yet versatile storage container.

Here is where knowledge of wood came into play. Until recent times, people who lived more closely to nature knew that different types of wood, oak, cedar, or pine for example, had qualities that were best suited for different uses. Much of the determination for use was whether the wood was hard or soft and whether the wood was tight grained or not. All this determined if the wood was impervious to water, a critical characteristic when it came to storage. When it came to barrels, the best wood by far was white oak. It was hard, tight grained, sturdy, and water resistant; the perfect barrel making material.

By the early 17th century, Western and Northern Europe were in a wood crisis. Most of the forests in the region had been long cleared and timbered off for building and fire wood, and what was left were scraggly, second growth trees hardly suited for much other than burning in fire places, still the common mode of heat. Though historical accounts of the European arrival in North America often focused on the fishery and furs, what most often stunned those who first gazed upon the shores of the continent were the trees. It is hard for us to imagine the impact on a people used to seeing a landscape devoid of trees to suddenly be in an environment dominated by wooden giants. Early English accounts of the forests of Southern New England praised them for the abundance and variety of wood to be harvested and two, Rev. Francis Higginson (1630) and William Wood (1634) praised in particular the abundance of oak.[2] Here was another commodity that could be harvested and sold at a hefty profit. When it came to barrel making, especially for the cod fishery, the shores of Southern New England were dominated by the perfect tree—the mighty white oak which, to this day, still thrives in the region with its northern limit being south-central Maine. If the Dutch wanted material for making barrels, here was the source.

Which brings us back to Totoket and the Dutch Fort. One conversation John and I constantly had was why would the Dutch, who had access to the entire coastline of Long Island Sound, choose Branford as a location of a fort that was now lost in the fog of time? The answers to our questions were always varied and not convincing; a safe harbor when there were many other more suitable options? An ideal location from which to trade with the local inhabitants for furs when there were better spots all along the coast? Was Totoket a place to capitalize on the production of wampum, the native beads made from local quahog and welk shells used in trade? Although there were historically large beds or middens of these shells located on the Branford River side of Indian Neck, wampum became a major item of production later in the 17th century and only after the arrival of the English in the area. Plus there are no known records of wampum production in Totoket. So why were the Dutch there?

The answer to that question will come a bit later. First, back to Adrian Block. Since the 300th anniversary of Block's voyage was just celebrated in 2014, it is only right that a brief description of his most important voyage be told. History notes that Block was an accomplished merchant and sea captain who had made many voyages on a global scale including four to the Americas in which his 1613-14 voyage is the most noteworthy for this story. In 1613 he sailed together with Hendrick Cristiaenz, another Dutch captain, in two ships to what is now New York Harbor on the heels of Hudson.[3] Upon arrival, the two captains soon had a falling out over the potential profits of furs obtained through trade with the local inhabitants. The situation grew worse with the arrival of a third Dutch ship under the command of a captain named Mossel.[4] There was then an accidental fire that destroyed Block's ship, the Tiger in New York Harbor which forced Block and his men to move to the island of Manhattan.

It was at that point that his crew mutinied, perhaps fearing the possibility of being stranded in this new and unknown land. Half of his crew agreed to sail off with Mossel while the others remained with Block for the winter months thus becoming the first recorded European residents of Manhattan. During that winter they busied themselves building a new ship named the *Onrust* (Restless) a small 42 foot vessel that would prove ideal for the shallow inlets and rivers along Long Island Sound. In the spring of 1614 they left Manhattan and sailed through the treacherous, rock strewn passage between what is now the East River and the western end of Long Island Sound, named Hellegat by the Dutch and today still known by the Anglicized version Hell's Gate. As Block and his crew sailed along the northern shore of the Sound, he charted and noted the various bays, rivers, and features he encountered giving names to many of them. Eventually he made it to the mouth of the Connecticut River which he designated the Versche (Fresh) River, no doubt for the extensive volume of fresh water that came down it during the annual spring flood. Block worked his way up the river past the location of present day Hartford, getting as far north as the Enfield Rapids, the site of the present town of Windsor Locks which will figure prominently in Milo Todd's story. Prevented from sailing further, Block returned to the Sound noting the many prosperous Native villages on either side.

Block then continued to work his way east along the Sound and sailed into Narragansett Bay, naming the largest island there Roode (Red) Island. While exiting Long Island Sound to begin his return voyage to Amsterdam, Block charted the island that still bears his name. Shortly after his return to The Netherlands, the Dutch government began a concerted effort to establish a foothold in the region and established The New Netherlands Company to do so, giving them a three year monopoly on trade. They established their base on Manhattan Island and thus was born the Dutch trading settlement of New Amsterdam. In time, the colony of New Netherlands would claim land from the South (Delaware) River to Cape Cod setting themselves up in direct competition with the English who by then were also moving to establish their claim to the continent's coast.

Block had probably not been the first in the waters off Totoket as Dutch ships were likely plying those waters by 1614 or earlier though the sparse records indicate that the merchants and captains they sent out kept the geographic locations of their trade in furs deliberately vague.[5] Former State Historian, Albert E. Van Dusen, writing in his meticulous history of Connecticut, noted that during the decade following Block's voyage, Dutch traders carried on an extensive trade with the natives of the region that had reached the volume of an estimated 10,000 beaver skins a year.[6] Evidence however does point to an even earlier Dutch presence. In an article written for the New Netherland Institute in 1974, Charlotte Wilcoxen of Harvard cited research that claimed that the Dutch had been trading along the New England coast since 1598. Wilcoxen also noted a letter written to William Bradford of Plymouth by a representative of the Dutch West India Company in 1627 that the Dutch had been trading in New England for twenty six years.[7] There was money to be made and the enterprising merchants of The Netherlands were the first to take advantage of the possibilities.

Even Adrian Block had been to the shores off of New England earlier. Jaap Jacobs of the University of St. Andrews in Scotland and a specialist on the early Dutch Republic and its colonies states in his 2005 study, *New Netherland: A Dutch Colony in Seventeenth Century America* that Block sailing for the Van Tweenhysen Company visited the Hudson region in 1612 and during that visit a fortification was built on what is now Castle Island near Albany which became Fort Nassau. Members of the crew remained there to trade while the ships were absent.[8] Jacobs visited our excavation in 1998 and 1999 and has suggested that the fort at Totoket may date in fact to that time as well.[9]

By 1620, the Dutch, using New Amsterdam as a base, established two well documented trading posts in Connecticut, one short lived post at the mouth of the Connecticut River on the west bank called Kievit's Hoek (Plover's Corner) in what is now the town of Old Saybrook and a more long lasting and permanent one along the same river in the southern section of the city of Hartford, still called Dutch Point to this day. Named Huys van Hoop (House of Hope),[10] it sought to capitalize on the trade in furs coming down the river from inland New England. It was eventually forced out by the English once they settled the town of Hartford and Wethersfield which was located directly to the south. But were there other trading posts? The historical record says no. The noted Harvard historian Bernard Bailyn in his 2012 study of the 17th century settlement of North America, *The Barbarous Years*, states however that by 1620 and prior to the formation of the West India Company in 1621, numerous Dutch entrepreneurs had established a variety of isolated trading posts, primitive farms, and temporary encampments throughout the region.[11] Was the outpost at Totoket one of them?

Stories on the Trail of a Yankee Millwright

The interesting thing about Block's expedition from the standpoint of the story of Totoket is that, as Block moved slowly along the coast, he charted and recorded important features. Upon his return to Europe, the information within his log and charts would have then been jealously guarded by The New Netherlands Company to dissuade possible competition, a standard practice at the time. Yet the information quickly leaked out as more and more ships in the coming years set sail from The Netherlands, England, and France all trying to get in on the growing bonanza of fish, furs, timber, and ultimately land. Block's charts eventually became public when a Dutch cartographer by the name of Willem Janzoon Blaeu published the first comprehensive map of the region in 1635, his *Nova Belgica et Anglia Nova*.[12] Based upon Block's 1614 expedition, the map shows the features of New York, Long Island Sound, Long Island, and Southern New England in great detail. Included are Nieu Amsterdam, the Noord (Hudson) River, the Versche River, and other landmarks as well as the names of native groups in their locations among them the Quirepeys (Quinnipiacs).

Blaeu labeled the Quinnipiac River the Rivier vande Rodenbergh where New Haven is today, the name Rodenbergh translating to Red Hills. To this day, the most prominent topographical features that can be seen of the New Haven area from Long Island Sound are the two massive red volcanic ridges that frame the city, East and West Peak; the Red Hills. Here however, is where Blaue's map gets a bit more interesting. Overall, Blaue was a bit stingy when it came to naming geological features on his map and as a result one gets a sense that those Block had noted were important. Thus, directly to the east of Rodenbergh, in the approximate location of Branford, is clearly shown a place called Roduyns which translates to Red Dunes. Why this and not countless other features, many more geographically significant?

Jan pulled his woolen cloak closer around his neck and shoulders as he gazed out sleepily onto the inland sea. In the distance he could make out the thin line of the long barrier island that hid this body of water from the ferocious Atlantic on its other side. He watched as the incoming waves broke on the many stony rock islands that revealed the low tide but it was turning now and the wind picked up with it. Though early April, the damp chill of the morning breeze off the water had kept him shivering all during his watch for any sign of the shallop making its way they had been told from the company base settlement on the island of Manhattan at the mouth of the North River to the west. He and his other five companions at the fort had been eating mostly native maize and salt cod since February and hoped some good Dutch beef, bread, and cheese would soon be their faire.

His thoughts drifted to when he first came to what was to be his home for the past five months following a harrowing and sickly voyage across the angry ocean from his home in Leiden. He had been recruited by the company as a cooper and though only 17 and an apprentice for only four years, he had eagerly jumped at the chance to experience the challenge and adventure of life in the newly planted company base in what was being called New Netherland. Here was an opportunity to see a new and unexplored world and he felt he would be a fool to not. He was the envy of all his friends though his mother was convinced he would die at the hands of the savages said to eat the flesh of any good Dutchman they could catch.

Jan recalled landing at the rowdy and bustling trade settlement on the tip of Manhattan Island that November day thinking how the bleak grays and browns of the season created a landscape like nothing he had seen before and how the damp breeze that seemed constant got into his bones in a way not even the cold winds of the North Sea back home ever did. Here was a place foreign to all his senses; the smells, sounds, and sights merging into a strange banquet that seemed at first overwhelming. But above all, it was the trees that he could not comprehend—majestic giants so old they seemed as old as the Earth itself as they towered above, touching heaven. As a cooper and woodworker, he imagined he had come to the Promised Land.

Within two days he and four other new company recruits were herded onto a coastal shallop by one of its officers and told they would be going east along the coast to a place called Totoket by the natives along with equipment and supplies for the winter. Their job they were told was to cut and saw the giant oaks for timber and his would be to make staves for the barrels the company needed for shipping. When asked what Totoket was like, the captain of the shallop just laughed.

Stories on the Trail of a Yankee Millwright

After a two day sail along a rocky and forested coast, Totoket appeared through a heavy mist and the little fortification on the crest of a red dune that would be his home seemed anything but welcoming. Its earthen walls had an unkempt look and the jagged posts that formed the wooden palisade above it had a haphazard look as if put in as an afterthought. The heavy damp air gave the entire scene a somber and cold appearance made even gloomier by the smoke from a chimney in a central building that shrouded everything in a hazy fog. As the small boat rounded the peninsula on the western side of the fort by oars, a small group of native men and women ran along the shore of the dune shouting as they waved and gestured. One of the crew swore as he rowed, cursing them as nothing but thieves and devils and pronouncing loudly that the sooner they were all gone the better. Jan had seen a few of the native men and women during his brief stay at Manhattan and found them fascinating; some proud and regal in their bearing and others who had succumbed to the temptations of the traders in alcohol seemed debauched and desperate. He wondered what these at Totoket would be like.

The shallop came to a halt at a small wharf in the estuary on the north side of the peninsula below the fort and directly across from a larger wharf on the far bank that also had what appeared to be a wooden warehouse near it. The estuary formed by a lazy tidal river, looped further off into the distance to the north into what looked to be a forested eternity. As Jan took in the scene he was startled by the gruff shouts and commands of an Englishman whose Dutch was poor but who got the message across. Petulant and arrogant to say the least and superior in his manner, this little Englishman Jan would soon learn likened himself king of this tiny wooded realm on the edge of this vast unknown world.

"Alright you plague ridden wretches, unload the supplies and step to it or the tide will turn and we will have to feed that scurvy crew" he bellowed as he sneered at the boat's crew with disdain. There was clearly no love lost on their part either as the captain, a tall thin Frenchman, snarled in return as he ordered his men to help. Jan and his comrades snapped to the order and the shallop was quickly unloaded only to be reloaded with bundles of wooden barrel staves.

"This is it? This is all they sent us?" the lout queried in disgust as he turned to the captain and accused him of trading the rest away to natives along the coast.

"Moulner, if it was not for the fact that the company keeps you here because you get results, I would run you through and feed you as bait while we fish our way back" the Frenchman said as he glared at his accuser.

"Well off with you and to hell with you all" Moulner responded with a dismissive wave of his arm. "With what you have brought we will be eating each other by January" as he motioned towards Jan. "That one's too boney for nothing but stew".

The rude man was Thomas Moulner, hired by the company to oversee the cutting of timber the company needed for ships, buildings, barrels, and export back to Europe. He was quarrelsome and offensive, but they knew he got results. Jan soon learned that the previous group of six workers had deserted him when a passing Dutch privateer had docked for a night and that he and his companions were their replacements. Moulner did fashion himself the master of Totoket and was quick with a curse, and only belligerent on a good day, on others—well, the bad were something else. But as November turned to December and winter came Jan learned to appreciate the ornery little man for he made them work for their keep, kept them alive that winter, and taught them the ways of this exotic land and its people.

Throughout the cold winter months Jan and the others cut the giant oaks and sawed them into manageable lengths, floated them down the river to the saw mill that ran with the tides turning them into boards and planks that could be shipped or made into staves which was Jan's responsibility and by April he imagined he had made thousands. It was hard and dangerous work but he knew he was experiencing a life in a world none of those back in Lieden would ever believe.

By late March the snow began to melt, the river rose with the melt, and the mud made cutting and hauling the timbers impossible. They worked bundling and stacking staves and planking for shipping and stayed busy trying to repair the equipment, the walls of the fort, and whatever Moulner ordered. Now that it was April, a shallop was scheduled to appear to bring supplies and return with a load of staves and lumber which was why Jan was standing watch. Two others were scheduled to follow and he hoped on the last he could leave Totoket for Manhattan Island and the village of what was now being called New Amsterdam they had been told. He thought perhaps he could catch work as a cooper there and just maybe in the future have his own cooperage. This new land was full of possibilities and opportunities. But would Moulner let him go?

Jan turned his back to the wind off the water and looked upon the tiny fortification with its parade or courtyard and small communal storehouse and lodging he had spent the five months in with the others. It was roughly octagonal in shape, with daub and wattle walls and a thatched roof. It was a ramshackle affair and hardly suited for the climate here at Totoket for it kept out neither the rain nor the cold. What he would give to be warm again he thought as he turned back towards the sea and the brightening horizon to the southeast. "At least it did not promise to rain today" he mused as he began to walk slowly along the western parapet of the wall, mostly to keep his legs from stiffening. As he walked he looked out across the small peninsula to the west and the wigwams of the Totokets that were arranged in a circular pattern in the distance, maybe 25 rods. Jan could see that some were occupied and some not as their habit had always been to disappear into the forested interior to escape the winter's cold to return with the warmth of spring.

Jan knew little about these people who God appeared to have abandoned to sickness and the disintegration of their way of life. Moulner had tried to keep them away though Jan would study and talk with them as best he could whenever he got the chance. They seemed a decent and proud people for the most part and he was often moved to pity by their suffering. Many he had been told, had already moved away in a vain attempt to escape the plagues the Dutch and others had brought and the demands of the arrogant and dangerous Pequots who not seeing a challenge in the small group of Dutchmen left them alone. But there were still these few here in Totoket who stubbornly held on because it was their home and that of their ancestors. If the Great Spirit determined they should pass from the Earth they often said, then this is from where they would leave.

Seeing the Past

"You forsaken son of a whore" yelled Moulner in his garbled Dutch, "the shallop's to be seen to the south west and not where your dreamy eyes are searching for one of your heathen tarts to bed!". Yes, Jan considered, perhaps it was time to move on.

As John and I walked west along the shore of Indian Neck, we came to a point where the elevation above the beach was significantly higher than either to the east or west, a run of maybe 150 to 200 yards prominently set 25 to 30 feet above the beach. Though partially obstructed by sea walls and large granite stones to help prevent erosion, it was clearly a high, sandy red cliff rising prominently above the beach. Perched on its crest were an old Victorian Era beach club and a private home. Was this Roduyns? To top it all off, the house had, of all things—a Dutch flag flying high on a full size flag pole. It was hard to believe, but it seemed Blaeu and our faith in Stiles had brought us to the site. And a Dutch flag to go with? As we excitedly retraced our path along the beach back to our car, reveling in our discovery, John and I decided to drive along the road to the approximate area where the beach club and home were, looking for tell-tale signs in the lawns that might give us any visual archeological clues knowing that close to 400 years can hide a lot. While John slowly drove, I held the Stiles and modern maps in my hands and as we approached the narrowest part of the neck that formed the peninsula, we realized we were at the approximate location Stiles had indicated the fort would be, and directly to our left was the beach club.

John stopped the car and we both approached the gated compound—locked. The century old club was buttoned up for the winter. As we glanced through the fence down a long grassy lawn we could just make out behind a tennis court a slightly raised area in the lawn, not far from the edge of the cliff. Often the remains of structures long gone leave a raised or sunken shadow on the surface, might this be it? To the right of the raised area, the club lawn was divided from the neighboring yard by a tall, thick hedge that looked like it had been there since the days of the Dutch so we turned and walked hurriedly along the road to the neighbor's driveway just to the right of the hedge. At first our view was blocked by a garage and another house close to the road, but as we peered up and around them from the road we could see the flag pole with the Dutch flag flapping in the breeze. John and I did not hesitate, up the drive we went.

By May, John had secured the eager and enthusiastic permission to begin an excavation from the owners of the home, Chet and Angelica Bentley. The Bentley's had always heard the rumors of a fort in the area, and family tradition had indicated it might have been where their home sat. Thus the flag. But that was all they knew. Angelica, who's family had owned the property since the mid 1800's, and her husband Chet provided us with as much background information as they could about the property including the fact that their current ranch-style home was the second on the lot, the first having burned in the 1970's. This was significant in that Chet recalled how the old gambrel style colonial had been torn down after the fire and quite a bit of site work had been done on the property. Unlike the neighboring inn property to the east of the hedge that divided the two lots, no raised area or berm existed on the Bentley lawn which indicated that on the surface any evidence of the fort had been scraped away during the demolition and building. The Bentley's assured us however that their new house sat on the very site of the old which allowed us to approach the dig with cautious optimism.

John had organized an archeological excavation that began in late June through a graduate course he was teaching at Wesleyan University that summer session, enthusiastic support of the local Branford Historical Society, the Town of Branford and a small cadre of volunteers of which I was one. Our goal was simple—to find evidence of the fort in the Bentley's lawn. The Owenego Inn, the private beach club next store, was off limits for now. We began planning our excavation by laying out a grid system of meter squares using a corner of the garage as our datum point off of which all measurements would be set. The grid formed a rectangle that was framed by the garage to the north, the hedge to the east, and part of the lawn leading to the house to the west. Ultimately, the southern end of the excavation area would be the edge of the red cliff itself which towered above the small beach and surf below. As we stood atop the red sandy soil that formed the edge of the shore, gazing out onto the Sound, John and I couldn't help but be drawn back to Block, Blaeu, and those early Dutch traders. Would we find evidence of their presence?

We did not have long to wait. We began our excavation by removing the turf from the grid near the garage, working our way along the hedge line towards the cliff. By hugging the hedge we felt we might best find signs of a structure that would have not been impacted by the site work done on the property back when the present house was built. But exactly what were we looking for? Prior to the dig that summer, John and I had spent time that spring researching what type of structure or battlement the Dutch might have built on the site. From existing historical evidence of forts built by the English and Dutch during the early 17th century in America and the Caribbean, it was most likely a small structure, square or roughly triangular, as little as 50 feet on a side. The walls were most likely earthen with a ditch or moat in front. In the corners, a raised area called a bastion would have jutted out, providing a place for a cannon. The earthen wall may well have been surmounted by a wooden wall, adding height to the overall structure so the defenders would have the advantage of firing down upon their foe if attacked. Even accounts of the fort at the tip of Manhattan as late as 1630 describe it as sod-walled. [13]

During the first few days of digging we followed a line hugging the hedge and excavated a series of test pits every meter with the hope of finding a hint from the past that would help identify whether or not any sign of the fort actually remained. Almost from the start we began to come across tantalizing clues as the soil began to reveal its secrets. When an earthen wall was constructed, for example, the remains of the wall as well as the trench that had been dug to create it should appear as different shades or even colors distinct from the undisturbed earth around them. The same would be true of the holes left by wooden posts that had been placed into the soil to support a structure or for that matter, any area disturbed by human activity. We did not have long to wait. By the third day of testing we had struck two interesting areas, one the remains of a possible structure and the other what promised to be a trench that had been back filled. Alongside it was an area of corresponding soil that hinted at what had once been a raised area of dirt. Had we found the wall?

As we pursued the shadow of earthen fill that defined what had once been the ditch that had been dug to create the wall it became clear that the wall formed a triangular structure that came to a head or point closest to the cliff edge. As excavations continued the next summer on both sides of the hedge, permission from the Owenego Inn having been secured, the remains of an earthen bastion were discovered on the Bentley side of the hedge and the shadow of the former wall moved off on a similar angle onto the inn's property. On both sides of the hedge, approximately 30 feet of the wall remained but the rest of the structure had been obliterated long ago. The bastion point, facing the Sound, was approximately ten feet on a side, small for any serious fortification, but large enough to have mounted a small canon from a ship to threaten any sea-born approach. Within this section as well as along what was the earthen section of the wall were post molds, the remains of posts that had been inserted into the mound onto which a wooden wall would have been attached.

The features uncovered indicated that this was not a large or permanent structure but more than likely a temporary one designed to last at most a few years. Perhaps this is the reason no documentation from the period detailing its existence has been found to date. But we had found proof of an early European presence and the shadow left by the wall they had built for protection aligned with research done on other early Dutch sites including Forts Orange and Nassau in New York as well as early English sites in Virginia. But it was what we found during those two summer digs inside the walls of the fort that convinced us that we had indeed found the remains of an early Dutch presence.

Inside what would have been the courtyard of the fort was an oddly shaped structure outlined by a chalky white material extending out from a rectangular feature, a possible hearth or fire place. About 1/3 of the outline of the structure remained, the rest having been scraped away when the Bentley's present home was built following the fire in the 1970's. At first it was a puzzle due to its shape and material. The chalky material that outlined the wall ran in lengths that varied from four to six feet and formed what could at best be described as a rough circular shape, really more octagonal in shape. This was something John and I were not familiar with having understood that most European structures, even if temporary, were built with right angles and usually square or rectangular. This was a mystery.

The chalky outline of the wall was also something neither of us were familiar with and along with the shape of the structure, called for more research. As we carefully excavated around the white outline, it became clear that the substance had fallen into a trench left by eventual rotting away of wooden timbers that had formed the base or temporary footing for a wall. Our hunch was that the chalky substance was in fact the remains of a typical European daub and wattle wall found throughout Northern and Western Europe at the time.

Because much of Western Europe had been denuded of trees by the start of the 16th century, many buildings throughout the region including the Netherlands were built with a technology that dated back to the time of the Romans and beyond. In order to build a sturdy wall while not using much wood, a frame of timbers was erected that would create the basic shape of the wall; a base or foundation, two vertical posts, and a header or plate timber across the top. Depending on the width of the wall, an additional timber or two might be set as posts inside the section of wall to provide stability and strength. Small, thin, pieces of long strips of wood called lath or wattle would then be woven like a basket between the posts to form the basic frame for the wall. Sometimes the wattle was actually made from long pieces of saplings or brush since their primary role was to form a surface onto which the daub could be secured.

The daub, a mixture of clay, sand, lime, and water was mixed together and then spread on and across the lath to form a plaster or stucco like surface that would then dry and form the permanent surface of the wall. The result was a hard wall covering that reflected the color of the mixture that had gone into making it and together with the timbers that framed it formed a substantial and relatively strong wall. This was certainly a building technology that a Dutch or other Western European would have been familiar with. Samples of the daub were sent to Philadelphia for analysis by *Powers and Company* who specialize in stone, brick, and surface preservation along with an entire host of other historic and structural preservation services. Owned by my brother Robert, they ran tests on the sample and it came back a mix of clay, sand, and lime. It was exactly what we had hoped for. Yet the mystery of the shape still remained.

Because only a section of the structure had survived, as we meticulously excavated what was left it became clear that the outline formed a hexagon like shape. Puzzled by this, we began to research whether or not this was a common form of temporary structure and at first were stymied by the lack of evidence. We did find a diagram however, of a fort built as a temporary encampment on the Caribbean island of Puerto Rico at Guayanilla Bay by the English in 1585 during an expedition against the Spanish led by Lord Richard Grenville that indicated structures of this type.[14] Drawn by John White who would later find fame as the leader of the ill-fated Roanoke Colony, as an artist White is still known for his meticulous accuracy for detail. At least we had visual confirmation. I also found an article detailing the creation and design of octagon houses in the mid-19th century United States that referenced the fact that the Dutch had built such structures in the Hudson Valley during the 17th century.[15] Was this what we had found?

The structure was intriguing and as we continued to slowly excavate in and around it that first and second year artifacts were found that indicated through association an early 17th century vintage. From within the hearth area two wrought iron nails of an early type were excavated along with a copper alloy button and a fragment of ceramic that came from a plate of what was at first of a mysterious type.[16] Research into Dutch ceramics of the period drew a possible correlation to late 16th and early 17th century majolica though the pattern with a series sharp blue pronged lines was of an unknown design. In 1999, five more fragments were found within the structure that dramatically fit together when assembled. To date the design and type have never been conclusively identified.[17] Charlotte Wilcoxen of Harvard University however, an expert on 17th century Dutch trade especially in ceramics, identified the clay, slip, and style as not European and suggested that they were likely either Turkish or Arabic in origin. It made sense. The Dutch, the consummate traders of the day, worked a global network. Artifacts found at Fort Orange where present day Albany stands came from forty eight different countries or locations around the world.[18] The existence of non-European ceramics at Totoket is thus not a stretch. The shards can be seen today, along with other artifacts from the fort, at the Branford Historical Society.

One interesting development, especially during the first summer of excavation was the absence of classic ceramic pipe fragments so frequently found in other 17th century Dutch and English sites as well as trade beads of European manufacture that were exchanged in trade with native people for furs. It turned out this lack, though initially seen as a negative factor, also led credence to the possibility of a very early date, possibly as early as the late 1590's or first two decades of the 1600's.[19] Since the Dutch did not begin production of clay pipes until the years 1609-10 the absence of these datable fragments adds further credence to a pre-1610 time period.[20] The signature long stemmed clay pipe quickly became a major trade item during the remainder of the 17th century. Other artifacts recovered during the excavation yielded further evidence to the fact that the fort structure in its entirety was an occupation site from the first decades of the 1600's or earlier. Did the lack of trade beads mean that the Dutch were not there to trade but to protect their source of timber to produce barrels? Two gun flints of European origin were found along with three lead shot/musket balls of the appropriate caliber for the era. What appears to be the pointed edge of a European pike, a spear-like weapon that was attached to a long shaft used to either jab or chop at an enemy was also found.

During the dig the summer of 1999, European manufactured glass trade beads were found along with a number of native shell wampum beads. These beads, it turns out, were also critical in helping to establish an approximate early 17th century date to the fort as the European made beads were introduced early in the century as important trade items with the native population. Taken as a whole, the artifact assemblage, along with the wall structure and the building inside, seemed to strongly support the claims of both Ezra Stiles and local oral tradition that the Dutch had established a fort and trading post in Branford early in the 1600's.

17th century English privateer, Sir Robert Dudley, published a map of the coast of Southern New England, Long Island, and the area around New York Harbor in 1646 that utilized information from the earlier Blaeu map. Obviously used for navigation purposes, Dudley's map carefully delineates points of land and islands as they would have been encountered from the water. He also details the dangerous shoals off of Cape Cod and those within the entrance to New York Harbor. Off what he still labeled Roduyns, was a series of three dotted arcs indicating shoals and rocks directly to the east of the site of the fort in an area that is still today dangerous to navigation centered around the Thimble Islands. Since Dudley, on his *Arcano del Mare* clearly utilized Dutch names and landmarks, his map gives further evidence to the idea that Roduyns was more than just a landmark for the early 17th century Dutch.

Bernard Bailyn offers one more intriguing element to this story. Beginning in 1621, a group of ethnic Walloon families from what is now Belgium petitioned the West India Company for permission to settle in either their new colony established at the mouth of the Amazon River in Brazil or in New Netherland. Having just been driven from the Amazon by the Portuguese, the company agreed to settle them in their North American holdings.[21] Despite the desire of the Walloons to be settled as a group, in 1624 they were distributed strategically instead in small groups on each of the major rivers claimed by the company from Delaware to Massachusetts. Consequently, two families and six men were sent to the mouth of the Connecticut River at Keivit's Hook.[22] There they remained until the company's governor, Willem Verhulst, was ordered to remove them in 1625.[23] There is no mention of where they might have gone. Did they end up on Indian Neck?

Does any of this really matter in the grand scheme of things? Does what happened four hundred years ago on an ancient sand dune overlooking Long Island Sound have a direct correlation to our lives? Once again, we are who we are, as a culture and people because of the past. For the residents of Branford, the story of the Dutch Fort is a proud chapter in the history of their community. The fort site, located on Indian Neck, is quite possibly the earliest European settlement in New England and certainly Connecticut. In it is the start of European domination of the region and its first link into a greater global world. In a time of accelerating globalization and all the economic and cultural impacts, both good and bad that it brings, it is interesting to look back to a time when a small group of men from The Netherlands brought with them a greater world connection that would transform a society and contribute to the eventual destruction of a Native American culture that had existed for thousands of years. If there is a lesson to be learned, it is that nothing is permanent. The currents of time will wash away even a stout fort on a sandy cliff and with it the new and promising world created there. In Totoket, the shadows of the past run deep into the red, sandy soil.

CHAPTER 3
The Promise

Like many New England communities, the village of Northford still harbors an occasional hint of its colonial past and for those willing to notice, those remnants are sign posts to a time gone forever. Despite the fact that the village, along with the rest of North Branford is now a modern commuter suburb, the surviving colonial era homes interspersed within later 19th and 20th century neighborhoods stand as silent sentinels guarding the secrets of their past lives. Together with the remaining farms that lie between and within the neighborhoods, one can catch a glimpse of what once was.

When first settled by residents of Branford as part of the North Farms during the 1690's and early 1700's, Northford had been purposely opened as an outlet for the expanding population of the shoreline town in their quest for more land to farm and other economic opportunities the new lands had to offer. Like most Puritan New England settlements during the 1600's, expansion into and settlement of additional land within the boundaries of the community's territory was a controlled process called a division in which each freeman within the town was given a portion of acreage based upon their current land holdings, family size, and in some cases the amount they had invested in the original settlement attempt. In Branford, these freemen, as share-holders in the community, were organized into three categories based on the value of their holdings in English Pounds; 500+, 200+, and 100.[1] Those with more would get more. What is now the southern section of North Branford was opened as the Third Division in 1692 and what became Northford in 1704 as the Fourth.[2]

North Branford and its northern village, Northford, remained part of Branford throughout the 18th century and the first three decades of the 19th, becoming a town in its own right in 1831 just three years before Milo Todd's birth. By then North Branford had become a prosperous and innovative community in many ways on the cutting edge of the new America being created at the time. Together with the many traditions brought to the town from their mother community of Branford, they began to shape institutions that were bringing them into that new age. But a return to Branford and the stories inherent to its 17th century journey is helpful in setting the scene for the life of her child.

As discussed earlier, Branford was, from 1638 on, part of the land that became the Puritan colony of New Haven. Yet prior to that time, what made it unique among the English plantations being settled in Connecticut during the following twenty years was the earlier presence of the Dutch. Were they still there in 1638 or after? There is no historical record to indicate they were but local tradition states that individuals were resident at the time. One thing for sure however, is that in 1638 three Englishmen were there. Robert Cogswell, Roger Knapp, and James Love were all squatters on the land and renounced all right to it when the purchase of Totoket from Montowese took place.[3] There was also another individual, Thomas Moulner living there at the time who agreed to sell his rights to land in Totoket though reserving the right to a lot when the plantation was actually settled. Isabel Calder, in her 1934 history of the New Haven Colony describes how Moulner, originally from Ipswich, England, repurchased a neck of land in 1639 and settled there becoming "a thorn in the flesh" of first the planters of New Haven and later those of Totoket. Still called Moulner's Neck today, it is directly across the Branford River to the west of Indian Neck within sight of the fort location. They eventually bought him out in 1651.[4]

Here is where it all gets a bit interesting. The record clearly states individual Europeans were living in Totoket in 1638, what were they doing there and why? What about Thomas Moulner? How had he obtained rights to land there previous to 1638 and the record clearly states he repurchased land on a neck of land in 1639. Why so close to Indian Neck, the location of the Dutch fort? What was it about Moulner that made him such a "thorn in the flesh"? Was he exercising what he believed to be a previous right now being threatened by the plans of the Puritan leaders of New Haven? Individuals like Moulner, Cogswell, Knapp, and Love do not fit into the tidy history of the Puritan settlement of New England. They were out livers, men outside the control of the planned and well-ordered Puritan settlement process. So why were they in Totoket?

Were they employees of the Dutch West India Company? Were they associated with or had they previously been associated with the fort? Oral tradition has it that Moulner operated a saw mill. If so, was there still a timbering operation and barrel production taking place? As a truly global trading enterprise, companies such as the Dutch West India Company employed sailors, craftsmen, and adventurers from throughout Europe with many Englishmen joining the ranks of their employees. In *The Barbarous Years,* Bailyn lists an extensive collection of employees from over eleven European locations working for the company.[5] Thus their presence working for the Dutch would not have been unusual. New Amsterdam, their probable base of operation, was a very international community with Europeans from many countries living and working there. Above all, the Dutch in 1638 were not ready to cede their interest in trade or sources of timber along the shores of Long Island Sound to the English despite the fact that the new English colony at Quinnipiac threatened it. There was a reason why the four were in Totoket and it certainly was not random.

There is one more intriguing twist to the story of the settlement of Totoket. In 1639, Theophilus Eaton, the Puritan minister and leader alongside of John Davenport in New Haven arranged for his brother, Samuel to receive a grant of land in Totoket. Samuel Eaton intended to bring from England a group of like-minded Puritan followers to establish a plantation there as part of the New Haven Colony.[6] Theophilus Eaton and Davenport must have wanted a trusted individual to take charge of the area. Why? Was it due to the presence of individuals unaffiliated with their colony? The plan fell apart however when Samuel returned to England in order to gather his congregation only to remain there and never return leaving Totoket in an unsettled state until a new plan was hatched five years later in 1644. Undoubtedly feeling pressure to establish a presence on land owned by the colony, the New Haven leadership negotiated with a group from Wethersfield in the Connecticut Colony to resettle under their supervision after another attempt to attract settlers had again failed.[7] Thus began the permanent English presence in Totoket. In 1653, after attracting additional settlers from New Haven and Southampton on Long Island, the name of the plantation was changed to Branford after Brentford, a town outside of London.[8]

With their land to the east now secured, the Puritan fathers could turn their attention to other matters. Plus, with Thomas Moulner gone after 1651 as well, they could focus on building the Puritan utopia they had left England to create. But the past can sometimes be more complicated than the official story states. The image of the heroic Puritans confronting a virgin wilderness sometimes doesn't fit. Branford is certainly a fine example.

Northford as a distinct community came into existence in 1745 when the Connecticut Colonial legislature gave those living there the right to organize their own church under the name of the Third Society of Branford.[9] But how was it that Northford along with the rest of Branford became a part of Connecticut? Most residents of Connecticut today do not realize that until 1664, the Connecticut Colony founded along the river of the same name and New Haven Colony along the shoreline from Guilford west to Greenwich were separate entities tied together only by the need to co-operate for defensive purposes with the other New England Puritan colonies of Plymouth, Massachusetts Bay, and New Hampshire. From the beginning they had serious political and theological differences as well as separate economic interests. The greatest divide however was over their visions of the role of the Puritan church in society with the more conservative New Haven disapproving of what they felt were the lax practices and standards of their Connecticut brethren.

By 1660, both had established additional plantations in the territory they claimed and had begun to move inland, New Haven in from the coast and Connecticut into eastern Connecticut and inland from the banks of the Connecticut River. But both had a problem—neither held an official charter or license to exist from the English government. This had been fine when the Puritan controlled Parliament in England had ruled under the leadership of Oliver Cromwell after deposing King Charles I during the English Civil War and then beheading him in 1649. Their Puritan friends protected them. All this changed following the death of Cromwell and the return of the dead king's son, Charles II to the thrown in 1660. In the eyes of the new king and his ministers, these two Puritan colonies were rouge and illegal. Plus, they harbored some of the radical Puritans who had fought Charles I and condemned him to death.

Connecticut Colony was quick to act. Under the leadership of their Governor, John Winthrop Jr., they decided to appeal to the king for a charter that would legitimize their existence and protect their interests. But it was a long shot and because of that the Governor himself went with the appeal to England where he remained for two years.[10] Winthrop was by then a leading figure in both colonies having helped New Haven establish the first ironworks in Connecticut, located where Lake Saltonstall is along the Branford/East Haven border in 1656.[11] Prior to his involvement in New Haven, Winthrop had established a plantation at what is now New London, Connecticut, which fell under the jurisdiction of Connecticut. He was also the son of the most influential man in New England at the time, Governor John Winthrop Sr. of Massachusetts Bay who had many important connections to powerful individuals within the King's new government.

Winthrop's mission proved to be a triumph of patience and diplomacy. After two years of carefully cultivating a network of powerful individuals who might support Connecticut's appeal for a charter, the King granted, in 1662 one so generous that it not only recognized the colony's existence, it also recognized the right of the colony to establish a level of self-government unheard of at the time. But the real bonus was the extent of the territory that now fell under Connecticut's control. The border to the east was now Narragansett Bay giving Connecticut claim to land nominally under the control of the Rhode Island and Providence Plantations Colony of Roger Williams. To the south, Long Island Sound would form the boundary, to the north Massachusetts, and to the west the "South Sea" or Pacific Ocean.[12] The extent of this western territory was undetermined but included the Dutch colony of New Netherland and its main settlement at New Amsterdam since the English government considered their presence a violation of the English right of discovery and claim to the territory. In future years, the lands included within the charter would lead to disputes with New York, Pennsylvania, and Rhode Island.

The Connecticut Charter was a disaster for New Haven. In it, the colony on the shores of Long Island and all its territory was completely absorbed into Connecticut. New Haven had been hesitant to protect its interests and now it was too late. On hearing of the charter, some of the New Haven Colony towns broke away and willing joined with Connecticut; Greenwich, Stamford, and Southold on Long Island. Guilford threatened to leave. Only Milford and Branford remained loyal.[13] Accepting their fate, New Haven's leaders entered into two years of negotiations with their now more powerful neighbor in the hopes of securing the best possible terms for their annexation. Many in the colony feared union with Connecticut would mean the demise of their more orthodox religious and political institutions and the establishment of what they saw as the more lenient, lax, and spiritually questionable ones of Connecticut. Some seriously considered leaving for New Netherland and were encouraged to do so by the Dutch West India Company.[14]

By 1664, circumstances had become even more dire for those hoping New Haven might somehow survive. A resurgent English monarchy had declared war on The Netherlands and had seized their North American holdings. New Netherland and their trading center of New Amsterdam were in the hands of the English. Charles II awarded the former Dutch colony to his brother, James the Duke of York, who through the work of a royal commission reorganized his new lands into the colonies of New York and New Jersey. Any idea of fleeing to the Dutch was gone and New York was under the watchful care of the Anglican Church of England, the very institution that had triggered the Puritan exodus to New England to begin with. Facing no alternative, the leaders of New Haven chose the lesser of two evils and voted to join Connecticut in 1664.

For some, these turn of events were more than they could stand as they felt the very salvation of their souls were now threatened. Under the leadership of the Puritan minister of Branford, Abraham Pierson, a plan to leave Connecticut completely was formulated and the disgruntled church members from Branford reached out to their fellow dissenters in surrounding communities. They would refuse to surrender to Connecticut and emigrate instead. Reaching agreement with the new English proprietors of New Jersey who had invested in the colony through the Duke of York, a location was chosen on the Passaic River where the dedicated group of unrepentant Puritans could establish their Bible State.[15] There they founded a community in 1666 they knew would uphold their religious ideals away from the corruption that had absorbed Branford. They named their new settlement New Ark.

Abraham Pierson was strident in his beliefs and had moved from England to America to make sure he could help those willing to follow him into the eternal bosom of the Lord. Now, after having first led his congregation to Southold on Long Island and then here in Branford he had thought they had finally arrived at a place where he and his followers could worship the Lord in a way that strictly followed the dictates of the Bible and the Calvinist doctrines that had transformed his understanding of what it meant to be a true follower of Christ.

Fresh out of Cambridge in 1632, Pierson had been harassed and chased from the pulpit for his radical Puritan beliefs early on in England by the representatives of the established Church and the King and in 1640 under threat of arrest found himself driven to New England and the opportunity to truly create God's Kingdom on Earth. That same year he gathered together a group of like-minded followers in Lynn, Massachusetts and led them to establish Southold on Long Island. Pierson had thought they had founded God's Kingdom there but by 1644 disputes within the congregation led him to seek, along with his most dedicated followers, a new haven where he could truly create his vision of a true Christian theocracy and where his flock might eagerly strive to serve the Lord instead of their own reward.

For twenty two years, Pierson pondered, he had served the people of Branford since first being asked to join his flock with those fleeing as refugees from the corrupt River Colony town of Wethersfield. Together, they strove to truly do the Lord's work and offer to others an example of a perfect Christian society. Now, as he sat writing his last sermon he would deliver to his congregation here in the Meeting House they had built with their own hands, a wave of righteous anger enveloped him.

"These apostates!" he said to no one in particular. "How they have sold their souls and those of the people God gave them the responsibility to guide into the Kingdom of Heaven" he fumed at the thought of what the leaders of the New Haven Colony had done. For two years Pierson had feared this day following news that King Charles had given Connecticut Colony dominion over New Haven and that the leaders of the colony had negotiated in vain to remain somehow independent. "They could have fought harder, they might have sought the guidance of the Almighty in this time of need but those charged with administering to God's Chosen have forsaken him and them for the monetary and worldly gain union will bring" he exclaimed to himself. "They will be forever damned".

Just then his son Abraham entered the room to check on who his father was talking with though well aware of his habit of speaking his thoughts. "Father, your passion for the truth has always made you a driven man, thus your decision to lead the people once again into exile is of no surprise to any. To speak of it from the pulpit will only reassure them of following you in your righteous quest to live in a community ruled exclusively by the word of God."

Young Abraham had accompanied his father and ten other men of the congregation earlier that year to what had formerly been Dutch land but which was now called New Jersey following its seizure in 1664 by the English along with the rest of New Netherland. They had found what they hoped would be their New Jerusalem at the mouth of the Passaic River and once permission from the new English proprietors, all friends of the Duke of York, had been secured, planning for the migration had begun in earnest knowing the inevitable outcome to New Haven's challenge.

"How might God's Kingdom ever come to be if those who are not full members of the church are allowed the same civic rights as God's People as Connecticut has allowed? We, the Elect of God, will always be a minority for the Lord chooses few and has determined through his grace that we and we alone should shape a community of true believers according to his plan. Now tell me son, how will this happen if those embraced by the devil are allowed to speak and take part in the administration of the Lord's Commonwealth? We shall all be like Godless Rhode Island."

Young Abraham put his hand on his father's shoulder, more to steady and calm him than anything else knowing how his passion for his work could at times overwhelm him and how the family and the community worried for his health. "Father, you know the majority of your flock is prepared to follow. They are only awaiting your word. They understand that this "Half-way Covenant" being talked of will be the ruin of God's Kingdom and they too seek exile over damnation".

"Tomorrow during the Sabbath Day sermon I will reiterate my fears once again and render unto them the choice. Stay in Connecticut and abandon God's work, or on to New Ark, the name I have chosen to name our new home for like Noah and his family, it is we who will save mankind from the devil and himself."

Thus was the rather complicated heritage of those who trekked northward out of Branford and into the new lands of the Third and Fourth Divisions. They had inherited a feisty sense of independence and purpose that would do them well as the 18th century unfolded and they worked to build a new community. They knew who they were and understood their past. They embraced it, learned from it, and built on it. As they did so, North Branford and then Northford were created under the watchful eyes of the town fathers who oversaw the process.

Yet this settlement by our standards was painfully slow as it was only the need for farmland for an expanding population that would lead members of the Branford community to turn their backs on Long Island Sound and move inland. It would take 101 years from the first settlement of Branford in 1644 until Northford was officially recognized as a community in 1745.

It is fun to speculate on what might have been the thoughts of those ardent families who labored to clear the land, plant their crops, build their homes, and try to recreate a society they had left a scant eight miles to the south. But on many of those first winter nights, the distance might have well have seemed like eighty. In New England and especially Connecticut, since individuals were not allowed to strike out on their own to settle new lands, the process was controlled by the mother community as has already been described. The entire process of creating these new officially sanctioned societies might take decades as land needed to be surveyed, allotted, cleared, built on, and made productive. Only then, and if there was deemed a large enough population by the colonial legislature, could a settlement be recognized as ready to be designated a church society and given permission to build a church and hire a minister. Until that point, the new community was linked to and dependent on the old. In colonial Connecticut there was no separation of church and state.

In the northern sections of Branford, the Second Society, now North Branford, was sanctioned by the Colony in 1725 and the Third Society, Northford in 1745.[16] Though still tied to Branford, they could raise their own taxes to support their churches and had a degree of autonomy over their own affairs including the supervision of their residents and church members. They could even raise and train their own militia to protect the community during times of danger. We can only imagine the pride and satisfaction community members must have felt in knowing they had created a new and prosperous society modeled on the old but with a character and personality of its own shaped by their efforts and dreams for the future.

By 1747, the wealth of North Branford and Northford was in their agricultural production of wheat, corn and rye along with cherries and apples. Large orchards were planted and cider and brandy were produced in great quantities.[17] During the first few decades of the 18th century a series of cider mills, grist mills and saw mills were built along the streams and rivers of the settlements laying the basis for later industrial development that would take place 100 years later. Roads had been constructed to carry produce to Branford to be shipped to markets that linked the two villages to the rest of the English Colonies and the Caribbean. This trade also brought African slaves to the community and by 1800 it is estimated around 50 freed blacks and slaves lived in the villages.[18] It was during this time that the Todd family arrived in Northford when Stephen Todd of Wallingford bought the lot and cider mill from Joseph Bradfield that Milo would later inherit from his father.[19] Thus by the eve of the American Revolution, Northford had become a prosperous agricultural community connected to the greater world beyond New England through its produce and trade. The promise of a new and prosperous life that had first brought their fathers to the New Haven Colony and Branford had been fulfilled. Life for most was comfortable, stable, and predictable. Under the watchful eye of church, family, and the community at large, the future looked promising as well. But all that would change.

CHAPTER 4
"There but for the Grace of God, goes I"

—John Bradford (1510-1555)

Thelus Todd was a fortunate young man. All his life he had lived in the shadow of Totoket Mountain surrounded by family and friends and the security that God in his wisdom had placed him in a land of plenty and opportunity. He had grown to his 18th year convinced in the inevitability of his destiny and despite the 7th year of the War for Independence and all the heartache, chaos, and uncertainties it had brought to the hamlet of Northford, he still believed that his future, along with that of his fellow villagers, would be bright and promising. Having recently joined the ranks of the Connecticut Militia as his older brother Thaddeus had six years before, he was now proud to do his part in the struggle that had lasted almost a third of his life. As he stood on the parapet of Fort Griswold on the Groton side of Thames River and looked across to the bustling harbor of New London, he could not help but feel pangs of anxious anticipation.

If the rumors were true he thought as he shielded his eyes from the glare of the late afternoon sun, then how might he fare in a fight if the troops of the King did come. Would he hold as trained or run as some do when a green militia is first confronted by battle hardened regulars? Would he make his family and village proud as others had? He hoped that he would. As a member of the militia, Thelus, like all others who were called up to serve as needed by the State, had as his charge the defense of the coast from incursions *by the British who still held New York. British ships of war routinely prowled Long Island Sound like angry sharks waiting for an opportunity to strike at the privateers and shipping that snuck out of this harbor to raid and capture unwary British merchantmen on their way to New York to supply the King's troops. Talk was rife that the generals in New York had decided it was time to teach those Yankee thorns in New London a lesson and so here he was, called into active duty and on station since early August, eager to do his part.*

Driving north on Interstate 95 along the coast of Connecticut on the way to Providence, Boston and Maine, many on the road have no idea of the momentous and tragic events that took place on September 6, 1781 as they begin to climb the expansive Gold Star Memorial Bridge that spans the Thames River from New London to Groton. In size and height the bridge is impressive as it extends over 6000 feet across the estuary that is formed by the Thames River as it meets Long Island Sound. As one crosses the bridge, New London, founded by John Winthrop Jr. in 1646[1], the governor who secured the Charter for Connecticut in 1662, is to the right. As one travels to the center and highest point of the bridge, it is hard not to gaze to the right towards Groton on the east bank of the river.

That shore, dominated by the Electric Boat complex, where our nation's nuclear submarines have been built since the 1950's, is a jumble of industrial and commercial buildings. Nothing about the view is aesthetically pleasing or interesting except for the shipyard. But, on a hill above the hodgepodge of nondescript buildings, sits an Egyptian Obelisk made of Connecticut granite, all but lost in the clutter of 20th century ephemera. It stands as a ghostly guardian of memory for on a warm September morning in 1781, the King's soldiers did in fact come.

It is fitting that the massive bridge, the largest structure in Connecticut with its two parallel spans and eleven lanes that dominate the landscape dwarfing both the city of New London and Groton as it arches across the river, is named as it is. Opened in 1943 in the midst of World War II, the Gold Star name was an honorable tribute to the mothers of the state who had by then lost sons in that conflict. Did those who chose the name know that they were also honoring the mothers of 85 others who had given their lives in defense of their country 122 years earlier? Now over seventy years later, the Gold Star as the locals call it, is still a marvel of 20th century engineering. Its sheer size all but hides the deep water harbor it crosses and the two port communities that cradle it, now mostly unnoticed by the motorists who climb the span. Yet that harbor was the very reason the British chose to strike in 1781.

New London, like many New England coastal ports during the Revolutionary War, became a base of operation against English shipping coming to and from North America. Because the United States lacked a navy and the resources to build one to take on the most powerful navy of the time, the states, especially those from New England, turned to an age old tool of war, the privateer. Privateers were legally sanctioned private ships of various sizes and types that armed themselves and attacked merchant ships of the enemy. Carrying a Letter of Marque, a license from the state government to attack and seize enemy shipping, the goal of a privateer was to seize a ship and return with it to a safe harbor, sell the cargo and the ship, and make a tidy profit. It was legal piracy; highly risky considering the power and might of the British Navy, but incredibly lucrative for those who succeeded. During the course of the war, Connecticut sent out between 200 and 300 privateers and New London had become a premier harbor for those privateers with easy access to Long Island Sound and the Atlantic Ocean beyond.[2] Plus, if threatened, ships could slip up the Thames River to the town of Norwich where the river narrowed and enemy warships would run into a gauntlet of gun fire.

Throughout the long years of war, New London and its privateers had been frequently threatened either by rumor or the presence of Royal Navy patrols but never assaulted. Fort Trumbull, built on the New London side of the harbor just south of the town was a simple blockhouse with cannon facing towards the Thames River as it entered the Sound. Named in honor of Connecticut's wartime governor, John Trumbull, the fortification was still being built in 1781 and thus had no defenses on the land side. Across the harbor on the eastern side and a bit further north was Fort Griswold, sitting prominently on a hill above the town of Groton. From this vantage point, called Groton Heights, this completed fortification commanded both the harbor and the surrounding countryside. Built with both earth and stone, Griswold presented a formidable obstacle if attacked. In design, it was roughly a square with triangular bastions on each corner facing the river and another projecting from the center of the wall on the east side. A deep trench surrounded the walls on three sides; the north, east and south. The walls were actually a series of two with the lower outer wall made of earth and faced with stone, then topped with long cedar pickets or sharpened poles projecting at an angle from it. The taller inner wall was made of earth and had openings called embrasures for cannon.[3] Outside the northern end a v-shaped earthen mound protected the gate into the fort. Taken together, Forts Trumbull and Griswold were placed to defend the harbor and behind them, the residents felt relatively secure as both were routinely garrisoned with a small number of local and state militia members on a rotating basis. If attacked, the plan was that their garrisons were to be quickly supplemented by up to 2000 local militia members. Thelus Todd was at Fort Griswold as part of the militia rotation.

Why did the British decide to attack in September, 1781? According to 19th century historian Frances Caulkins, a number of factors came into play that determined the decision by Sir Henry Clinton, the British commander in New York, to order an attack to take place. New London privateers had become a serious irritant to British shipping and a large amount of goods and merchandise from the West Indies and Europe had been seized of late and brought to the warehouses there along with military supplies that helped keep American armies in the field. The *Hannah*, a merchant ship captured a little south of Long Island bound for New York from London was the real prize.[4] She had been captured by the *Minerva* and her cargo said to be the most valuable sent to America during the war, was seen by the British as an exasperating loss with a value of over $400,000.00.[5] The cargo included a large number of personal supplies for the British officers in New York, including those of Clinton himself. This affront, along with the considerable number of privateers present and operating from the port, seems to have been the trigger that launched the assault.

Apparently, New London was also targeted as a diversionary tactic to draw the Continental Army of George Washington, stationed outside of New York, away from a possible move towards Virginia where the British commander there, Lord Cornwallis, following his campaign through South and North Carolina had recently arrived. A strike against New London might also draw the French Army, under the Comte D'Rochambeu out of their base in Rhode Island and prevent a possible link-up with Washington.[6] The deep water harbor of New London if taken and held, might also serve as a launching point for an invasion of central New England and a base for an expected British flotilla scheduled to arrive the following spring.[7] Clinton had by 1781 established a policy of utilizing the resources of his navy to conduct lightening like surgical raids along the American coast and had recently dispatched former American general Benedict Arnold on a number of devastating raids along the Virginia coast and an attack on New London would certainly fit the pattern.[8]

Benedict Arnold, whose name today is synonymous with traitor, had been until September of 1780 a true American hero. Born and raised in Norwich, Connecticut, just up the Thames River from New London, Arnold had been a successful merchant, sending ships out into the Atlantic trade prior to the outbreak of war in 1775. After Lexington and Concord, he traveled to Boston to offer his services and quickly established himself as a vital and dynamic leader in the new Continental Army with the capture of Fort Ticonderoga in New York and his heroic actions in the ill-fated invasion of Canada in 1776. Here in Connecticut, he led the American effort in 1777 to repulse a major attack by the British in the western part of the state at the Battle of Ridgefield, inflicting heavy casualties on the enemy and discouraging further attacks there for the remainder of the war. Arnold is also credited with turning the tide in the Battle of Saratoga in up-state New York during the summer of that same year and for all intents and purposes thwarting the plans of the British to seize the Hudson Valley and cut New England off from the rest of the states. Up until then, Arnold's accomplishments were the stuff of legend. And he knew it.

So what happened? Despite all he had done for the American cause, Arnold was time and again overlooked for promotion and although he did obtain the rank of Major General, the Continental Congress routinely passed him over for a higher rank and post for those he considered lesser men. By 1778 he had come to resent how he was being treated, was in debt, and had fallen under the influence of his pro-British second wife, Peggy Shippen.[9] Adding to his frustration was his strong dislike of the French alliance the victory at Saratoga had helped to bring about. Unappreciated, disillusioned, and desperate, Benedict Arnold switched sides.

The story is still shocking. Having been assigned the post of commander of the important American fortress at West Point on the Hudson River, Arnold entered into secret negotiations to turn over the fort to the British. When his accomplice on the British side, Major Andre was captured with papers on him that revealed the plot, Arnold fled to the British in New York City and was quickly offered a position in the British Army. With the rank of Brigadier General, a position that had eluded him on the American side, he threw himself whole-heartedly into the fray in the service of his former enemies. And he was not alone. Many Americans had remained loyal to the King and were serving in the British Army in Loyalist units. Some of these units would play a significant role in the attack on New London and Groton Heights.

For Henry Clinton, Arnold was the logical choice to command the expedition against New London and strike at what he had termed a "Den of Serpents". Intimately familiar with the Long Island Sound, New London's harbor and the Thames River, Arnold knew the area in a way no British officer did and it would be a true test of the Norwich native's loyalty and commitment. One can only imagine what the conversation between Clinton and Arnold might have been like and what thoughts must have run through Arnold's mind when ordered to lead the expedition and prepare for an attack on his boyhood home and most certainly neighbors, friends and acquaintances. For Benedict Arnold it must have been the ultimate break with the land and people he had fought so hard to defend for six hard years. How lonely he must have felt knowing that his countrymen now held him in hatred and disgust and that this raid would only reinforce their enmity. And the British? Would they ever truly trust him?

Arnold's plan was to strike New London under cover of darkness, destroy the ships, warehouses, wharfs, public buildings, stores, and the forts on both sides of the river, then depart by morning before a sizable force of local militia could be assembled to confront his soldiers.[10] He knew both Forts Trumbull and Griswold were manned by a small number of militiamen so resistance he hoped would be minimal. This turned out to be true as both garrisons were seldom if ever full as most men capable of bearing arms were either already with the army and thus away, had signed on with privateers, or were home harvesting their crops.[11] The British expedition, consisting of a fleet of 32 ships and 1700 men, was assembled and moved slowly along the northern shore of Long Island coming to a halt just ten miles opposite the mouth of the Thames the evening of September 5th. Such a large force of ships must have been seen moving up the Sound by the local Sea Coast Guards of Connecticut who watched for and tracked British ship movements, but no warning was apparently sent to New London or if it was, it was dismissed as just another false alarm.[12] According to Frances Caulkins, so many false alarms and faints of attacks had been made during the course of the war by the British Navy that if word had been received of their presence, the news certainly did not raise any unusual precautions.[13]

For Arnold and the British however, once his force was assembled just off Long Island, all there was left was to wait for darkness and a favorable wind to carry the ships across the Sound. As the evening darkened, the nightly off-shore breeze began to carry the ships and transports across the ten miles of water but uncharacteristically, around 1:00 AM, it stopped and shifted from the north and the mouth of the River. This all but stranded the ships and left them to slowly struggle towards the Connecticut shore closing in on the mouth of the Thames around 9:00 AM, six hours later than planned.[14] The element of surprise had been lost. Yet Arnold proceeded with his two pronged attack, landing one part of his force on the New London side below Fort Trumbull near the light house about ½ mile from today's Ocean Beach then known as Brown's Gate.[15] This contingent, led by Arnold himself, was made up of British Regulars and American Loyalist units and a small group of Hessian mercenaries numbering all together around 900 men.[16] Their plan was to proceed to Fort Trumbull, neutralize it, and move on to the town to destroy the shipping and warehouses.

The second prong of Arnold's attack was on the Groton side of the Thames and landed near the tip of Avery Point. This force consisted of around 800 men under the command of Lt. Col. Edmund Eyre an experienced veteran of battles throughout North America and Europe. His force consisted of two regiments of British Regulars, a unit of New Jersey Loyalists, and Hessian mercenaries. Their plan was to quickly secure what they believed was the undermanned Fort Griswold and then halt any ships including privateers from fleeing up the Thames to Norwich by using the cannon captured in the fort as well as the artillery they had with them.[17]

By the light of dawn, the British transports making their way towards the west bank of the Thames had been seen and word was quickly sent to the defenders at Trumbull and Griswold. The overall commander of the defensive forces, Col. William Ledyard, ordered the customary alarm of two cannon to be fired from Fort Griswold. This was not only to alert the local residents of the impending attack, but to let those in outlying farms and villages, even people in Norwich, know of the need to send help. All in the region understood that the firing of two guns at fixed intervals was a call for assistance and if a third was added, it became a signal of celebration and that a victory had taken place or a captured prize was being brought into the harbor by one of the privateers. Evidently Arnold knew of this custom for he ordered a third gun to be fired from one of his warships thus negating the alarm and ensuring a delay to any aid arriving from beyond the two towns he was targeting.[18]

Col. Ledyard was in trouble and he knew it. Fort Trumbull was garrisoned by only 23 men under the command of New London native

Captain Adam Shapley and he had on hand at Fort Griswold only 150, far from the compliment of 300 men needed to properly defend it. [19] With the enemy upon them, he knew Shapley at least would be unable to hold as Trumbull was all but defenseless from the land side. New London was doomed. With the sound of the alarm guns, despite Arnold's third, the startled residents of New London and Groton awakened to the quickly spreading news of the assault and panic ensued as desperate citizens grabbed what they could from their homes and began to flee with their families. In her *History of New London*, Frances Caulkins sets the scene in her classic Victorian prose:

> "In the town, consternation and fright were suddenly let loose. No sooner were the terrible alarm guns heard, than the startled citizens, leaping from their beds, made to send their families and portable and most valuable goods. Throngs of women and children were dismissed into the fields and woods, some without food, and others with a piece of bread or a biscuit in their hands. Women laden with bags and pillow-cases, or driving a cow before them, with an infant in their arms, or perhaps on horseback with a bed under them, and various utensils dangling at the side; boys with stockings slung like wallets over their shoulders, containing the money, papers, and other small valuables of the family; carts laden with furniture; dogs and household animals, looking strange and panic-struck; pallid faces and trembling limbs—such were the scenes presented on all the roads leading into the country. Many of these groups wandered all day in the woods and at night found shelter in the scattered farmhouses and barns." [20]

As the British approached Fort Trumbull on the land side, Captain Shapley turned a canon to confront them, fired a round in defiance as had been directed by Col. Ledyard earlier in the morning, then spiked his guns and told his men to evacuate to the Groton side of the river. As the British soldiers charged the fort, Shapley and his men fled to the river and into several row boats to make their way across the Thames.[21] They were fired on by British ships by then in the Thames and a number were killed and wounded, the rest making it safely across.

Arnold's main force proceeded into the town and was divided in order to move into various parts of New London with the hope of meeting little resistance as they began the process of destroying designated targets. Some units were sent to destroy the warehouses along the wharves and to burn any ships found there. Other units were assigned to confront and eliminate any force that might appear in opposition and in the process raid the homes of known military and patriot leaders. Small groups of New Londoners did form and one gathered on a hill above the town and began to fire on the British before being driven off. One town resident, John Hempstead, later gave an account of his part in this action and how having been awakened by the alarm grabbed his musket and cartridge box and prepared to hurry to a pre-arranged meeting place. Upon leaping on his horse, he recalled "…after I got under way my wife called to me pretty loud. I stopt my hors and asked her what she wanted. Her answer was not to let me hear that you are shot in the back."[22] Since there was no designated leader, and many of the men were unarmed, their efforts were at best nothing more than an irritant for the raiding troops though individuals kept up a harassing fire throughout the time the British troops remained in the city.

As Arnold's troops began to move through the town, a unit of New Jersey Loyalists began to ransack houses as they proceeded towards the wharves despite being under sporadic fire from those militia and citizens who were able to offer some resistance. The plundering soon got out of hand as some homes were either accidently or purposely set on fire. The Loyalists had seized an American piece of artillery from a small battlement on a hill above New London called by the locals Fort Nonsense for its placement and viability, and brought it towards the wharves to use against the ships that were beginning to make their escape up the Thames. At first the fleeing vessels found their escape all but impossible due to a light wind blowing down from the north but just as the Loyalists set up the artillery piece to fire upon them the wind shifted and allowed many to set sail and escape to safer waters up the river.[23] They were fired at by British ships lower down the Thames but no pursuit was initiated undoubtedly because the plan had been for the ships to be fired upon if escaping by the guns of Fort Griswold once it had been taken. This did not happen as the assault on Griswold had not yet taken place.

As the British troops began to their work of firing the warehouses and ships still tied to the wharf, including the *Hannah*, which was set on fire and adrift, they soon moved to private homes and shops torching everything as they went.[24] The result was a great conflagration that before it was over consumed over 140 buildings; 65 homes, 31 stores and warehouses, 18 shops, 20 barns, 9 public buildings, and 12 ships.[25] While his troops were involved in their work, Arnold climbed to a high point within the town to get a view of Fort Griswold across the river. By then his forces on the other bank had not yet seized the fort and from his observation, he had surmised that it was being held by a greater force than he had hoped. Knowing that his objectives in New London were being met and that some of the shipping and privateers had by then escaped his grasp, he surmised that a potentially costly assault on Griswold would be pointless. He sent word to Col. Eyre to call off the assault.[26] But it was too late.

Eyre's force after landing at Avery Point, became entangled in a woods and swamp as they moved towards Griswold and thus their progress towards the fort was slowed by the difficulty his New Jersey Loyalists were having dragging their artillery through the muck and thickets.[27] By the time they did break through and arrived before the fort, the purpose of their assault had become moot. But not having yet received word from Arnold, Eyre moved his men into position deploying units to the south, east, and north in preparation for the assault. Col. Ledyard, in overall command at the fort had on hand 150 militiamen and citizen volunteers including those who had come across from Fort Trumbull. The majority were local Groton men who had responded to the initial alarm earlier that day or once the assault on New London had begun.[28]

Around noon, Col. Eyre sent a Captain Beckwith up to the fort to demand its unconditional surrender. Ledyard called a meeting with his officers and discussed their situation prior to sending an answer back with Beckwith. They understood they did not have a garrison on hand strong enough to repel an assault but felt they could hold out long enough for the hundreds of regional militia that would surely arrive in their relief.[29] Ledyard thus sent an answer to Beckwith, that they would not surrender. It turns out Ledyard was right about the militia, hundreds did in fact turn out. But, as they began to move towards the fort and its relief, the sight of the heavily armed British Regulars and Hessian mercenaries caused them to hesitate and remain hidden. They were unsure of what action they should take; some hoping that Ledyard's men would come out of the fort and join them in open combat against the British knowing that in such a battle all would be accorded rights under the rules of war and not be put to death if they survived. They all knew this would not be the case if they joined their comrades in the fort.[30] Some felt to take on such a well-trained and sizable force would be foolhardy and opted to wait and see. They remained hidden in the woods.

When told of Ledyard's response, a surprised Eyre sent word that if obliged to storm the fort, no quarter according to the laws of war would be given. Surely he must have felt, Ledyard understood his position was untenable. Col. Ledyard's final response to Eyre's message was: "We shall not surrender the fort, let the consequences be what they may".[31] With that, the fate of so many was sealed. The order to call off the assault had not yet arrived and as Eyre's men began to move forward, Arnold later said he feared another Bunker Hill where the British won the day but at a terrible cost.

As Eyre ordered the attack and as his troops moved forward on three sides, Ledyard told his men to hold their fire until the British were close, hoping to maximize the damage their volley might do. The British moved silently towards Griswold from the north, east, and south, like a scarlet wave bent on engulfing it. The only sound to shatter the quiet were the shouts of officers as the disciplined troops of the King wheeled into action, moving as one, eerily setting the stage for the ferocious chaos that was soon to overwhelm them and the defenders. A sudden booming roar of a sole Griswold canon broke the silence and sprayed the British line to the east with grape-shot that ripped a wide hole in their formation as twenty men fell. With that, the battle began.

The first British advance was checked by a withering fire from the fort yet goaded on by their officers they continued on despite their casualties. Col. Eyre fell mortally wounded while encouraging his men forward. In the words of one of Griswold's defenders, Stephen Hempstead, the first two assaults were "repulsed with great slaughter".[32] But the British, rallied twice by Major Montgomery who had assumed command, continued their charge for a third time. As he led his men up onto the walls, Montgomery met his end stabbed by one of the fort's two free African-American defenders, Jordan Freeman, who was himself quickly killed by the now enraged attackers.[33] While this assault was taking place, a tragic accident took place that would lead the British troops to believe they had been deceived by the fort's garrison. According to Hempstead, during this attack "a shot cut the halyards of the flag and it fell to the ground".[34] The British, thinking the flag had been lowered in surrender, surged forward only to be met by continued American fire.

This fourth assault overwhelmed the defenders as the British poured over the eastern and southern walls. A small group opened the gate to the fort and detachments of Regulars flooded in. To this point, the British had suffered a high number of casualties while the Americans but a few. But this was to change. On seeing the fort gate breached and the enemy flooding over two walls, Col. Ledyard made a fateful decision. While fighting was still continuing inside the fort, Ledyard realized that further resistance would be fruitless and gave the order to lay down arms and surrender Griswold to the enemy hoping to save the lives of his men. In his account of that moment, Stephen Hempstead described how upon hearing his Colonel's order "We did so, but they continued firing upon us… marching in and firing by platoons upon those who were retreating to the magazine and barrack-rooms for safety".

Hempstead then goes on to tell, in chilling detail, what happened next. The commander of the New Jersey Loyalists, Colonel Beckwith, cried out "who commands this garrison?" Ledyard, who was standing near Hempstead stepped forward to proclaim "I did sir, but you do now" offering the hilt of his sword with the point towards himself in a universal symbol of surrender.[36] At that instant, Hempstead says, he perceived a soldier about to bayonet him from behind. Weaponless, he turned to partially deflect the blow with his hand and was stabbed in the upper right hip just below the abdomen. Forced to the ground by the blow, the next thing Hempstead remembered was the sight of Colonel Ledyard lying beside him, having been run through the heart by his own sword.[37]

Another surviving witness, recounting the death of Ledyard in 1832, fifty one years later, adds dramatic flourish to the story. Thomas Hertell stated:

> "On entering the works the officer, on whom had devolved the command of the remnant of the British forces, demanded, "Who Commands this fort?" The gallant Col. Ledyard advancing answered, "Sir, I had that honor but now you have", and presented the hilt of his sword to the victor, who demanded, "Do you know the rules of war?" "Certainly", said Col. Ledyard. "Then", replied the savage victor, "You rebel, prepare for death", and immediately with Col. Ledyard's sword run him through the body."[38]

A general massacre then ensued as the angered British and Loyalist troops fell on their outnumbered and mostly unarmed foe. Another survivor, Rufus Avery, remembered how the British began to move through the parade ground of the fort firing by platoon into the defenseless Americans and freely bayoneting others. Avery stated "I believe there was not less than five or six hundred men of the enemy on the parade in the fort. They killed and wounded nearly every man in the fort as quick as they could, which was done in about one minute. I expected my time to come with the rest."[39] Miraculously, three attempts to bayonet him failed. Stephen Hempstead recounted how "…the bayonet was freely used even on those who were helplessly wounded and in the agonies of death."[40] As the maddened soldiers moved through the fort and into the barracks and magazine in the hunt for those taking shelter in them one British officer had seen enough and began to demand that the slaughter stop. According to another witness to the massacre, George Middleton, that one officer began to cry "Stop! Stop!" "In the name of heaven I say stop, my soul cannot bear it".[41] With that it was over.

Prior to those brutal moments inside Fort Griswold, the Americans had lost only six men and eighteen wounded. By the time the killing had ended, eighty-five in all lay dead and another thirty-five were wounded, many mortally. Forty were taken prisoner to New York, most according to Hempstead slightly wounded.[42] A handful of men had somehow escaped the chaos by scaling the wall and running towards the woods to the north and east. The British losses were high as well, of the 800 Eyre sent into the battle, 48 were killed and another 145 were wounded.[43]

What happened next is best described by the survivors. Stephen Hempstead explained how once the killing had ended the British soldiers began to "plunder us of everything we had, and left us literally naked." They moved those still alive, both wounded and not into a group in front of the barracks in the sun and left them there without water or medical attention for over an hour.[44] Rufus Avery, another survivor described what happened as well, stating: "They did not bayonet many after they ceased firing their guns. I was amongst them all the time, and they very soon left off killing, and then stripping and robbing the dead and wounded. They then ordered each one of us to march out to the northeast of the parade, and those that could not go themselves, from their wounds, were to be helped by those that were well. We poor prisoners were taken out on the parade, and every man ordered to sit down immediately, and if not obeyed at once the bayonet was to be put into him."[45]

The officer who had assumed command of the British forces at Griswold, Major Bromfield of the New Jersey Loyalists, decided to blow up the powder and munitions still in the magazine and thus felt it prudent to evacuate the fort and ordered the wounded to be moved. The American wounded were placed in an ammunition wagon to do so and thus began the final tragedy to befall the defenders of Fort Griswold.[46] Again those there best tell what occurred. Stephen Hempstead, one of the wounded placed in the ammunition wagon recalled: "Those that could stand were then paraded to the landing, while those who could not, of which I was one, were put in the ammunition wagons, and taken to the brow of the hill, which was very steep and at least 100 rods in descent, from which it was permitted to run down by itself, but was arrested in its course, near the river, by an apple tree." Hempstead went on to describe the experience: "The pain and anguish we all endured in this rapid descent, as the wagon jumped and jostled over rocks and holes, is inconceivable; and the jar in its arrest was like bursting the cords of life asunder, and caused us to shriek with almost supernatural force".[47]

Rufus Avery witnessed the wagon careen down the hill and had a bit of a different take on the incident. Avery recounted that as the British soldiers began to pull the wagon out of the fort, they reached the brow of the hill where they lost control of it. Avery said that "… they began to put themselves in a position to hold it back with all their power. They found it too much for them to do; they released their hold on the wagon as quick as possible to prevent being run over by the wagon themselves leaving it to run down the hill at great speed. It ran about twelve rods to a large apple-tree stump, and both shafts of the wagon struck very hard, and hurt the wounded men very much."[48] According to Avery, soldiers nearby came to the aid of those tossed from the wagon by the impact as well as those still inside and brought them to a nearby home, there those too hurt or wounded to take back to New York as prisoners were paroled.[49]

Hempstead recalled what occurred after the wagons tumult a bit differently. He said they were left in the wagon after its crash for about an hour before "our humane conquerors hunted us up when we were again paraded and laid on the beach, preparatory to embarkation". It was only through the intercession of Col. Ledyard's brother, Ebenezer Ledyard, that the British agreed to leave those too hurt behind and moved them to a neighboring house.[50] Hempstead was one left behind. Rufus Avery was taken to New York with the other 29 survivors of the battle and exchanged for British prisoners a number of days later.[51]

By mid to late afternoon Arnold's men began their withdrawal from both sides of the Thames as they began to embark on transports for waiting ships. They had buried their dead in Fort Griswold which had delayed the destruction of the powder magazine and had left the American bodies to be claimed by their families. New London, along with its wharves and shipping that had not escaped, was left in smoldering ashes. As a leaderless militia from surrounding towns began to gather on the outskirts of both communities, Fort Griswold was quickly left and the magazine never blown. The trail of gunpowder that was supposedly left to ignite the explosion was put out by either the blood soaked ground or a local person who bravely entered the fort to extinguish the flames.[52]

A fire however, had begun to engulf the barracks and as soon as the British had left for their ships residents and others began to approach the fort. According to Frances Caulkins, a Major Peters from Norwich managed to put out the flames and thus save the fire from eventually reaching the magazine and thus causing an explosion that surely would have destroyed the fort and all who lay there to be retrieved by their loved ones.[53] All that evening, family and friends came in search of those they feared lost. Here Caulkins described the scene: "Women and children assembled before the morning dawn, with torches in their hands, examining the dead and wounded in search of their friends. They passed the light from face to face, but so bloody and mangled were they—their features so distorted with the energy of resistance, or the convulsion of pain, that in many cases the wife could not identify her husband or the mother her son. When a mournful recognition did take place, piteous were the groans and lamentations that succeeded. Forty widows had been made that day, all residing near the scene of action. A woman, searching for her husband among the slain, cleansed the gore from more than thirty faces before she found the remains she sought."[54]

One can only begin to imagine what the dawn of September 7th brought residents of Groton and New London as they started to face the reality of what had befallen their communities. The disaster hung like a heavy fog on both sides of the Thames as the traumatized families returned to where their homes had once stood or came to the realization that a loved one was gone. Help from surrounding communities began to arrive as militia and citizens from as far away as Rhode Island came to lend what aid they could and prepare to thwart a possible return of the British; help too late to save New London or those who had fallen at Griswold. In time, Connecticut would make inquiries into why members of surrounding militias had not responded more effectively or in a more timely matter to assist against Arnold's attack on New London and the defense at Fort Griswold. Eventually, thirty eight militia commanders from surrounding communities would be court-martialed for their ineffective roles.[55]

As an old man and grandfather, Ebenezer can still remember that day as clearly as if he was still experiencing it and its terrible end. Even now he might cry out in the middle of the night and startle Martha awake and it was sixty years since. He was just a boy, fifteen and technically too young for the militia, but there was a need in Preston for members with so many gone and he was a good size for his age and strong as an ox his father would say, so he was admitted with the family thinking it would never come to him being in a fight.

But there he was, crouching with his neighbors and family members, his cousins Caleb and John, his uncle Martin and his brother Thomas, and all the others sheltered in the trees watching as the Redcoats formed their lines to the east of Griswold. "We could hit them now and get them running" whispered Ebenezer's uncle. "They would turn tail and run being caught between us and the fort. There must be near five hundred of us now, just look down in that ravine and over towards that knoll" he said with a growing sense of frustration. "I guess the captains know what they are doing".

Ebenezer could see their captain, Samuel Barnes huddling with the officers of the other militia units and it was clear that an argument was taking place. Some were gesturing while others, one could tell even from a distance, were animated in making their opinion heard. All this as the shouts of the British officers could be heard above the drums that were leading the enemy soldiers into position, flags flying and the sun glistening

Stories on the Trail of a Yankee Millwright

and reflecting off their bayonets like so many sparks of fire. Above all, what Ebenezer remembers, was the silence. It was ominous and smothering for it told of what was soon to follow. Except for the drums and the shouts of the officers, not a sound came from the wood where they lay waiting, the line of red moving between them and the fort and in the fort itself though one could see men moving into position on the battlement, they too were silent in anticipation. Yes, Ebenezer so often later would remember, it was the silence that was so profound and powerful.

As the King's soldiers formed their ranks and waited, it was clear that they waited only for the order to attack, but they waited what for Ebenezer even now thinking back was hours. "Why do they wait?" whispered John, newly married just this past month. "What holds them back?"

Martin responded, "Perhaps there is a negotiation taking place for there are hardly more than one hundred inside and they know they can't hold".

"But with our help they can" answered John who some said was too eager at times for a fight or an argument.

"Remember what the captain said when we first gathered this morning by the Meeting House" his uncle replied, if we fight while Ledyard and the boys still sit in Griswold then by the rules of war we too can be put to death as there will be no quarter but only death. That's what keeps us here with our tails between our legs and while Captain Barnes and the others sort it out".

No sooner had Martin finished when word came down the line, whispered man to man, that the militia was to hold and not engage and under no circumstances fire on the British. Ebenezer could feel the frustration and fear of those around him but he too though surprised by the order was relieved for he remembered thinking at that moment that he was surely going to die. Just then the smothering silence was abruptly broken by the roar of one of Griswold's cannon which it could be seen, cut through a line of Regulars as if a scythe on harvest day. With that the battle was joined as the first line of soldiers moved towards the outer wall of the fort and its sharpened pickets. They were quickly followed by a second line while and third held its position.

"Now" Ebenezer recalled his cousin had shouted, hoping to move them all forward in an assault that would stun the British line and win the day.

"John, its best you close that mouth of yours or you might be shot for disobeying orders" Martin responded sternly. He had fought the British before on Long Island in the defense of New York early in the war and knew how lack of discipline among some troops had helped to lose the day. "We wait".

The firing from the fort and those attacking seemed to go on forever though reality was Ebenezer remembered, it was over so quickly despite the fact that the first assaults were turned back by Ledyard and his men. But suddenly it ended as the fort's colors were lowered in a signal of surrender just as the King's troops flowed over the walls like a wave crashing over rocks in a storm. Paralyzed by this sudden turn of events, Ebenezer realized the gathered militia and its leaders knew not how to react and it is clear now through the luxury of time they fully anticipated to see Ledyard and the defenders marched out as prisoners of war. But it became clear something horrifying was taking place instead.

A repeated firing of volleys took place inside and shouting and screaming could be heard. Up and down the militia line "no quarter" was murmured as it became understood what was happening. "We must do something" said some while others began to softly pray.

"Hold men" the colonel from Norwich was heard to say, "For there is nothing now we can do for those boys now unless dying yourself is on your mind."

"Or killing those bastards" said John to the consternation of his uncle.

Then in an instant it was quiet except for an occasional order shouted from within Griswold. It was an eternity it seemed until the King's own began to march out of the fort and a small line of surviving defenders now prisoners joined them. Then a wagon full of men clearly wounded followed and soon it was obvious that the British had returned to their ships but not before the last few ran from the gate and the smell of burning powder drifted towards the woods.

"They're to blow the magazine" Martin cried out and before he could stop me, Ebenezer still proudly recalls, I ran towards the fort intent on stopping the line of flaming powder from reaching the precious stores of ammunition and destroying the fort. It was only after I had stopped the flame by breaking the line of powder with my foot that I actually saw what had happened inside

Griswold. Bodies were everywhere, grisly and mangled, bloody and many stripped near naked. Most lay where they had been killed and to this day it is this that haunts me. A scene from hell and we could have stopped it. John was right. So I still wake in the night; all those dead and the shame of it.

The raid, one of the last chapters in the American War for Independence, was for the British a questionable victory. Though partially successful in their effort to strike at the privateer base of New London, it had come at a high cost with over 200 casualties. It failed to turn Washington and Rochambeu away from their march to Virginia and the eventual surrender of the British at Yorktown a month later. For all intents and purposes, the war would soon draw to a close though American independence would not be recognized by the British government until almost two years later in 1783. New London and Groton would recover and become by the start of the 19th century one of the nation's leading whaling, fishing, and ship-building ports bringing with it a level of prosperity that would propel them well into the 20th century. But the citizens of New London and Groton would never forget the events of that fateful day when the soldiers of the King did arrive. On the first anniversary of the raid, they marked the occasion with solemn tributes and ceremonies which would continue yearly well into the next century. By 1830, through a subscription lottery, money was raised for a permanent monument to be erected at Fort Griswold to memorialize those who had fought and fallen there. In 1881, a centennial celebration lasting days complete with patriotic orations, poetry, and music marked Arnold's raid and the Battle of Groton Heights. By then, one hundred years later, both had entered the realm of myth, memory, and nostalgic patriotism. The local community continued to honor the memory by preserving the fort site and in 1953 Fort Griswold became a Connecticut State Park. Today, Fort Griswold State Park is open seasonally and the fort, memorial, and story of what happened on September 6, 1781 are maintained by the Connecticut Department of Energy and Environmental Protection (DEEP).[56]

But what of Thelus Todd?

CHAPTER 5
Myths through Time

Thelus Todd was indeed a fortunate young man. According to family lore, while serving with Colonel Ledyard at New London and Groton Heights as part of his militia rotation, he began to suffer from an unspecified illness after six weeks. Two days before Arnold's assault, he was sent home on a medical furlough and more than likely arrived back in Northford the day of the attack. Call it fate, chance, or luck; Thelus had avoided what more than likely would have been his death and though circumstance had spared him, one cannot avoid thinking that the impact of the tragedy of Groton Heights would shadow and influence the rest of his life.

How might he have felt when news of the massacre at Fort Griswold arrived at his sickbed one can only imagine. Thelus certainly must have grieved the loss of his comrades but did he feel the guilt a survivor often feels carrying the burden of the deaths of others while he still lived? Was Thelus angry? Was he relieved? How did his family and neighbors react? These answers we will never know. But this we do know; Thelus went on to marry, have a family, and live a long, productive, and prosperous life. He would live to see his grandchildren, Milo among them.

In 1890, amidst the flush of patriotic and nostalgic nationalism that accompanied the cultural movement known as Colonial Revival in the United States, *The National Society of Daughters of the American Revolution* was founded and an early chapter was started in Connecticut.[1]

Organized by women who were the daughters and granddaughters of men who fought in the Revolution, the society was dedicated to keeping the memory and lessons of their struggles alive for future generations. The Daughters viewed the role their fathers played in the Revolution through the distance of years and hoped to keep alive the meaning and remembrance of their sacrifice and to offer it as a template of patriotic virtue to a nation they saw as being engulfed by immigrants with no connection to their shared and hallowed past. In the introduction to the 1904 book about the Connecticut Chapter of the D.A.R., *Chapter Sketches: Connecticut Daughters of the American Revolution: Patriot's Daughters*, Rose E. Cleveland wrote about the importance of keeping the memory of the Revolution alive. Cleveland said that "There never was anything more worthwhile than the American Revolution; and there is nothing more worthwhile than the realizing of it, in all its unending consequence, and realizing it all the time".[2] One of the founding members of the Connecticut and the Meriden, Connecticut Chapters was the daughter of Thelus Todd, Mary Todd Hall. Her story and that of Thelus were included in *Chapter Sketches*.

Looking through *Chapter Sketches*, it is clear that the book was designed to help those now removed by more than 120 years to remember the individual sacrifices and accomplishments of those who had fought to protect their homes and secure American independence. In doing so the women of the Connecticut chapter hoped to foster for the reader a personal connection with the past and keep the memory of their fathers alive. They must have sensed that the lessons of the Revolution were fading with the years and hoped, just like those who celebrated the centennial of the Battle of Groton Heights, that they might be relearned by the present generation. How many residents of Connecticut, Groton, or Northford are today aware of how the struggles and sacrifices of their predecessors helped shape our today? Many certainly can recite general facts about the Revolution; they may know about Yorktown, Lexington and Concord, or George Washington. But does what happened locally matter?

STORIES ON THE TRAIL OF A YANKEE MILLWRIGHT

What if there had never been a Revolution or the British had seized New London and used it as a base to subjugate New England? What if those who had fallen at Groton Heights, both American and British, had lived instead? What would have been their contributions to society? Might there have been a great inventor, composer, or poet among them? Would one have become a leader of his people? And what of the children they never had? We will never know. What may seem to us from the vantage of time, a minor yet tragic incident in the struggle between nations, has in reality been truly life altering for every generation that has followed including our own.

Our sense of the past is shaped by our level of awareness and *The Daughters of the American Revolution* were determined to rekindle an awareness of the values that they had come to believe their fathers had in some cases died for. For the *Daughters*, these were the values that shaped their America and their sense of the past was captured in *Chapter Sketches*. Each Patriot's Daughter is raised on a pedestal along with their father as paragons of those virtues they hoped to convey. Mary Todd Hall was no exception. In telling the story of father and daughter, their legitimate Puritan pedigree is described along with the courageous role of the Patriot father in saving our nation.

In *Chapter Sketches*, the Todd story begins with the telling of how Thelus served with Colonel Ledyard at Fort Griswold prior Arnold's assault and how taking ill, he was sent home just before the raid. Nothing more is said about his service.[3] Next is an account explaining that Thelus was the son of Jonah Todd and a descendant of Christopher Todd who came first to Boston in 1637 and then settled in New Haven in 1638 as one that planation's original members. Pedigree established.

Jonah Todd was a goldsmith in New Haven and thus a highly skilled and relatively wealthy artisan who during the war served the revolutionary cause by making gunlocks. In this work Jonah was assisted by his youngest son Thelus until he came of the age to serve in the militia.[4] Mrs. Hall, the account goes on to say, remembered as a young girl going to the shop of her grandfather and hearing of the work done there during the war thus creating a personal connection to that noble effort. The Todd contribution to the struggle for independence continues with a mention of Jonah's two older sons, both unnamed, and how they had enlisted early in the war and worked as artificers until its end. An artificer in the 18th century was an inventor of sorts whose skills in metallurgy allowed them to create tools or devices to serve a specific purpose. One helped to forge the huge iron chain that was strung across the Hudson River below West Point to prevent the passage of British Warships.[5] The omission of the names of these two brothers of Thelus is interesting. Do they not fit the image of the patriot hero? In all this however, we have come full circle: New Haven, West Point, Benedict Arnold, and Fort Griswold. The past is often a web of connections.

The past can sometimes also get lost in the telling and can at times be interpreted or manipulated by those of the present to convey a message suited to their needs. The facts can be blurred, the story repackaged, and lessons reshaped over time. This often happens when oral history is passed down from generation to generation and the story of Thelus Todd I fear, was an example of just such a tale. I first came across his story while researching Milo Todd's mill site with a reference to his furlough from Fort Griswold mentioned in the *History of North Branford and Northford*.[6] But that was it. Unfortunately militia records from the period are not always reliable or complete and I could not find Thelus on the roles of either active members of the militia during the war or later as a State or Federal pensioner. I did find numerous references to his older brother Thaddeus as both a militia member and a pensioner, but no Thelus. It was a bit perplexing. Yet there was the reference to his service in the *Chapter Sketches*. Was this, I began to think, the fanciful recollections of an elderly matron caught up in the patriotic zeal of the Colonial Revival?

 Further research turned up few other clues, but eventually another account, most surely based on family tradition, came to light while researching Milo's later life. A reference to the service at Fort Griswold and furlough of Thelus in *The Year Book of the Connecticut Society of the*

Stories on the Trail of a Yankee Millwright

Sons of the American Revolution was part of the biographical material that accompanied Milo's admission into the Society in 1896.[7] This document went on to say that Thelus was later discharged at the end of the war. Like that of Mary Todd Hall, Milo's aunt, this account was also based on family tradition. I still needed proof.

One of the things about the past is if you keep looking, something will eventually turn up and for me and the Todd family, it finally did. In records found on line of Revolutionary War pension applications I discovered through the National Archives mention of Thelus Todd's service. A fellow militia member of Thelus, Wait Munson of Wallingford, Connecticut had applied for a pension from the State of Connecticut in 1835. His testimony on behalf of his friend was the following:

> "I Thelus Todd of the town of Wallingford 72 years, depose and saith that Wait Munson of Wallingford in said New Haven County now a resident in Barkhamsted in Litchfield County in sd state was drafted as a soldier three months tour to serve in the Revolutionary War at New London and did serve with me and was discharged according to law. I was served under Capt. Bryant and Lt. Bunnell in the year 1779 or 1780 in the same company and regiment that Wait Munson served in." Wallingford, March 5, 1835

This testimony, though proof of Todd's service in the militia, raised a number of questions. In it he states he is a resident of Wallingford, a town directly to the west of Northford. Also, he states his time of service in the militia to be 1779 or 1780, not 1781 when the Battle of Groton Heights took place. Records clearly show that Thelus never applied for a pension as a veteran from either Connecticut or the United States. His grandson's application to join *The Sons of the Revolution* along with the testimony above state that Thelus did enroll in the militia from Wallingford, and not Northford.[8] It also turns out that the Todd family did own considerable tracts of land in Wallingford and may have at that time claimed it as their primary residence. But what of the discrepancy in the dates of service? Based on his testimony in 1835, Todd did in fact serve in the militia but not at New London in 1781. A listing of those who died in the battle by the *Connecticut Gazette*, September 21, 1781 revealed that there were only 2 casualties from outside of the immediate Groton-New London area. The newspaper listed 59 men from Groton, 14 from New London, 3 from Stonington, 1 from Preston, and 2 negroes. The only men to have died at the fort from beyond the region were two from Long Island.[9] Clearly, there is no evidence here of the presence of militia from beyond the immediate area. According to Jonathan Lincoln, the Park Manager for Fort Griswold State Park, there were no out of the region militia members stationed at the fort prior to the British attack.[10]

Was the story of his chance sickness and thus rescue from possible death on September 6, 1781 a fabrication created over time to enhance the family prestige during the 19th century? Was Milo simply following the lead of his aunt? By 1896 Milo was working in the insurance industry in Hartford and a family link through his grandfather to the Revolution and Fort Griswold could only have furthered his ambitions in an increasingly class and ethnicity conscious industry and culture. It seems we may never know the true story.

But does it matter? In many ways, no. But once again, the tale of Thelus Todd and Fort Griswold shows how though facts do matter, the reality created by their fabrication, manipulation, or maybe just their absence does as well. Regardless, the myth or legend of Thelus Todd and Arnold's assault now live in the realm of our collective awareness of the past. They both carry the burden of our understanding of who we are.

Another example of how the past and our view of it can change over time is the story of the soldier credited with the slaying of the British officer, Major Montgomery, on the walls of Fort Griswold, Jordan Freeman. A free black man according to most accounts, Freeman was the "body servant" of Colonel Ledyard and thus at the fort in that capacity. His presence there, along with another American of African descent Lambert Latham, raise some interesting questions about race, slavery, the Revolution, and our ability or in some cases inability to deal with

Stories on the Trail of a Yankee Millwright

these issues when looking back at our history.

Both Freeman and Latham had spent a good part of their lives as what was then called "servants". The term goes to the very heart of the reluctance of New Englanders, especially during the 19th and 20th Centuries, to recognize or acknowledge the fact that many prominent individuals and families had slaves as far back as the 1630's. Somehow the label servant sounds so much more palatable than slave. When both men fought and died at Fort Griswold however, Jordan Freeman did so as a free man but it is not clear whether Lambert Latham was. In all likelihood not. The story of these two men also reveals how over the years since their deaths our view towards race, slavery, and their meaning has evolved.

What first piqued my curiosity about these two men was the story of the death of the British Major Montgomery. In most modern accounts, Jordan Freeman is given either the credit or partial credit for the act. Why the discrepancies? Eye witness accounts are also conflicted. Adding to the mystery is the fact that a monument with a brass plaque depicting Freeman stabbing Montgomery with a long spear-like weapon called a pike has been placed on a stone at the approximate spot where Montgomery died. On the plaque is inscribed "The death of Major William Montgomery while leading the British attack on the fort at this point".[11] Furthermore, Freeman is shown dramatically stabbing the Major, while another militiaman kneels and fires his musket and a second is poised to climb up to confront the enemy. Three British soldiers are seen behind Montgomery. There is no mention of Jordan Freeman though his depiction does appear to portray a man of African ethnicity. The plaque led to another question—was the monument placed to honor the death of the British Major? When was the monument placed in the fort and who commissioned it? More important, it clearly recognizes the heroic act of Freeman, yet why is he not acknowledged?

The story of Jordan Freeman and Lambert Latham is as old as that of New England. Most Americans today do not associate slavery with New England but in countless ways, slavery and links to that institution were just as important to the region during the 18th and early 19th centuries as it was to the American South. In their comprehensive study of slavery in Connecticut titled *Complicity*, *The Hartford Courant* on September 29, 2002 published the story of slavery in Connecticut and made it for the first time known to the general public. In *Complicity*, it is detailed as to how slavery played a major role in the development of first the Colony of Connecticut and later the State, leading up to the War Between the States in 1861.[12] In *Complicity* it is explained how slavery helped build Connecticut and how the institution played an important role in creating its general prosperity during the Colonial Era and after, where slaves were located within the state including a town by town inventory, the importance of slavery within the economy, and the cultural impact of the institution including the rise of the abolitionist movement, and slavery's lasting legacy. When published, *Complicity* was a powerful shock to many of the popular notion that slavery had been a Southern issue settled nobly by Abraham Lincoln, the Northern States, and the Civil War.

Within the first decade of the 17th century English colonization of Connecticut, slavery was a fact of life. It had become common in the European colonies in the Caribbean, Central, and South America since the 16th century as a handy solution to the chronic problem of enough labor to produce the sugar or other commodities that generated tremendous wealth for European overlords. By the late 17th century, following the Pequot War (1637) and then King Philip's War (1675-8), thousands of Native Americans in Connecticut and the other English Colonies of Southern New England were enslaved in retribution by the victors. According to Professor Margaret Newell from Ohio State University in an article on the subject in *Complicity*, it was all but impossible to travel through New England at the time without finding Native men, women, and children working as farm laborers or domestic servants.[13] Having defeated those they saw as savages, the Puritans saw little reason not to enslave the survivors of both devastating wars and in the process save their souls through the civilizing mission of Christianity and the English way of life. The existence of this system of Native enslavement made the transition to African slavery all the more easier.

Stories on the Trail of a Yankee Millwright

For many of the wealthier Connecticut colonists, the possession of a slave or two, besides solving the problem of a consistent labor shortage, also was a formidable status symbol. House "servants" and field "hands" became the norm for many as the 18th century progressed and by the time of the first census of the United States in 1790, there were 2,648 slaves listed in Connecticut.[14] Slave numbers were broken down by town and county, by the name of the owner, and by the number of slaves owned. It is interesting to note however, that the total number of slaves in Connecticut by then had dropped by over half when compared to a list compiled from the *Public Records of the Colony of Connecticut* in 1774 in a 1999 doctoral dissertation by Guocun Yang. Then the number of people held as slaves was 5,101.[15] In 1774, during the life time of Jordan Freeman and Lambert Latham, the three communities with the greatest number of slaves were New London with 316, New Haven 262, and Norwich with 234. Groton had 174 making the triangle formed by New London, Norwich, and Groton along the Thames River the largest concentration of slaves in the colony.[16]

The reasons for the growth in African slavery in Connecticut during the 18th century were a complex mix of cultural, religious, and economic factors but the main driving force was the colony's economic connection to the system of trade establish by the British during the 17th and 18th Centuries. An intricate network of exchange between the British Isles, the Caribbean, Africa, and the American Colonies created an opportunity for industrious Connecticut farmers and merchants to lock themselves into that system bringing with it a level of unprecedented prosperity. As part of the Triangle Trade of molasses, rum, and slaves that operated between New England, the Caribbean, and Africa, Connecticut prospered by providing food crops and livestock to the sugar colonies of the Caribbean, brought molasses back home to process into rum, and then traded that liquor in Africa for slaves to feed the constant demand for labor on the sugar plantations.[17] According to his article in *Complicity* titled "The Plantation Next Door," Joel Lang points out that Connecticut's trade with the colonies of the West Indies was so great that for a while after the Revolution, it was double that of

Boston's.[18] What port was in the center of it all? New London. Jordan Freeman and Lambert Latham were part of that system.

Recent archeological and archival work in New London County has revealed that like some areas in neighboring Rhode Island, large farms or plantations worked by gangs of slaves were quite prevalent. In "The Plantation Next Door," Lang documents the research done by archeologists Jerry Sawyer and Warren Perry in what is now Salem, Connecticut, just north of Norwich and New London, of a large plantation of 4,000 acres owned by the Browne family beginning in the early 17th century and how it was worked extensively by large numbers of African slaves, some accounts have put the number at sixty slave families.[19] It turns out this plantation system was relatively common for the region, producing the food needed to feed the slave labor in the Caribbean that could be shipped directly out of New London and Norwich.

The number of slaves in Connecticut peaked during the 1770's and with independence from Great Britain a gradual end to the institution in the state began. In 1784, the State passed a gradual emancipation act that began the process, allowing black and mixed race children born into slavery after March 1st of that year to be freed at age 25. Three years later, in 1787, the legislature voted to extend the slave trade in Connecticut for another 20 years then abruptly in 1788, there appears to have been a change in attitude. The importation into the state of African slaves was prohibited and fines were set for slave trading or forcibly removing freed blacks or Native Americans from the state.[20] However, slavery as an institution remained well into the 19th century until Connecticut, in 1848, became the last New England state to outlaw the practice. This act did have a codicil however, it freed all slaves except those 64 years old or older.[21] Obviously, this was seen as a gesture of kindness.

Connecticut by then had emancipated the majority of its slaves partly due to the efforts of abolitionists who pushed the State and Federal governments to end the practice and the simple truth that the institution was no longer economically practical. By 1848, Connecticut had become one of the leading centers of the burgeoning Industrial Revolution and throughout the state textile mills popped up along streams and rivers

Stories on the Trail of a Yankee Millwright

first spinning wool into thread and fabric, but quickly changing to the abundant amount of cotton imported from the slave worked plantations and farms of the American South. As a result, during this period of rapid industrialization, the number of slaves in the United States grew to 1.5 million in 1820 and 3.9 million in 1860, all feeding the insatiable desire of Connecticut and other New England textile mills for more cotton.[22] Connecticut may have freed her slaves, but her mills kept the institution viable and growing elsewhere. It is ironic that a state that now prides itself, and justifiably so, for fighting mightily to end slavery in the United States had been so intricately and intimately responsible for a good amount of its explosive growth prior to the Civil War.

Jordan Freeman and Lambert Latham were the descendants of Africans brought to Connecticut earlier in the 18th century. Freeman was born into slavery in 1732, the third son a slave named Oxford and Temperance, a biracial woman.[23] The parentage of Temperance is unknown, though intermarriage between Africans and Native Americans in Southeastern Connecticut was common. Both his parents were "servants" of Richard Lord of Lyme, Connecticut just to the west of New London. Freeman was eventually sold to John Ledyard of New London and in 1755, while still a slave, married Lilly, a servant of a woman from New London. Ownership of Freeman then was passed on to Ledyard's son, Colonel William Ledyard who made him his "body servant" or personal valet.[24] Apparently prior to the Revolution, Ledyard freed Jordan Freeman and from that point on employed him as his valet. Most accounts state that there was a strong bond of friendship between the two and that Freeman voluntarily went to Fort Griswold with his employer.

Less is known about Lambert Latham though all sources state he was a servant of a Captain William Latham of Groton and was most likely not a free man as Jordan Freeman was. Lambert, or Lambo as he was also known by, obviously carried the last name of his master, a standard practice when naming slaves. According to an account first published in an abolitionist pamphlet called *The Colored Patriots of the Revolution* in 1855, William Anderson of New London, whose grandmother was the sister of Lambert, witnessed the seventy second anniversary ceremony of the Battle of Groton Heights at which there was no mention of his great uncle or Jordan Freeman. Dismayed by the omission, Anderson wrote an account of what he understood to be the contribution of his great uncle and Freeman.

According to Anderson, on the morning of the attack Lambert was in a field tending cattle with Captain Latham when the alarm sounded and was told to return the cattle to the barn while his master returned to the house. Once the cattle had been secured, Lambert went to the house and from there to the fort having been told by Mrs. Latham that Captain Latham had since left to join his comrades there. Lambert left for the fort and joined his owner just before the British assault.[25] Other accounts vary as to where and what Lambert did before arriving at Fort Griswold, most saying that he helped the family of the Captain get to safety and upon completing that task, grabbed a musket and hurried to help repel the attack.[26] Tradition in the Latham family states that Lambert fought valiantly by his master's side rapidly loading and firing his musket despite the fact that he suffered a severe wound to his hand and was praised for his effort by Captain Latham who said "stick to 'em, Lambo". Lambert supposedly replied "Yes massa, kill 'em every time".[27]

Here is where things get interesting. According to Anderson, Lambert had survived the British assault on Griswold and was near Colonel Ledyard when he made his gesture of surrender to the British officer, Major Bromfield. What happened next is not in any other accounts of the death of Colonel Ledyard and speaks to the reality of race relations at the time and after. Anderson states that as soon as Ledyard offered his sword to Bromfield and was stabbed in the heart with it, Lambert thrust his bayonet into the officer. He was then immediately killed by enraged British soldiers, suffering thirty three bayonet wounds and thus, in the words of his nephew, "fell nobly avenging the death of his commander". William Anderson then attested that this information had been given to him by two survivors of the battle.[28] Here he was, the man who avenged the cold blooded killing of the heroic Ledyard, and hardly a mention. Interesting. As attitudes towards race have changed in the late 20th century, research has righted this wrong and Lambert Latham now has his place in the pantheon of patriots.

The heroic role Jordan Freeman played in the battle is also now recognized as well and as the servant of Colonel Ledyard, his story has always been more known. By the start of the 20th century, his act of stabbing Major Montgomery was generally acknowledged and in 1911, when the memorial stone and plaque were placed on the wall of the fort, it was clear through its depiction that Freeman was responsible. However, did he act alone or was the killing of Montgomery also committed by another as so many of the 18th and 19th century sources claim? Stephen Hempstead, one of the survivors of the battle and massacre, does not mention Jordan Freeman at all and gives credit of the slaying of Montgomery to Captain Shapley who had led his men to Fort Griswold following the evacuation of Fort Trumbull. Another witness to the battle, George Middleton stated that Freeman and Captain Shapley together speared the Major[30] while Benedict Arnold in his report to General Clinton noted that he was killed by Jordan Freeman and a lieutenant named Henry Williams.[31] If there is mention of Freeman's death, it is that he died quickly afterward by bayonet.[32]

In 1826 the State of Connecticut and local committees began the process of erecting the memorial to those who fought and died in the battle and the first rendition of the obelisk was commissioned and dedicated in 1830. On the monument is a list of the men who fell at the fort and on the very bottom of the list, after a substantial space, are listed the names of the two colored soldiers; Jordan Freeman and "Sambo" Latham. The placement of the names of these two men who gave their lives just as their white brethren in a separate space and designation says volumes about the attitude of the white majority in Connecticut at the time. 1830 was during the height of slavery in America and slaves still were common, though decreasingly so, in Connecticut. African-Americans like Jordan Freeman, though free, were discriminated against and marginalized in society. To list Latham and Freeman together with the others was simply unthinkable and beyond any acceptable societal norm. Even the fact that Lambert's name would be listed as "Sambo" instead of his nickname Lambo was completely acceptable at the time since Sambo in the 19th century was a common derogatory name for African Americans, both slave and free.

The 19th century abolitionist Parker Pillsbury, wrote to his fellow abolitionist William Cooper Nell in indignation over the treatment of Freeman and Latham on the monument in 1851. In his letter he wrote of their placement on the monument saying:

> "It is difficult to say why. They were not the last in the fight. When Major Montgomery was lifted upon the walls of the fort by his soldiers, flourishing his sword and calling on them to follow him, Jordan Freeman received him on the point of a pike, and pinned him dead to the earth. And the name of Jordan Freeman stands away down, last on the list of heroes, perhaps the greatest of them all."
>
> "Yours with becoming indignation, Parker Pillsbury."[33]

It is interesting to note that by the last decade before a Civil War that would tear the United States apart, those that were working hard to bring slavery to an end had begun to look for and find examples of African American patriots to use in their cause. If abolitionists had their way, Latham and Freeman would not to be forgotten.

As previously noted, William Anderson, the relative of Lambert Latham attended the seventy second anniversary of the battle in 1853 and his reaction to the treatment of his great uncle and Jordan Freeman was quickly taken up by the abolitionists in their cause to end slavery. This was the start of the effort to bring about an acknowledgement long overdue. Throughout the second half of the 19th century as Connecticut and the United States began to settle into the era of racial segregation that followed the Civil War and Reconstruction, the centennial of the Battle of Groton Heights was celebrated and the monument was added to and rededicated. Once again, there was no mention Freeman and Lambert as the cultural and societal landscape would never have allowed it. But times and attitudes were changing. In 1911, Connecticut, a local organization called the Fort Griswold Commission, and the Anna Warner Bailey Chapter of the Daughters of the Revolution erected the Memorial Gates that now grace the entrance to Fort Griswold. A series of plaques honoring those who fought in the battle were commissioned and placed on them. Also on the wall, where tradition said Montgomery fell, was placed the memorial boulder and plaque showing Jordan Freeman in the act of stabbing the Major.[35] Connecticut it appeared, was almost ready to place Jordan Freeman and Lambert Latham in with the other heroes they were continuing to honor.

When I asked Jonathan Lincoln, the Park Manager, why the stone and plaque but no mention of Freeman by name, he reminded me of the level of prejudice that still existed in 1911 among many state residents. It was, he said, significant that the depiction of Jordan Freeman, as prominent as it is, was incorporated onto the memorial. But to place his name on it, might have been seen as too much. Thus the inscription about the death of Major Montgomery as if the memorial was for him.[36] When it came to wrestling with the legacy of slavery and racism in Connecticut, it was sadly all about baby steps. Now, at the start of the 21st century, the story of Jordan Freeman and Lambo Latham has been fully integrated into the narrative of the Battle of Groton Heights. It has taken almost another 100 years, but their story is now our story as well.

"So much sorrow" William reflected as he stood to the side of the large ceremonial gathering, listening to the grand orations of the dignitaries gathered to honor the fallen heroes of Griswold. Here it was 1853 and despite all the years that had passed, the events of that terrible day were still a raw and painful memory for the communities of Groton and New London and he appreciated and understood both the sorrow and expressions of pride that surrounded and humanized the events marking the anniversary.

Yet for William, there was a hollow feeling and even a bitterness in his heart as well that he knew no others gathered on the heights under the shadow of the grand sandstone monument overlooking Groton, the harbor and New London to the west could experience or understand. Here he was, the grand-nephew of one who died heroically within these walls, perhaps even valiantly, and his name along with the other colored man, Jordan Freeman, was not even an afterthought. And here he was, separated off to the side in order not to stand with and mix with those whites honoring their patriot dead. Seventy two years Anderson thought to himself, had anything changed?

William surveyed the crowd gathered and recognized in it those who supported abolition, those that did not, and those who did not care one way or the other. After all, though experiencing prosperous times, the two communities snug along the Thames were still small towns and everyone knew everyone else. As a free colored man with an education, Anderson knew that the issue of slavery was beginning to tear the country apart and he wondered if slavery did end would free men like himself ever be accepted as equals in a place like this or anywhere for that matter? He faced prejudice and discrimination on a daily basis as he worked in Hempstead's store as a clerk or as he went about his everyday routines. He had his doubts.

As the speeches and readings drew to an end, it was announced that in solemn tribute to those who had died so gloriously in the cause of freedom, their names would each be read followed by prayer to the Almighty and a moment of silence. "I wonder if this is the time uncle Lambert's name will be among them" thought William knowing full well the answer to his question. He had grown up hearing the story of his uncle's heroic role in the fighting at Fort Griswold and his valiant slaying of the British officer who killed Colonel Ledyard. His grandmother had told the story over and over saying "lest we forget". As an adult, he was determined not to and even ten years ago he had talked with two old veterans who had survived the massacre in Griswold who verified his grandmother's account. Yet, when he approached the planning committee for this anniversary occasion he was politely but sternly rebuffed.

As the last of the speaker ended his eloquent oration and the reading of the names of the dead was about to begin, William had a sudden urge to yell out— "but wait!". But he didn't and he felt an anger well up inside him not just for the continued injustice heaped upon his uncle Lambert and Jordan Freeman, but anger at himself as well for not having the courage to speak out and say what needed to be said.

CHAPTER 6
The Athens of Connecticut

When my good friend and Northford historian Gordon Miller threw himself into the study of his village's past, he did so with a gusto and enthusiasm that clearly showed his pride of place. To Gordon, there was no better place to be from or part of than Northford and he attacked his research as only a man on a mission of joyous discovery could. Little did I know that when I agreed to meet with him to discuss conducting an archeological dig at Industrial Site Number 3 that he would start me along on this journey into the past. Like most non-residents, Northford, it seemed to me, was just a sleepy New England hamlet that was haphazardly reinventing itself into yet another late 20th century commuter suburb. But as we sat in a local coffee shop and Gordon began to regale me with stories of the industrial history of his village in what I quickly learned was vintage Gordon enthusiasm, my interest grew. He handed me a study of industrial sites he had done for the Totoket Historical Society[1] that outlined all the early industrial locations and activity at each and the topic of our talk turned to why Northford and what had happened?

As I drove home from my meeting with Gordon, quite surprised but interested in what he had shared, I stopped by Site Number 3 to take a look as he had suggested. Gordon had already secured permission from the owner for us to investigate the location where the Todd family had once had a series of small mills as part of the town's brief but prosperous 19th century industrial heyday. Climbing the guard rail that divided the site from the busy state road, pushing through a tangle of thorny wild roses and second growth saplings, I found myself on a slight hill looking down on a small, meandering stream strewn with the scattered stone debris of a former dam and buildings. My first reaction was that whatever mill was here had to be small since the flow of water was little more than a trickle. But as I surveyed the site I realized how undisturbed it appeared to be; this could be an interesting dig.

The Northford Thelus Todd returned to after the Revolution was transformed within his lifetime from a sleepy agricultural village to an incubator of industrial innovation and change. That change was what so excited Gordon. There was something unique to the character of the community during those years that allowed for a blossoming of creativity that Gordon had actively pursued for many years and in 1997 he wrote a paper for the Totoket Historical Society that detailed what he believed was the cause. In the paper, which appeared in the *Journal of The New Haven Colony Historical Society*, Volume 43, Number 2.[2] Miller identified what he believed to be the answer. By utilizing research and letters from two 19th century residents of Northford, the Reverend Jonathan Maltby and the Reverend Elijah C. Pierce, he was able to establish that one of the keys to the flourishing of the village was the unusually high number of Yale graduates proportional to the size of the population. This Miller stated, was the direct result of an environment within the community that encouraged direct participation in education and learning that was inspired by an extraordinary series of ministers who served at the local Congregational church.[3]

In the introduction to the paper, Gordon quoted the Reverend Maltby who said of the series of Yale graduates that "They were no ordinary men... They were the most remarkable men which the world ever produced. They lived for a nobler end... for a higher destiny than that have ever lived. These are the men to whom New England owes her religion with all the blessings civil, social, & literary that follow in its train."[4] Though many of those alluded to by Maltby went into the ministry, others went on to serve their community and elsewhere in a variety of professions as the Reverend Elijah Pierce stated when he said "few parishes in the State and perhaps none of equal population, have given to the world so large a number of liberally educated men—so goodly a number of emigrant sons, who have served their generation in the varied fields of professional labor as Northford."[5] Miller added a comparison of Northford to other Connecticut communities during the period as to the number of Yale graduates in number and percentage to the total population and the numbers certainly support the idea that something different was indeed happening in the village.

Northford it turns out, had a far greater percentage of Yale graduates per the population than any other town at 5.2% with the next highest being from Norwich with 1.9%.[6] With an average population of 500 residents per year during the period 1768 to 1826, Northford had a total of 26 graduates from Yale by Maltby's estimate and 31 by that of the Reverend Pierce. Of Maltby's 26 listed, 8 remained ordained and practicing ministers throughout their lives while the remaining 18 pursued other professions; 6 as doctors, 2 as lawyers, 3 as government officials, 2 as businessmen, 1 as a scientist, 1 as a publisher, 1 as a soldier, 1 as a missionary, and 1 as a priest.[7] Both the Reverends Maltby and Pierce firmly proclaimed that it was the strong influence of the ministers and the Congregational Church that shaped the community and encouraged an educated populace. Maltby stated that it was the tradition handed down from their forefathers who were intelligent and educated men, "accustomed to leaders of university training and naturally desirous of the like privileges for their children" that made such a degree of success possible.[8]

This attitude towards education and service permeated 18th and 19th century Northford according to Gordon and it apparently had a strong influence on even those that did not pursue an education outside the confines of the village. This manifested itself in a level of creativity and entrepreneurial success far beyond the bounds of a community of its size leading Miller to christen Northford the "Athens of Connecticut", likening it to the ancient Greek city that had a level of influence well beyond its size and numbers.

As already stated, the Northford of Thelus Todd following the Revolutionary War continued to be a relatively prosperous agricultural community tied into outside domestic and even foreign markets through well-established trade systems that re-established themselves after the war. The Todd family, having purchased the mill site and cider mill along the Pistapaug Stream back in the 1740's were well positioned to take advantage of the growing prosperity that followed peace and Thelus appears to have obtained the property through his grandfather Stephen's (1702-1772) and father's ownership. By 1786, Jonah Todd (1731-1803) had moved to Woodbridge, Connecticut and Thelus purchased the mill site that year for 150 English Pounds. The record states that Thelus purchased "two certain pieces of land lying and being situated in the North part of the society of Northford… together with a dwelling house, shops, and cyder mill thereon standing".[9]

Interestingly, Thelus, like his father, had remained officially residents of Wallingford just to the east while owning the Northford mill and this pattern of ownership was fairly typical of an extended family's web of economic activity that included a mix of farming the land, raising livestock, and pursuing either a craft or ownership of a shop, mill or store where merchandise could be produced, sold or bartered. Extended families functioned as one economic entity to the benefit of all usually under the leadership of a patriarch, in this case Stephen and then Jonah Todd. During the 18th and 19th Centuries, many Northford families operated in such a manner and resided or maintained properties in the eastern part of Wallingford due to its close proximity and the relatively easy access between the two communities. Sometime between 1835, when Thelus gave his deposition in support of his fellow militiaman, Wait Munson, and his death in 1846, however, he moved his residence to Northford.[10]

Like most early New England and Connecticut communities, the first mills to be established once the settlement process began were sawmills and gristmills, both vital to the economic survival of the residents whose

Stories on the Trail of a Yankee Millwright

most important purpose was aiding in their subsistence and eventually the ability to sell to an outside market. Northford was no exception and according to the *History of North Branford and Northford*, the first sawmill was built in Northford in 1707 along the Farm River south of the current village center.[11] From that year on, an increasing number of both types of mills were built as need required and they were quickly joined by fulling and carding mills for the processing of wool.[12] Once orchards were established during the 18th century, cider mills were built to produce hard (alcoholic) cider every fall, the drink of choice for New Englanders and beyond for most of the 18th and 19th Centuries. The production of cider was what brought the Todd's to Northford from Wallingford in 1747.

By the first few decades of the 19th century the bucolic world of farms, saw, and grist mills began to change as the industrial revolution swept through Connecticut and the rest of New England and Northford was caught up in the torrent of innovation and transformation it brought. It seemed any stream or river large enough to dam and set up a water wheel to power the new machines of the age was a potential site for a manufacturing operation and the opportunities presented by this new mode of production instantly appealed to the entrepreneurial spirit of Connecticut Yankees. Spurred on first by the introduction of wool and cotton textile manufacturing during the first few decades of the century, by 1845 an impressive variety of items were being produced in Connecticut. Items made of brass, Britannia ware, buttons, clocks, coaches and wagons, textiles, hats, caps, muffs, hollow ware, machinery, iron, and tools were being manufactured throughout the state.[13] Of those on the list, Northford would produce brass, Britannia ware, buttons, wagons, machinery, tools and more.

There was something about the character of residents of Connecticut during the 19th century that seemed ready made for the adventure and challenges the Industrial Revolution would bring. Connecticut historian Ellsworth Grant wrote of this character in his history of the state called *The Miracle of Connecticut*, in which he shared the Frenchman Alexis de Tocqueville's impression of the Connecticut Yankee. De Tocqueville, author of the classic commentary on the early United States titled *Democracy in America* (1835) praised Connecticut and its reputation for ingenuity, pioneering efforts in education, the missionary zeal of its teachers and ministers, and the contributions of its public servants who helped shape the political institutions of the young republic.[14] It seems that Gordon Miller was on to something when it came to Northford.

Mr. Grant went on to state that the source of de Tocqueville's praise of Connecticut were the "hard working, inventive farmers, artisans, and entrepreneurs who made the state the manufacturing center of New England".[15] It was that inventiveness that would propel Connecticut and the tiny village of Northford into the forefront of the manufacturing revolution and to highlight this point Grant went on to quote a mid-19th century English observer who was struck by the prolific inventiveness of Connecticut's citizens. In his observation, Daniel Pigeon wrote:

> "He is usually a Yankee of Yankees by birth, and of a temperament thoughtful to dreaminess. His natural bent is strong toward mechanical pursuits, and he finds his way very early in life into the workshop… he cherishes a fixed idea of creating a monopoly in some branch of manufacture by establishing an overwhelming superiority over the methods of production already existing…To "get up" a machine, or a series of machines, for this purpose, is his one aim and ambition. If he succeeds, supported by patents and the ready aid which capital gives to promising novelties… he may revolutionize an industry, forcing opponents who produce in the old way altogether out of the market, while benefiting the consumer and making his own fortune at the same time. The workshops of Massachusetts, Rhode Island, and especially Connecticut are full of such men".[16]

It turned out that Northford had its share of such men and two families in particular, the Maltbys and the Fowlers produced a number of them. The Maltby family by the start of the 19th century had been residents of Branford and Northford since the 1600's. By the early 1830's, Julius

Stories on the Trail of a Yankee Millwright

Maltby (1788-1872), a cooper by trade, began to experiment with the production of buttons out of bone, ivory, and wood and eventually by the 1850's also formed a partnership with his brother Samuel to design farm implements and the machines to manufacture them.[17] But it was his son, Epaphras Chapman Maltby (1828-?) who put the village on the map and helped propel it into the industrial age.

Having been given the rather enigmatic first name of Epaphras, from an early age Maltby called himself Chapman. Like his inventive father, Chapman did not limit himself to creative nomenclature, but struck out in his own right even as a young man to make a name for himself in the new world of manufacturing to become the epitome of the Connecticut Yankee Daniel Pigeon had found so fascinating. Taking over the manufacture of buttons from his father around 1850, Chapman soon expanded production at his factory along the Farm River just off the road north to Durham and Middletown to include axe handles and wooden spoons. He also became one of the more famous Yankee Peddlers of Connecticut keeping as many as four peddler's carts loaded with items for sale on the road at one time.[18]

One of Chapman Maltby's best innovations was the invention of the coconut shell dipper for use in drawing water from buckets and tubs. In a time before plumbing for running water, most water used in the home or in production had to be drawn from wells. Either wooden or metal dippers, usually made from tin, were most commonly used to ladle the water from buckets. Chapman was already making them from wood when he came across the novel idea of making them from coconut shells. Coconuts had long been brought to Connecticut on ships returning from trade in the Caribbean so access was relatively easy. Maltby cut the top off the coconut, scrapped out the contents, polished the shell, then added a rim and either a wooden handle or a metal one made of Britannia which was an alloy made from tin, copper and occasionally bismuth or zinc.[19] These dippers proved to be extremely popular for their durability and novelty and sold for $3.50 for plain dippers and $3.75 for those with Britannia.[20] Within no time he expanded the size of his shop along the Farm River, known as the "brick shop", into a brick factory.[21]

As production of the dippers increased, a disagreeable by-product became a growing and unpleasant source of nuisance and irritation to the residents of Northford. Because the contents from each coconut used to make a dipper were, when scrapped out, tossed out a window of the shop, over time the growing pile of rotting meat began to develop a putrefied odor that the entire village found quite objectionable. Tradition has it that Maltby's carpenter and wheelwright, George Scranton Sr., came up with the idea that instead of letting the coconut meat rot, why not sell it as a food and thus rid the factory and the neighborhood of the malevolent smell.[22] The coconut meat was consequently dried and shred and quickly became a popular treat across Connecticut and even New York. The confectionery delicacy, known as Maltby's Shredded Coconut, became so popular that promoters from New York approached Chapman with the idea of moving his operation to the city to take advantage of the large market there. Julius however, thought the idea of getting involved with New York entrepreneurs a risky mistake and forbade his son to pick up and move production. When another New Yorker began to manufacture and sell large quantities of shredded coconut similar to Maltby's he also refused to allow his son to take legal action against him.[23]

The Maltby's were thus satisfied, or at least Julius was, to make their delicacy and net $100 a day while the bulk of the market was captured by their competitor. Twenty six years later, a degree of satisfaction was gained for Chapman when *Maltby's Shredded Coconut* won first prize at the 1876 Philadelphia Centennial Exhibition. Epaphras Chapman Maltby might have become a very wealthy man if not for the wishes of his father, and the entire episode reveals much about how families in the 19th century still functioned as patriarchal economic entities.

By the 1860's Maltby's interests had begun to change as he sold his factory to a company called Smith & Cowles who continued to produce his dippers and in 1878, as part of a new company called Maltby, Stevens, and Curtis, moved to Shelton, Connecticut.[25] But Northford residents were far from done and the spirit of invention continued. Though Smith and Cowles continued to produce the coconut dippers, their true success came from the invention, patent, and manufacture of the first self-operating horse hay rake.[26] By the time Chapman Maltby had left for Shelton , the baton of invention had been passed to his cousins, the Fowlers.

Julius Maltby's grandmother was Elizabeth Fowler and through this connection a family bond existed. His cousin, Maltby Fowler (1780-1855), moved from Milford, Connecticut to Northford where he established a wagon factory along the Farm River. According to *The History of North Branford and Northford*, Fowler built the first four-wheeled wagon in the state.[27] Maltby Fowler married Loly Todd (1785-1869), a niece of Thelus Todd, and together they had six sons; William, George, De Grasse, Horace, Frederick, and Thaddeus. All told, father and sons would create and patent seventeen machines or inventions that would lead to the manufacture of a wide variety of products. Here is a list of the machines invented by each family member:

Maltby:	Machine for making buttons
	Machine for making pocket combs
Frederick:	Machine for drawing out brass tubing
	Machine for turning out 6,000 screws per minute
	Machine for making cigars
Frederick along with Isaac Bartholomew;	
	First machine invented for making perforated tin ware
Horace:	Embossed rolls for making silk hats
	Original Dies for pin-making machines
De Grasse:	Machine for making cigarettes
Thaddeus:	Machine for making horseshoe nails
De Grasse and Thaddeus:	
	Pin-making machines
	Machine for sticking pins into pin-paper
	Machine for making hairpins
	Machine for washing clothes
George:	Machine for making tin lamps
	Machine for making platinum rivets

De Grasse and George:
> Power press with a slide box and eccentric ring

In the hot-bed of the Industrial Revolution, many of the Fowler's inventions had a significant impact on society at the time, starting with pin-making and pin-to paper machines. Common pins had always been in demand but required sometimes as many as 18 steps by hand in their creation. It was a tedious and time consuming process with the result being a high price for even a small number of pins. Herbert Miller states the cost of pins in pre-Revolution America was seven shillings, six pence for twelve hand-made pin,[28] the equivalent of $40.00 today. In Gordon Miller's survey of Northford Industrial sites, a Dr. John Howe of New York is credited with inventing the first practical machine that created a pin in one operation in 1831 and his was soon followed by one invented in Poughkeepsie, NY by the Slocum and Jellson Company and another by the Fowlers in Northford in 1840. Of these, that of the Fowlers supposedly worked the best turning out 120 pins per minute.[29] Thaddeus Fowler went on to invent a machine to package pins by inserting them into paper, a procedure also pioneered by Dr. Howe. Prior to this, pins had to be inserted by hand, an extremely inefficient and time consuming process.[30]

But the world of pin production was a bit prickly. Dr. Howe sued the Fowlers in Federal Court in New Haven for patent infringement after moving his manufacturing operation to Derby, Connecticut in the Naugatuck River Valley. The court ruled in favor of Howe and as a result the Fowlers turned over seven parcels of land in Northford to Howe in payment of damages.[31] This may have caused the Fowlers to become disillusioned with the pin industry for in 1842 they sold their operation to the Brown and Elton Company who moved it to Waterbury, Connecticut also in the Naugatuck Valley which was quickly becoming the center for pin production in the United States. But by then Thaddeus had moved on to create his horseshoe nail making machine which revolutionized the horseshoeing industry. Before this machine, nails were hand made by blacksmiths, often on an as needed basis. In an era where horsepower provided the major source of land transportation, machine production of nails was truly transformational in making the shoeing of horses much more efficient. These machines, manufactured by the Fowler's Paug Manufacturing Company along the Farm River, also became the center of the production of tin ware making machinery.[31] Another Fowler business, the Northford Manufacturing Company, produced what they touted as high quality "japanned and stamped tin ware" along with rivets, perforated tin, and cash box locks.[32] A third company, Northford Hook and Eye Co., produced a wide variety of clasps and fasteners used in the clothing and hardware industries.

The diversity of inventions, machinery, and businesses created by the Maltbys and Fowlers alone propelled Northford into the forefront of industrial production in Connecticut and by the 1860's it seemed that the little village was destined to grow into a major manufacturing center.[33] This was the Northford of Milo Todd's childhood who, having been born in 1834, was growing up in the shadow of the dynamic Maltby and Fowler families whose shops and factories lay just down the road from his home and his grandfather's gristmill and cider mill. Milo's father, also named Thelus (1802-1861), operated the gristmill alongside his father but this heart was in farming and it appears he never dreamed of doing more with the mill site he inherited. But Milo had bigger plans. He had been caught up in the energy and excitement along the Farm River and wanted to be part of it.

So what happened to Northford's industrial boom? Beginning in the 1840's, plans had begun to build a railroad line from New Haven to Boston that would by-pass the already established coastal route. This direct or "airline" would be the shortest route between New York and Boston, cutting through the Connecticut countryside from New Haven, through Northford, to Middletown where it would cross the Connecticut River and diagonally move on through Eastern Connecticut to the rising textile manufacturing center of Willimantic, then from there on to Boston. The line would cut hours off the trip and provide much needed rail service to the developing industrial centers all along its route, Northford included. From the beginning, the planned route would take the railroad through the village and would be a boost to all the enterprises there as materials and finished products could be shipped in bulk by rail as opposed to the lesser volume carried by horse drawn wagons. By 1851, as funds began to be raised for the construction of what became known as the Air Line, increased prosperity seemed to be in the offering for the village and its ambitious and inventive entrepreneurs.[33]

But the anticipated bonanza envisioned by the coming of the Air Line was dashed in 1867 when the route abruptly moved 2 1/2 miles to the west through the Clintonville section of the neighboring town of North Haven, completely by-passing Northford. The reasons for the shift were never known though powerful interests in other communities may have promoted the move. Regardless, Northford and her industrialists were left in the lurch, cut off from a vital transportation link into their future. By 1873, when the Air Line began operation, Northford was a dying community.[34] But there were other factors as well. The reality was that the increasing demand for products was more than the factories and shops of the village could produce as their primary source of energy, the Farm River was for all intents and purposes a stream incapable of providing the amount of volume in water power needed to allow for expansion. Most of the operations in order to compete with manufacturers elsewhere, were forced to relocate or the owners, the Maltbys and Fowlers among them, sold their businesses to outside interests who then moved them to more advantageous locations.

Northford, as an industrial incubator could not compete with the factories in the state's cities and towns located on larger rivers with their sources of water power like the Quinnipiac, Naugatuck, Willimantic, Quinibaug, and Housatonic. Investors from large urban centers as far away as Chicago either purchased the machinery from Northford's factories, their patents, or in some cases simply began manufacturing the machines and products without patent rights. By 1890, Northford's industrial era was over. Yet one member of the Maltby family would obtain international fame not as a minister, inventor, or industrialist, but as a champion bicycle rider. Epaphras Chapman Maltby's son Wilburt earned the title of Champion Trick Cycle Rider of the World as he performed all over the United States and Europe before enthusiastic crowds and even royalty[34] but this was years after the family had moved from the village to Shelton, Connecticut

The story of Northford's brief blossoming as a center of education and invention speaks powerfully to how individuals, rooted in a sense of place and nurtured within a community that embraces the future while maintaining an awareness of its past, can become beacons of positive change. In the end, the industrial age, in many ways a child of the village, quickly outgrew the tiny hamlet tucked in along the ledges of Totoket Mountain. Like its ancient namesake, the Athens of Connecticut drifted into a quiet complacency while clinging to the story of its former glory.

CHAPTER 7
For Want of Water

Milo sat and stared out the window of the new mill building he had recently erected next to the old gristmill and shop. His eyes wandered along the penstock he had constructed to bring water down into the new metal tub wheel he had installed to replace the old wooden water wheel of his father and grandfather. This, he had been told by that slick salesman from Hartford, would solve his problem. Now here he sat, $5000.00 in debt to that banker from New Haven, and he still could not run his machines to the extent he needed. The water ran, but the flow was insufficient to provide enough torque to power all this new and pricey machinery. This was a problem he needed to solve.

Milo Todd had grown up in the shadow of the Maltby's and Fowler's just down the road and as a boy no doubt saw how their creativity, drive, and initiative had transformed the village and their family's fortunes. By the time he was a young man, he must have wanted to be part of all the excitement and wealth the industrial boom was bringing and felt he had everything he needed to do so at his fingertips. His grandfather Thelus had died when he was 12 years old in 1846 and by then his father had long been running the gristmill along the stream that emptied out of Pistapaug Pond up a ways past the Wallingford line. The Paug's flow of water had never been strong but a series of low stone and earthen dams had been rebuilt over the years to capture enough water into the small mill pond to run the great wooden wheel that turned the gristmill stones that ground their neighbor's corn and wheat into flour. The mill ran mostly in the late summer and fall leaving Milo's father content with that seasonal role as his heart lay in farming and livestock and not the explosion of innovation taking place just down the Farm River from their mill.

Thelus (1802-1861) was the third child and second son of Thelus Todd and Irene Rogers (1766-1860) who had in total five children. Wyllis (1798) was the oldest followed by Rebecca (1800), Thelus, Mary (1805) and Esther (1808). Unlike the elder Todd, young Thelus lived his entire adult life in Northford in the house that his family had owned adjacent to the cider and gristmill since the 1740's though he also owned land in eastern Wallingford and like most Northford families at the time, had strong family ties and property interests there. By the time his son Milo was in his early 20's, he seemed happy to let him run the gristmill and experiment in the shop attached to it with other endeavors.

Thelus had married Antoinette Harrison (1809-1848) and had settled into a comfortable life as a farmer and livestock dealer. He and Antoinette had seven children, Milo was the second child and son. Tragically, Milo's older brother, Apollos Edward (1831-1834) died three months before his birth leaving Milo as the oldest child of the family and the only boy. His sisters were Venelia (1836), Matilda (1838), Miranda (1841), Delia (1843), and Bertha (1845) and with his mother's death in 1848, fourteen year old Milo must have felt a certain amount of responsibility for helping to raise his younger siblings. How much this played in his later quest to become a success in the industrial age is pure conjecture yet I cannot help but feel, with his father content to work the land, he might have felt driven to do more. When his youngest sister, Bertha Sirena, married into the Fowler family,[1] certainly Milo must have felt even more pressure to succeed.

His father Thelus had made quite a name for himself locally as a cattle dealer and each fall traveled to upstate New York to purchase grass fed cattle that he drove to Northford to sell to local farmers. They in turn would fatten them with hay and corn during the winter and sell them in the New Haven market for a sizable profit. In Earl May's book about the silver industry in Connecticut, *A Century of Silver*, it was said that Thelus had a lot of "get up and get".[2] Good for Thelus, good for his neighbors. It took twenty one days to drive the herd down from New York and it must have been quite an adventure for Milo when he began to accompany his father on these annual drives. The experience certainly must have opened his eyes to the greater world beyond his home village as the great herd slowly made its way through New York and Connecticut to the waiting pens of Northford and Wallingford.

Thelus apparently led the quintessential gentleman farmer life in Northford and Wallingford and was well respected as a person and as a breeder of prize winning livestock. In 1839 he represented North Branford in the Connecticut Legislature, certainly a sign of the level of esteem his neighbors held for him.[3] But according to some information found in the archives of the Connecticut State Agricultural Society, breeding livestock must have been his passion. In 1855, Thelus came in 2nd place with his 3 year old oxen, winning a $6.00 premium.[4] He also came in first place for a "pen" of six lambs and second for another five netting premiums of $5.00 and $4.00. A notation stated that the lambs were "a cross of long wooled and native sheep and that all had been fed with grain two weeks before the competition".[5] Not only was Thelus accomplished in his breeding, he was obviously savvy in his skill of showing his prize winning animals. In another category, Thelus was also awarded $2.00 along with three other competitors for his "beautiful specimens of pears" though he exhibited an insufficient number to earn a premium.[6] Here was a man who loved the traditional fruits of the soil and not the frenetic future being embraced by his son.
So what was Milo up to?

It is unclear when Milo actually took over the running of the gristmill from his father but all indications are that he had by the early 1850's. In *A Century of Silver*, Earl May in describing Thelus as "enterprising" also mentions that Milo managed the gristmill successfully by "cutting corners" a skill that would serve him well as he sought to expand into other production opportunities.[7] As Gordon and I, along with our of eager volunteers, began our archeological investigation in the fall of 1992, we quickly came across some of Milo's early efforts at transforming the family gristmill and shop on the Paug into those other operations he hoped would elevate him into the entrepreneurial realm of his neighbors as we began to excavate the area that we identified as the site of the gristmill.

The gristmill was built along an area where the stream turned almost 90 degrees just below where the dam had once stood. A stone retaining wall still partially stood against the shallow northern bank of the stream and had survived years of neglect and flooding. It framed part of what remained of a pit where the great wooden water wheel of the mill once sat. Water would have been directed down through a gate from the dam into this area to push the paddles of the wheel as it flowed under it; a classic type of water wheel called an undershot wheel. This type of mechanism was common in an area with a limited flow of water since it was how fast the water moved as well as its volume that created the force necessary to push or turn the wheel. The amount of force and thus the power that the water struck the paddles of the wheel with was also dictated by how far down in distance the water dropped from the dam to the wheel. This height was critical; the taller the drop, the more force the water would have. At the Todd mill, the height was probably between four and six feet, not very impressive by the hydraulic standards of the day.

The dam itself by our estimations was a small affair, less than six feet tall and fifty feet across, creating a rather shallow mill pond behind it, which though long gone, would have encompassed a total area of only a quarter to one half acre. The size of both the dam and the pond were dictated by the relatively low lying banks of the stream and the low elevation of the surrounding land it flowed through which would have been prone to flooding if a taller dam had been built. But, because the gristmill was a seasonal operation, the low and limited volume of the water flow was sufficient to power and turn the grinding stones needed to turn corn and wheat into flour.

Stories on the Trail of a Yankee Millwright

Directly below the gristmill site and along the eastern bank where the Paug turned its 90 degrees to the south was a slight and gently sloping hill that rose to the relative height of the roadway that formed the eastern boundary of the property. Here, near the gristmill and attached roughly at a right angle to it was the location of the original shop identified in land records. This may have been the original site of the 18th century cider mill but more important to this story, appears to be where Milo tried a number of different enterprises before settling on one in particular.

Unknown to most residents of Connecticut today, the state during the early 19th century was a center of bone and ivory button and comb production. Bone from livestock, usually cattle and hogs, had long been cut up and used as handles for a variety of items and tools and during the early 1800's became a major material in the production of buttons. Trade with Africa also brought to Connecticut, along with slaves, ivory which quickly replaced bone as the material of choice for the production of buttons, combs, handles, and other items and implements. Ivory was harder than relatively soft bone, held its white color whereas bone turned brown over time, and was more expensive and thus more fashionable. The lower Connecticut River Valley, centered around the Ivoryton section of Essex in particular, became a center for this industry. But shops producing these products turned up elsewhere in the state and this appears to be the industry Milo first tried to develop. Excavations in the shop area in 1992 and again in 1993 unearthed not only a quantity of bone buttons, but pieces of cattle bone that had been cut into sections, sawed into strips, then from the strips buttons cut and shaped. This would have meant that the Todd's would have had to have invested in machinery, driven by water power, to do the sawing and shaping of the buttons. Milo must have also experimented with ivory as well as a number of buttons of that material were also found. But without a reliable source for ivory, and knowing his bone buttons just couldn't compete, it appears Milo abandoned button production.

In the same area, and in a slightly higher layer of the excavation, we uncovered artifacts associated with the production of leather strapping and other products.[8] In an archeological excavation, each area investigated is slowly scrapped of its dirt by hand using small masonry trowels. The dirt removed is then sifted through screens revealing artifacts. Theoretically, unless the site has been extensively disturbed, the deeper layers of excavation should reveal older artifacts and those closer to the surface newer. This was definitely the case in the shop and gristmill areas as the bone and ivory artifacts were deepest, followed next in depth by leather artifacts. These leather pieces varied from scraps and cuttings to whole belts and straps, some still held together with brass or copper rivets.[9] Some of these pieces were possibly used to run machinery in the shop since leather straps were attached to drive shafts and wheels that got their power from the water wheel, but most seemed to have been associated with production. Milo had abandoned bone buttons and had begun making belts and straps for the new industrial machinery transforming his village and state. But this too seems to have ended relatively quickly since it must have become obvious he could not compete with larger operations establishing themselves elsewhere, especially in Middletown to the north where the Russell Company was producing belting on a much larger scale.

Thus by the mid-1850's, having experimented with production in bone, ivory, and leather and still longing to be part of the diversity of manufacturing and invention taking place around him in Northford, Todd finally found an industry unique to the area that would hopefully propel him into the local manufacturing class. He had settled on the production of paper which was in high demand in a growing national economy. But this meant a sizable investment in machinery, materials, and the construction of a new building alongside the family gristmill and shop.[10] To do so, Milo turned to a new tool increasingly used by enterprising business men in the burgeoning industrial economy; a loan from a bank. Such an untraditional and risky move must have been frowned upon by his staid Yankee father; mortgaging the mill site and buildings to take a gamble on a new and unproven enterprise?

"I know father is skeptical and even worried that I have created a serious

mistake" Milo reflected, becoming a bit annoyed and frustrated but at the same time sympathetic to the misgivings of his father about his securing the loan from Townshend Bank. "What if", Milo recalled, "What if was all he could ask when we discussed the risk. What if? Well… you will lose the mill" Thelus repeated emphatically. "He just couldn't see the opportunity that was presenting itself here. Milo reworked their endless conversations in his head. "Paper, will be my niche and a way to move beyond the limitations of a life of the gentleman farmer he so wants me to be. He just does not and has never understood and in his mind is confident I will eventually come to my senses".

His rig bounced a bit on the ruts as he climbed the hill on the outskirts of the village of North Haven towards the North Branford line and they reminded him of the rut he had increasingly felt he was trapped in when dealing with all the circumstances that had led him to work so hard to make his way into the industrial future. With few financial resources, he had tried to take advantage of what was available to him and had found that though he was able to turn to the various raw materials that were a by-product of farming in Northford such as the bone of cattle for buttons or the skin of their hides for leather making, those efforts had proved inadequate due to much more established competition and the limitations of his production abilities.

He had been thankful to the Maltbys for selling him their old bone shaving and button equipment at a reasonable price and remembers his father's reluctance even then to loan him the money. "Milo", he had said, "let this be a chance for you to get this through your system and see what the life of a manufacturer is really like". Milo thought about the feeling of excitement and anticipation he felt despite those foreboding words as he set the machines up in the old cider mill that he converted into his shop. He recalled that it would be November soon and when the annual slaughter of livestock for meat for the winter began he would be able to secure enough bone to begin producing. "All I needed was one more small loan from father to pay for the bones and that was like pulling his teeth," Milo smiled at the memory. "But he helped me out and I was grateful and able to start making buttons by December".

He remembered how Chapman Maltby had counselled him about having to deal with unknowns when it came to industry and unfortunately for Milo he was hit with a series of unfortunate ones by January. Despite Chapman's offer to sell the buttons through his peddlers, a cold January and February caused his mill pond and wheel to constantly freeze up and he spent more time chopping ice than making buttons. Then April brought so much rain that the pond overflowed and all but destroyed the old wooden wheel and its penstock keeping him from producing until May and by then Chapman's wagons were loaded with products and gone. By June and July he was still having power problems when that talkative merchant from Essex came through the village and stopped at his shop. Milo remembered how Hayden, his name was, looked at him and straight away said "bone is a thing of the past young man its ivory now that every woman wants. I can provide you with the ivory blanks you need son for a start-up fee of only $400.00".

Of course he had turned to his father once again who this time was emphatic in his denial but Milo was able to scrape together $150.00 and the Essexman on his way through the next time was more than happy to provide him with a small amount of ivory to begin making the buttons that were changing the market. But of course ivory was much harder than bone and all the blades for his equipment had to be replaced which once again he was fortunate enough to get for a "future consideration" from Chapman. By the autumn however, he saw that despite his best efforts, he would never be able to obtain the ivory in the amounts he needed and he began to think of an alternative product to manufacture.

Milo knew that leather production might be a viable alternative and with a number of local tanneries in the area he decided to focus on the production of belts of all types but with an emphasis on those for the growing number of machines that the new industrial economy was demanding to provide power from water wheels and even the new steam boilers he had seen in New Haven and elsewhere. He made contacts with the tanneries up in neighboring Durham and even in Guilford and found them mostly eager to provide him with the treated leather he would need though all claimed they were limited by the number of hides they could procure from the local farmers. "I knew I was a newcomer to this and that as a result I'd be low on their list for availability" Milo remembered, "and that was the case. And with limited capital to pay up-front for the hides, many looked to others who could buy more in bulk". After one year of production, again Milo realized he could not compete with larger and better financed operations. Plus he recalled, it was always the power; there just wasn't enough especially with the old wooden wheel patched together as it was.

He had "borrowed" the cutting and stitching equipment from Chapman with the idea that he could return it and he was grateful to Maltby for his generosity and even though it was old and not used by the Maltby's for years had worked well when the water gave him enough energy. This had led Milo to confront two issues; first and foremost what other line of production might he go into that would make his success and how could he obtain a reliable source of power. The answer to the first came one day when he was working the stones and grinding Jim Bennett's corn and Jacob, the son of the general store owner and post master for Northford dropped by with a package from his uncle in New Haven. As he began to unwrap the parcel, it came to him he remembered fondly and he shouted out with certainty to the whirling mill stones "of course – paper! There's a great demand I have often heard and I can obtain all the straw locally I need, even from father's fields. I will just need to learn a bit about the business and come up with a plan to finance the project". Milo knew the Maltbys and Fowlers both at times obtained loans to provide them with the money they needed and he thought to himself, "that's the modern way, I'll speak with Chapman".

Now here he was, on his way back from New Haven having met with the bankers his uncle Ambrose knew and Milo felt his future was finally going to be a manufacturer of high quality straw wrapping paper. He had presented his business plan to them and they were interested, of course with the gristmill property as collateral which was something his father had cautioned against. "But he had turned the property over to me so it was mine to use as I saw fit" he thought with a slight pang of guilt. "With this loan I too am on my way to becoming a successful manufacturer" as another series of ruts in the road jostled the wagon and shook him to his bones.

Todd must have felt that this was his chance, and in 1857 he mortgaged the mill, shop, and property for $5,000.00 with the Townsend Savings Bank of New Haven.[11] Paper making during the mid-19th century was going through a series of rapid changes that were transforming not only the production capabilities of manufacturers, but increasing the demand which all were struggling to meet. This Milo must have believed, was an excellent opportunity. In a hope to make his new enterprise successful, he decided to enter a particular niche which would allow him to take advantage of a local resource that was readily available, field grown straw. Straw paper was in great demand as wrapping paper for all sorts of products and was a critical commodity when it came to shipping in a pre-plastic age. It was strong, durable, and profitable for the producer. But in order to manufacture enough of a volume to produce that profit, he needed specific pieces of machinery and equipment, a larger building to house them in, and enough power to run them. Hence the loan.

Paper making required various steps that until the late 18th century had changed little since the Chinese had invented the process during the 2nd century. Production began with a source of fibers that were crushed and pulverized into a pulp that was then combined with water and put into a vat with a wire mesh. As the paper began to dry, a sizing was added to assist in the binding of the pulp into a firm sheet. The result when dried was a sheet of paper.[12] From its beginnings with the Chinese, the main source of fiber for making paper were rags or textile waste and this continued well into the 19th century when rags and other fibers were replaced eventually by wood pulp.[13] Like the Chinese, European paper makers during the Middle Ages also experimented with a variety of plant fibers such as tree bark, hemp, rope, flax and any other fibrous materials. By the time of the Revolution, American paper makers were experimenting with any fiber available although rags were still the most common and sought after source. Rag paper was smooth, durable and long-lasting, qualities that made it desirable for all types of printing whether for books, newspapers or any other item made from paper.

By the time Todd opened his paper making mill sometime around 1857-8, he was able to take advantage of advances in the technology of paper making that the ancient Chinese could never have imagined. Until the 18th century, most paper was made by hand as the Chinese had by beating the rag pulp in a water filled vat and then applying the mixture to a mold. By the late 1700's, European and American paper manufacturers were using a rag engine invented by the Dutch to speed up the pulping process commonly called a hollander. This engine or beater was essentially a tub filled with water and rags which were beaten to a pulp by a set of rotating blades that were powered by a water wheel.[14] The pulp was then transferred to a mold and then, while still damp, moved to a felt lined press that would press out and absorb the remaining moisture. By the time Todd built his paper mill, this press would have been powered mechanically by water as well and he may even have replaced the vat and press system with a vacuumed wire cylinder connected to the vat that did the job of the mold and press.[15] Regardless of which process Milo might have used, once pressed, the sheet was then fed to a mechanized cylinder that would combine the sheets into a large paper roll. The result was the production of up to nine reams of paper or 4,500 sheets of paper in a day.[16]

By the first few decades of the 1800's, the demand for paper began to outstrip the supply and the price steadily rose between 1810 and 1830 leading to an increased number of producers which in turn increased the supply and consequently drove the cost down over the next decade.[17] This up and down price was dictated by the availability of rags and the efficacy of introducing other fibers into the process. The Panic of 1837 apparently also had a significant impact on the demand for paper, the price, and its manufacture as many of the producers that had loans from banks were driven out of business when the lending institutions they were tied to failed seemingly over-night.[18] Two decades later, was the memory of this economic disaster still fresh in the mind of Thelus when his son broached the idea of a loan for his planned new enterprise?

The Panic of 1837 did lead surviving manufacturers, particularly in New England, to diversify their fiber sources as, short on cash and not able to purchase rags, they turned to the waste materials from the local fishing fleets. Paper makers were able to obtain old manila rope, rag-bale ropes, hemp sails, and scraps of canvass and combined these with yarn, burlap, and fibers from jute, flax, and hemp.[19] The result was a hodgepodge of lessor quality but serviceable paper. Wrapping paper remained in demand however and as demand for all types increased by the early 1850's, the price for all began to rise.[20] By 1857, when Milo signed the papers for his loan, the future of the paper industry looked bright.

The making of straw paper in the United States began almost by accident. In 1827, a farmer in Meadville, Pennsylvania discovered while making potash that when he lined the potash hopper with straw as a step in the process of making it, the straw became crushed. The subsequent pulp looked like it might have paper making possibilities so he brought a sample to a local paper maker by the name of John Shyrock. Shyrock experimented with the straw pulp, mixing it with rags, and the result was a new type of paper that quickly spread throughout the industry.[21] The standard mix became 60% straw and 40% rag which was probably the mixture that Milo would have used. As Todd eagerly began production, he certainly had access to enough harvested straw from his father's fields as well as those of other local farmers. His biggest problem in terms of materials and production would have been the same faced by all paper makers; an adequate supply of rags, or so he thought.

Exactly when the paper mill began production is difficult to tell, but by the outbreak of the Civil War in 1861, it appears Milo was producing paper. As in most large scale conflicts, shortages of many commodities tend to develop quickly as the demands of the war effort take precedent over consumer markets and apparently there soon developed a shortage of straw wrapping paper.[22] His timing it turned out was perfect. Among the new pieces of equipment he had purchased and installed in his recently built factory was a new type of water wheel that would power his expensive machinery called a turbine. Developed in both Europe and the United States during the early decades of the 19th century, these horizontal wheels were descendants of an earlier form used for centuries in places where the volume of water tended to be low called a tub wheel. A tub wheel was a simple horizontal wheel with paddles inside a wooden tub that would spin at a much faster rate than the traditional larger water wheel when struck by the water channeled into it. The result was a much greater amount of power in relation to the size of the wheel. The development of the new more sophisticated turbine wheels were a direct result of the upsurge in industrial development in the United States prior to the Civil War and its demand for greater amounts of power.[23]

Unlike wooden tub wheels, all the parts of these turbine type wheels were made of iron which added to the durability but also to the ability of the wheel to tolerate much greater pressure as the paddles were now struck by water with much greater force. This also included the housing or circular tub that contained the wheel. All told, the average metal turbine could provide up to 25% more power than a traditionally designed undershot wheel like the one that apparently had been used at the Todd grist mill.[25] The remnants of the circular housing for Milo's turbine, found during the excavation of the new factory building in 1994, revealed that the horizontal wheel had a diameter of two and a half feet. The water to spin it would have been brought to it by the construction of a wooden penstock from the top of the dam that would have dropped the water directly into the turbine.[26] Though small in size, everything Milo hoped to achieve was dependent upon this new device. The water if channeled and directed correctly against the paddles or wings of the metal wheel would provide enough power to run his expensive machinery despite the limitations of his water supply.

From the start it turned out however, Milo Todd's nemesis persisted. His attempts at production suffered repeatedly from the lack of a sufficient amount of water to consistently run his paper making machines despite the investment in the turbine.[27] During the age of water power, seasonal changes in water supply were a common problem and most manufacturers or millers understood that there would be times when there would be too little water, too much water, or frozen water. This was just the way it was. By the middle of the 19th century, steam engines began to augment and often replace water power to solve this problem but this only replaced the problems of water supply with the new problem of finding enough of a wood supply to boil the water that drove the steam engine. By the 1860's, Connecticut like much of the rest of Southern New England, had been stripped of its forests and wood supply. What was left was carefully husbanded for building material, heating, and cooking. This lack of wood for steam power was eventually alleviated by the importation into the state of coal from Pennsylvania and beyond. But his was expensive and a manufacturer needed to be located near a port where it could be brought in by ship or along the expanding network of railroads by which it could be brought in in bulk. We already know what happened to Northford in that regard. At any rate, already in debt to the Townsend Bank, Todd was apparently not in a position to experiment with steam.

Although challenged by the problem of water, Milo's paper making venture appeared to be successful enough to allow him to maintain production throughout most of the decade of the 1860's no doubt due to the demand for wrapping paper and undoubtedly his ability to coax as much power as he could from his meager source of water. Todd even entered into a partnership at some point during that decade with Chapman Maltby and the Northford Manufacturing Company to obtain ownership of the Pistapaug Pond in East Wallingford, the source of water flowing into the stream that brought his factory the power it had. His ownership included 1/3rd control of the dam at the Pond which regulated the flow of water. This he must have thought would allow him the ability to obtain as much water out of the dam as possible to run his business yet the reality was that his millpond which held his operational supply was too small and shallow to make a difference. A larger or taller dam might have stored more water but was impossible to build in that it would have flooded his neighbor's fields; obviously not an option. In an age of riparian rights, as the right to water and its control were called, problems associated with property rights and flooding were a constant source of legal entanglements and battles.

Despite his water related limitations, Milo persevered and became successful enough to find himself in a position to ask Cornelia Cook of East Wallingford to marry him which she did in February, 1865. In the 19th century, men did not marry traditionally unless they were established well enough financially to provide for a wife and family and Todd, ever conscious of becoming a success, would not have done so otherwise. Interestingly, their first child, Lillie Antoinette, was born one month later on March 23rd, giving us a glimpse into the fact that customarily marriages were more often than not dictated more by economic considerations than cultural morality associated with pregnancy.[28] Also, was this a possible indication that Todd's income associated with the paper mill was inconsistent and meager enough to postpone the marriage until a time when he and Cornelia's family felt more comfortable with his ability to support her and the child?

The issue of Lillie Todd's birth opens up some interesting insights into the changing moral codes surrounding marriage and pregnancy in mid-19th century New England. During the 18th century it was not at all unusual for women to be pregnant at the time of their marriage as rules associated with courtship were by later Victorian and 20th century standards much different. In the 1780's and 1790's studies have shown that roughly one-third of all women were pregnant at the time of their wedding and contrary to popular belief, sexual intercourse prior to marriage appears to have been the norm. Pregnancy appears to have simply accelerated and assured the inevitability that a marriage would take place due to community and parental pressure.[29] Rural communities in particular seemed to by custom look the other way and tolerate early pregnancies as part of the courtship ritual as long as the mother and child in the end were provided for in the proper manner which meant marriage.[30] This may come as a surprise for us schooled as we are in the Hawthornian tradition of *The Scarlet Letter* but on second thought, in insular communities like Northford and East Wallingford where there were few marriage options, what was the choice?

The late date of the marriage of Cornelia and Milo may also speak to an underlying reluctance on the part of one of the parties or family to see such a union. We will never know. But 1865 was a year on the cusp of new social moirés being established during what became known as the Victorian Age and the old custom of pregnancy before marriage was quickly disappearing, especially among the middle class and aspiring entrepreneurs such as Milo Todd. By the 1860's, a cult of Motherhood was developing in which the woman became the beacon of morality within the context of the home and family. Sexual abstinence before marriage became the ideal, preserving the sanctity of the union and elevating the wife and future mother into the virginal realm depicted in the cult of motherhood sweeping through the middle and upper classes.[31] In 1868, as Todd began his odyssey across Connecticut while pursuing his dreams of success, the social codes associated with the Victorian Era would come to play an important role in his future life choices.

In 1867, Cornelia and Milo's second child, Clara Maria was born and tragically, she died at the age of nine on December 2, 1876. Their third child, another daughter named Alice Clarilla, had been born three months before her sister's death in September.[32] Nothing is known about the circumstances of Clara's death; had she suffered from a long illness or was it an accident? But the long period between the birth of Alice and that of her older siblings may indicate that Clara may have been ill for a long time with not much chance of recovery. Or was Alice an "accident"? Milo and Cornelia had been there before. Whatever the circumstances, the Todd family had by then moved to Windsor Locks, Connecticut far from their families in Northford and Wallingford.

So, in 1868, Milo Todd had been married for three years, had two daughters, and had established himself in the paper making industry in Connecticut. He still faced the constant problem of not enough water power to produce paper in the amounts that would bring him to the next level. He was stuck and knew a change needed to be made. According to Earl May in *A Century of Silver*, that change came in the person of Mr. David S. Stevens of Wallingford, Connecticut. Stevens had learned the cutlery trade at a factory in the town of Prospect, Connecticut and had moved on to produce knives, forks, and spoons at another in Bristol. By 1868, he was operating a factory of his own manufacturing flatware in a shop located in an area called Quinnie that straddled the North Haven—Wallingford line at the head of the tidewater of the Quinnipiac River. Milo had heard he might be interested in a swap of properties. But for Todd, the real draw was the river and the power he could draw from it.

It is not clear what precipitated Steven's move to Northford but on

September 11, 1868 he purchased two pieces of property from Todd for $3000.00. The first was made up of nine acres, a dwelling house, and all the buildings on it. This must have been the Todd home. The second parcel was a "¼ acre lot, more or less with Factory building standing there on. Also the water power, raceway, with the privilege of repairing and maintaining the dam on land of said Thelus Todd". Milo also sold to Stevens his 1/3rd interest in Pistapaugh Pond.[33] Stevens quickly moved his silver plating and cutlery business to the Todd mill site and began production of spoons, knives, and forks in the factory building built by Todd to house his paper manufactury. Apparently the low volume of water did not impact his operation since the requirements for his machinery were apparently much less.

On November 6, 1868, North Haven Land Records show an entry registering the sale and transfer of the Stevens property to Milo Todd. Included in the sale were "9 acres, factory buildings, dwelling houses and other buildings…" More important for Todd was the following provision: "…all water power and privileges on the Quinnipiac River".[34] In return, Todd paid Stevens $9,500.00, a substantial sum at the time. He must have felt that the location where he was to create his future was worth the price and as he turned his back on Northford and his family's past, Milo must have felt himself at the entrance into the exciting, dynamic, and limitless world of the industrial explosion he had for so long yearned to be part of.

CHAPTER 8
Silver Sparkings

David Sterne Stevens (1823-1896) had for many years been part of the vibrant and expanding cutlery industry in Connecticut and by 1868 he must have realized that although his Britannia works was as good as anyone else's, his operation was becoming dwarfed by the larger companies that had blossomed along the Quinnipiac in Wallingford and further north in Meriden. The move to Northford perhaps was an attempt to stabilize his place in the market away from the frenzied pace being established by his competitors. Stevens would continue to produce cutlery in Milo's factory building along the Paug until 1879 and he eventually retired to Virginia in 1883. His son Elizur (1851-1926) had married Harriet (1852-1905), the daughter of Chapman Maltby, and in 1879 entered into a partnership with his father-in-law and became part of the firm of Maltby, Stevens, & Curtis. The business, located in Shelton, Connecticut was eventually moved to Wallingford. They became a leading supplier for many years of flatware for the Wm. Rogers Company of Hartford, key innovators in the electro-plating of silver onto Britannia ware.[1]

When David retired and Elizur moved the business permanently to Shelton, activity at the Todd/Stevens site came to an end. A slow, permanent period of decline set in as the cutlery factory, the early shop, and gristmill were abandoned and left to decay. Over the years, the elements and vandalism would exact their toll and 150 years of life vanished. All that was left were a scattering of artifacts under layers of soil, broken foundations, a blown out dam, and the silent ghosts of memory standing vigil over what had once been the vibrant home of hopes and dreams.

During our excavations in 1993 and 1994 at the Todd/Stevens Site we came across a substantial number of artifacts associated with the Stevens operation. We were able to establish which steps in the cutlery process took place where within the building as we slowly dug and sifted through the earth where the factory had stood. Perhaps at this point it would be best to describe how the spoons, knives, and forks were produced along with a bit of the history of the industry.

During the mid to late 19th century, Connecticut became the leading center for the production of Britannia, German Silver, and silver-plated cutlery. Prior to that time, the state had long been an important leader in the production of pewter and tin ware items which included some cutlery and these all became the basic fare of the famous Yankee Peddlers of the era. These travelling merchants wandered the roads throughout the state, region, and even as far as the Mississippi River hawking the wares produced by the state's tin and pewter shops. Those shops, located mostly in the central part of Connecticut in Berlin, Meriden, Wallingford, and a number of other towns churned out what seemed to be an endless supply for the carts of the peddlers. By the 1840's, many of the shops had grown into factories such as the one operated by Stevens and were producing a type of cutlery called Britannia ware while beginning to experiment with another type called German silver.[2]

Exactly when Britannia ware began to be manufactured in Connecticut is uncertain but it was first made in England around 1770. It is a pewter-like alloy made of 92% tin, 6% antimony, and 2% copper.[3] Unlike pewter that was made up of 80% tin and 20% lead, britannia metal contained no lead, was harder and firmer in its texture, and when polished had a better luster that lasted much longer.[4] Experiments producing Britannia were first made in Meriden, Connecticut during the first decade of the 19th century and by the 1820's two brothers from the Yalesville section of Wallingford, Charles and Hiram Yale, brought a few artisans from England to their pewter factory along the Quinnipiac River and began to manufacture the new type of cutlery. The popularity of the new ware, carried far and wide by the peddlers, spread quickly and demand triggered the establishment of dozens of new factories throughout central Connecticut. Seemingly overnight Wallingford and Meriden became the hub of this expanding industry.

The process of making Britannia metal was a step up in sophistication from that of pewter in both chemical formula and technique. Unlike pewter which is cast, Britannia is heated, spun into sheets, then when cooled items would be stamped out of the sheet. This allowed for a faster rate of production as now rough forms of the cutlery called blanks were stamped out of the cold sheets and then reworked and shaped into the desired knife, fork, or spoon. As popular as Britannia ware became, by the 1850's it started to lose some of its luster due to the introduction of German silver, discovered in the early 19th century by the German chemist E.A. Geitner. An alloy of copper, zinc, and nickel, German silver was even tougher than Britannia in its hardness and resistance to corrosion. The exact mixture of the alloy would depend on the intended use, the formula ranged from 50% to 61% copper, 17.2% to 19% zinc, and 21.1% to 30% nickel.[5] More important however was that it had high electrical resistance which was crucial in the next phase in the cutlery industry introduced into Connecticut by the Rogers brothers.

By the 1840's, brothers William, Asa, and Simeon Rogers, were well established as silversmiths, watch makers, and jewelers. Inventive and always looking for new products to sell from their shop, they had learned about a method to coat Britannia or German silver with silver through the process of electro-plating. Called the Elkington Process, it had stirred much interest at home in England and in the United States among inventive and scientific types and William began to experiment with it only to improve upon it in 1847.[6] Through this new process, the Rogers brothers were able to create cutlery that looked like silver but was stronger and more durable, held its shine longer, and was affordable for the growing number of middle class Americans yearning for the status symbols their rising wealth and prosperity could bring them.[7]

The process of silver-plating as introduced by the Rogers was relatively simple. Earthen vessels or tubs were filled with an alkaline plating solution (containing cyanide) and below them were two other tubs, one containing a plate of copper and one of zinc. These two tubs would produce an electrical or galvanic current used in the process. To begin the electro-plating, as it became known, a bar of silver was suspended in the alkaline solution at one end of the tub and at the other end a knife or other utensil formed from either the German Silver or Britannia alloy was suspended. A copper wire was brought up from each of the tubs containing the zinc and copper; one was put in contact with the silver and the other with the knife. The electrical charge transmitted through the solution would then dissolve the silver which passed through the alkaline solution and reappeared as a coating on the knife.[8] This revolutionary process of electro-plating was quickly understood by the Rogers brothers as a technique that might completely transform the cutlery industry but they lacked one crucial ingredient in the process; capital. In this new industrial age, ideas counted for nothing without the money to make them a reality. The brothers turned to Meriden.[9]

Under the leadership of Horace and Dennis Wilcox, seven small Britannia and German silver manufacturers in Meriden had organized into one large entity named the Meriden Britannia Company in 1852. The firm came to dominate much of the market producing Britannia and German silver ware and soon forged an agreement with the Rogers brothers to supply them with the Britannia and German silver cutlery or blanks for their silver plating process.[10] Meriden Britannia and the Rogers Brothers soon refined the silver-plating process and developed it into a more sophisticated operation on an industrial scale. The simple earthen tubs were replaced by large enamel lined iron vats, the solution became a mix of potassium cyanide and granulated silver in distilled water, and the electric charge necessary to the process was delivered from a device known as a dynamo.[11] The entire plating operation became more scientific and exact leading to a greater output of finished products. The use of this more highly developed plating process led to an explosion of large silver-plating manufacturers in the Meriden-

Stories on the Trail of a Yankee Millwright

Wallingford area as companies such as Wallace & Simpson, Hall, Elton, & Company, Charles Parker, and the Rogers Brothers themselves joined the scramble to capture market share.[12] Yet none matched the size and production volume of Meriden Britannia which eventually absorbed most of their competitors including the Rogers Brothers and Maltby, Stevens, & Curtis. This industrial giant by 1898 became known as The International Silver Company with a global market second to none.[13] Through the first half of the 20th century, International Silver dominated the industry and employed at its height thousands of workers locally and throughout the United States and Canada. Headquartered in Meriden, it gave the city its nickname, *The Silver City*.

When Milo Todd and David Stevens agreed to their swap of mill sites in 1868, the great era of growth and consolidation in the cutlery industry was in full swing and both must have had distinctly different reactions to it. Stevens, by moving to Northford, seems to have wanted to move away while Todd by relocating to the Quinnipiac River just south of the action, must have been excited and intrigued to be so close hoping to become part of it all. Years later, David's grandson and president of the International Silver Corporation, Evarts Chapman Stevens (1885-1956), reflecting on his family's role in the silver industry, described the family puzzlement at the move by his grandfather by stating "…for some reason which I haven't been able to fathom, my grandfather sold his property at Quinnie and moved his family to the village of Northford, six miles to the east, where he continued to operate a small plant on a mill privilege which he acquired in that town".[14] To the successful leader of an international corporation in the 20th century, his grandfather's act of turning his back on the action on the Quinnipiac was incomprehensible. Yet Stevens appears to have done fine for himself in his new location and from the evidence we found in our excavations, he produced many of the Britannia blanks required by the big silver-plating manufacturers and did some silver plating himself.

The 1870 U.S. Census gives us a snapshot look at the Stevens operation a year or so after moving it to Northford. In the listing, Stevens is identified as a spoon manufacturer utilizing 25h.p. of water from one wheel. The census also lists that he had a total of 12 machines associated with spoon making and that he employed 22 males 16 years or older, 1 female 16 or older, and 5 children. The report also states that the business was active twelve months out of the year and had a stock of tin, antimony and copper.[15] As the decade unfolded, it turned out the business probably did not grow much beyond this point and that by 1879 it was but a shadow of itself. Was it once again the problem of water supply that had driven Milo to leave his ancestral home?

During our archeological investigation of the factory site a number of Britannia blanks and cuttings were uncovered, some very crudely shaped in the form of the utensil whether a knife, spoon, or fork and some ready for buffing and finishing or silver plating. Along with the blanks and cuttings we also found two sheets of 1/8 inch thick Britannia. Our dig also revealed a surprising and interesting aspect of the Stevens operation in that many of these skeletons or utensils ready for plating were made of a mix of copper and nickel as opposed to Britannia and or German silver. If so, had Stevens found his market niche by turning out less durable and possibly less expensive flatware?[16]

Among other artifacts unearthed were a complete spoon, a four tined fork, and a number of broken parts of both made from German silver. A German silver spoon bowl and its stem were also found in the circular metal housing of the turbine water wheel.[17] Another significant find was the discovery of a dozen or so small six sided glass bottles about three inches in height. They were found in a cluster in one corner of the factory area and from their shape it is evident that they were designed to be packed together in a box so as to not be tipped. Gordon and I surmised that these must have contained the dangerous cyanide used in the plating process. Thankfully all were empty and without tops, the contents having been used and the bottles more than likely had been packed for a return to the supplier.[18] We also unearthed the remains of a brick furnace and surrounding floor that was where the metals used were melted to start the production process. The furnace contained a number of burned artifacts and pieces of coal.[19]

In the collection of the Totoket Historical Society is a diary of one of

Steven's workers during this period. Frank Wight kept a journal of his activities and work from January 1st to December 29th, 1879. It reflects in his simple notations, the vagaries of working in the shop and how he often was forced to seek other work to supplement that at the factory. An interesting aspect of Wight's account is that he was employed by the Stevens family the last year of their production on the Paug and his diary reflects the fact that work there was winding down. It also appears that Wight did not like the work there or working for the Stevens's.[20]

Wight's diary is chronological by day with often substantial gaps in between entries. It does show the varying jobs he performed but his primary role appears to be buffing the finished utensils. He noted:

January 4:	(went) to air line (railroad) depot 890 lbs. of coal
January 8:	Buffed spoons
January 13:	worked on tin spoons
April 9:	worked overtime. Hope it is the last day I shall buff
April 10:	moved the buffing lathe in the cutting down room
May 20-24:	worked today Deck did not work
July 28-31:	worked in the shop today
August 22:	got the machines all running today[21]

From his entries, it appears that Frank was a relatively unskilled worker, more of a laborer than a craftsman. While employed by the factory, he wrote that he turned twenty nine (February 22) a relatively late age for a man without a skill or true occupation. This may in fact reflect the changing economic circumstances and decline that had enveloped Northford by the late 1870's. In his diary, it is quite clear that he had to supplement his income and work by helping out local farmers and working in other shops employed for the most part as a day-laborer. Much of the outside work was done with or for a co-worker named Deck. The easy transition to work in a mill or on the farm captures the degree in which the two very different parts of the economy were still integrated in a small rural community like Northford which even in the 1870's, was more like the early mill towns of the first part of the century than the latter half. This easy movement back and forth would not have been found in the larger industrial towns and cities of Connecticut and the region.

> January 1:   Went up the mountain with Deck and got a load of wood
> January 11:   no work in shop—helped get ice
> April 12:   Went to Wallingford with Deck for pigs this afternoon
> April 13:   helped Deck get out the manure from the cow shed
> April 16:   worked for fuller today
> April 23:   Went to work at the rivet shop today
> May 30:   Decoration to day. Got two loads of wood
> June 8:   went strawberien to day
> June 9-11:   sick today did not work
> July 10:   got in three loads of hay
> July 12:   sowed turnips today and put ashes on corn
> July 16:   two loads of hay ready to go in the barn but they got wet
> July 17:   went claming this afternoon
> July 26:   Went to New Haven …and sold some chickings
> August 7:   went hucklebering this morning
> September 12:   commenced digging my potatoes to day
> September 21:   helped brake the colt[22]

Although the Stevens shop used coal as Frank Wight's journal indicates, it must have been purely for the furnace we found during our archeological investigation used to heat the metals. As for power to run the various machines used in the production of the utensils, Stevens relied on the often insufficient water supply that had plagued Milo all those years. Wight's diary shows what a problem this was during their last year of operation. Low or no water meant no work. Under those circumstances, the Stevens factory could not even dream of competing against the giants on the Quinnipiac. October of 1879 seems to have been particularly dry as Frank recorded:

> October 9:   Worked till half past three—had to stop for water

October 10: No work today—no water
October 11: Worked today
October 14: Worked till noon—no water
October 15: Worked till half past three—no water
October 16: Worked today—drawed the water most all but the pond[23]

The weather also had an impact on work along the Paug as too much water, cold, or heat could also shut things down. Unlike October, August must have been a wet month as the little stream overflowed and Wight wrote that on the night of the 18th water flooded into the shop and it took until the 22nd to get the machines running again.[24] As for problems caused by the temperature, winter's cold could freeze up the water supply making it impossible to run the machinery as must have been the case on January 21st when Wight recorded that the temperature was 14 below zero. On the opposite end of the scale, he noted on June 27th that it was "hot as the divel".[25] What must it have been like in the shop with that type of heat and little ventilation? As part of an advisory on silver plating in *Metal Working Illustrated* published in 1907, it is stated emphatically that ventilation is vital "… because all the exhalations of gas from the solutions are extremely poisonous and soon debilitate the strongest workmen when fresh air is absent". They go on to say that an even temperature is important for the proper working of the solutions and that employees do better and more work when "… the shop is well ventilated and comfortably warm".[26]

Weather extremes must have limited production for Stevens and added to grumbling by his workers as reflected at least on Wight's part, in his diary. On a number of occasions he writes of his displeasure or anxiety in regard to his work and future with the company. Twice he complains about his pay and how little it is and the amount and frequency must have been due to his limited hours at the factory or the fact that production was coming to an end. He wrote:

January 14: smallest pay I have got since I was a boy

September 4: got paied—the first time in three months[27]

His anxiety over the closing of the factory was evident as early as January when he wrote:

January 15: don't know how long I will have work
January 17: wish I had a nuther job—don't like the work it hurts my eyes
January 18: hope I will get a nuther job before I get out of work[28]

Wight did lose his job twice during the year but evidently was rehired shortly after the first time. On April 15th he noted he "got through up to the shop" but was back after working elsewhere by May 16th. The second time was permanent however as on October 27th he records "was made a free man today".[29]

It was obvious to Wight as early as January 18th that the factory might close as he wrote anxiously, as noted above, that he was hoping to find another job before he was out of work. On March 6th he wrote "they think they will not go to Birmingham with the spoon works".[30] They must have been the Stevens' and Birmingham was the section of Shelton that Elizur Stevens moved the operation to when he helped form Maltby, Stevens, and Curtis that year. Was there hesitation on the part of David and Elizur at that point? By March 12th however the decision had been made as Wight writes that "they took the cutting down lathes down today" and on the 18th he states "Bill __?__ and Bill __?__ and Bob Stephens went to Birmingham today".[31] This may very well have marked the start of production for Maltby, Stevens, and Curtis in their new home.

What happened to Frank Wight after the Stevens' closed the factory is not known. He may have eventually found himself employed at one of the surviving shops and factories in Northford, became a farm laborer, or drifted to Wallingford or Meriden where his experience may have landed him a job in one of the flatware factories there. As for the Stevens family, Elizur's branch went on to have an illustrious career in the flatware industry, first with Maltby, Stevens, and Curtis and after when it was absorbed into Meriden Britannia and eventually International Silver. As previously mentioned, David Stevens retired to property he bought along the Rappahannock River in Virginia following the closure of the Northford factory.[32] Two of his other sons however would take their creative and entrepreneurial skills in a completely different direction.

David S. Stevens Jr. and Henry M. Stevens probably worked in their father's shop after it moved to Northford though by 1871 they had begun to experiment with the printing of calling cards for businessmen. Their efforts soon branched into the printing and production of Christmas and Valentine's Day cards. The two it was said had a creative and artistic nature and an understanding of mass psychology that helped in regard to creating the two types of cards as well as for making "sparking" cards. Sparking cards were cards that young men, often too shy to approach a young lady in person, would send as a means of initiating a possible relationship.[33] They became extremely popular during the Victorian era when rather strict codes of morality and behavior were seen as proper and even mandatory when it came to relations between men and women. But it was their production of Christmas cards by 1877 that really propelled the brothers into the forefront of a trendy phenomenon that was sweeping the nation.[34]

Christmas cards first began to appear in the 1840's as a greeting and exchange of good will between neighbors and friends during the holiday just as it began to shake off the old Puritan restrictions on public celebration in New England. Important to this trend were changes in postal charges which had previously been the burden of the recipient. Now the sender simply paid a set price for what was sent. Post cards were also introduced in 1870 which provided an even less expensive way to send holiday wishes and cheer.[35] It was the opportunity inherent in this new and growing practice that the two Stevens brothers grasped and by the late 70's they certainly must have needed greater space than what was offered to them in their father's spoon factory. There is no mention of their presence in Frank Wight's 1879 diary so they must have already secured another location for their card printing operation by then. In

March of 1880 the brothers purchased from Chapman Maltby his old mill on the Farm River and it is more than likely that they had already been using space in the mill owned by their older brother-in-law for a number of years.[36]

The Stevens Brothers employed over fifty workers in 1880 and were producing highly ornamental and fancy Christmas cards that became immensely popular across the entire country. They had also created a local cottage industry in which women and children cut scraps of paper, fabric, lace, and other materials for trimming and pasting on to the fancy and elaborate creations that the public demanded. (May 1947, 129) These cards featured a wide range of images and symbols with the most popular being robins, evergreens, ivy, mistletoe, poinsettias, religious images, presents, holiday feasts, and of course St. Nicholas. [37]

The popularity of these fancifully trimmed cards continued into the 1890's and by then the Stevens Brothers Company had opened a second factory in Wallingford, reflecting no doubt the need to be near the main New Haven to Hartford railroad line that ran through the center of that town in order to receive the volume of paper needed to produce the cards and to ship out the thousands produced.[38]

Still, during the decade of the 1890's, Northford became known as "the Christmas Card Center of the World" as the Stevens Brothers struggled to keep up with the demand insisted on by the American public. Their success spawned over 25 local competitors who even though they were competing directly with the larger enterprise on the Farm River, also performed work jobbed out to them.[39] But the future was in the cards so to speak. The move to Wallingford was an acknowledgement that production costs were too high when it came to remaining in Northford and competitors elsewhere in the country and in Germany and England were chipping away at their market share.[40] The Stevens brothers closed their operation on the Farm River and by the early 1900's, the last spark of industry in Northford was gone.

Elizur Stevens, after the move to Shelton in 1879 to run the new firm of Maltby, Stevens, and Curtis, built the company quickly into a leading supplier of flatware for the Rogers Company. Undeterred by a fire that destroyed the factory building in 1883, he moved the entire operation to the old Hall, Elton, and Company factory on the Quinnipiac River in Wallingford and went back into production.[41] The building, located on a pond called Community Lake formed by a dam on the Quinnipiac, had recently been owned by the Wallingford branch of the Oneida Community, a utopian religious society headquartered in upstate New York. In moving to the Hall and Elton shop, Elizur had come full circle; when he first worked for his father as a young man in Quinnie, his father's factory had been a chief supplier of Britannia blanks to Hall, Elton and Company.[42] All roads it seemed, led back to the Quinnipiac.

When Maltby, Stevens, and Curtis was absorbed into Meriden Britannia which then became International Silver, Elizur played a prominent role in both company's growth and leadership. He brought his son, Evarts Chapman Stevens (1885-1956) into the business and the younger Stevens rose through the ranks to become president of The International Silver Corporation from 1935 until 1946.[43] What David Stevens might have thought of his grandson rising to the top of the industry he had helped to establish but also fled from is anyone's guess, but I would like to believe he would have viewed his success with a mix of pride in his achievement and wonder at the sheer scale of the business he came to supervise.

During the 1880's and 90's, Meriden Britannia continued to buy up and absorb competitors in the flatware industry and in 1898 renamed itself The International Silver Company and although an international operation, focused much of its production in the Meriden area. The small twenty to thirty man, one storied shops of David Steven's era had by then been replaced with colossal four storied brick giants employing hundreds of workers. Men and women seeking jobs from throughout the region flocked to the factories and were increasingly joined by immigrants from Germany, Ireland, and the Slavic regions of Europe, especially Poland. By 1910, Meriden and to a lesser extent Wallingford, had grown into a vibrant, cosmopolitan community of diverse ethnic neighborhoods all chasing the promise of the American Dream the factories had to offer.

The city continued to grow during the first half of the 20th century as later immigrant groups such as Italians, African-Americans from the U.S. South, and after World War II waves of job-seekers from Puerto Rico flocked to Meriden. As the city grew, so did the wealth of its middle and upper classes who managed the factories or owned auxiliary businesses that provided services in order to meet the ever growing demands of the industry and the increasingly affluent population. Builders and developers strained to meet the demand for housing and the cityscape took on the appearance of a confident and wealthy Victorian community made up of the high-style mansions of the wealthy, the tidy and tasteful homes of the middle class, and the two and three family houses of the working class. This was the Meriden of Evarts Chapman Stevens as he presided over what must have seemed to everyone a remarkable dream men like Stevens had molded into a reality through their drive, ambition, and determination; a world of unlimited progress, wealth and possibilities. It was truly Meriden's silver age.

Elizur stopped for a moment to take in the view from the top floor of the newly constructed and operating four story brick factory. It stretched nearly a city block and sat over- looking the intersection of East Main and Broad Streets which was becoming an area of elegant and modern Victorian homes and it all, he reminded himself, was a legacy of what he and the other officers of Meriden Britannia had created. Yes indeed, he thought with pride, as he gazed west towards Meriden Mountain in the far distance realizing he was almost as high up as its peak. Stevens smiled when he somewhat arrogantly surmised that yes, we are capable of building monuments equal to those of nature and even nature's God.

"Here it is, 1893", he said as he turned to his secretary. "We have come a long way from our beginnings haven't we Arthur" he said to the attentive young man who stood respectfully two steps behind. "In little more than fifteen years we have transformed that valley below us from a collection of small villages and farms into this modern city we see before us. Is there no limit to what the future may hold?" he stated with pride as Arthur fumbled

with his note pad and hesitated to interrupt Mr. Stevens and inform him he had a meeting to attend in five minutes.

"Yes sir. The possibilities for the future are endless" Arthur said as he found himself suddenly reminiscing as well about the day he had announced to his family of his being hired as Mr. Steven's secretary. His parents, both immigrants from Germany had come to Meriden in the hopes of finding work and his father had found it first with the Charles Parker Company and then with Meriden Britannia. His parents had struggled and worked hard and insisted he stay in school and become an "American" and in that way find himself a fine middle class job. "You do not want to work with your hands like me when you have such a fine mind my son" Arthur recalled his father would always say. "Stay in school and make your mother and me proud". So he had and for that he was now eternally grateful that he was not allowed to leave at 13 like so many of his fellow German friends who thought of nothing other than work in the factories, beer, and girls.

Just then Elizur turned and said "are we late for our meeting Arthur?"

"No not yet sir" was his reply, "we do have four minutes and it is in the administrative offices just below on the second floor" as he quickly glanced at his pocket watch, a gift from Mr. Stevens for his loyal service to him and the company.

"Well, let's make haste Arthur, I do not want to be the cause of a delay. As you know, the key to our success has always been timely efficiency in all aspects of this operation from the top down". Arthur smiled as he thought how often he had heard him say that phrase and how Mr. Stevens actually lived it and expected all at Meriden Britannia to do the same.

As they walked to the stairwell the noisy hum of the machines on the floor and the singular focus of each worker operating them brought a feeling of pride to Elizur. This is efficiency of production, each man doing his part thought Stevens as he followed Arthur into the stairway. As he descended the steps his thoughts returned to those days working besides his father back at Quinnie and Northford, never imagining then the full potential of this industry that they had both been pioneers in. If only father might see this wonder of manufacturing, what would he think? And wouldn't Chapman be amazed and proud as well as he thought of his father-in-law who had convinced him to leave Northford and take their newly formed company to Shelton saying "the future lies elsewhere and it is there that Maltby, Stevens, and Curtis will make its mark". And so it was despite the devastating fire and the move to Wallingford into that old factory built by the Communists.

But he also remembered the words of both his father and Chapman, "…remember Elizur, its product development, efficiency of production, and marketing that make the difference" and how he had taken them to heart and lived those words every day. Some call me driven and that may be so, he thought, but that advice has served me and Meriden Britannia well. Arthur opened the door to the meeting and all present rose to their feet from their chairs around a large ornately carved oak table. "Good afternoon Mr. Stevens they stated in unison.

What happened? World War II for starters. Like all industrial giants at the time, International Silver retooled its production to meet the needs of the U.S. Government and the Armed Forces. Insilco, the name by which the company had become informally known, continued to produce flatware but the customer was no longer the discerning American housewife, but the U.S. Military. During the war the company produced an estimated 250,000,000 pieces for the Army and Navy.[44] But they also turned their expertise in chemicals that had continued to refine their flatware products into research and production of incendiary bombs and hundreds of other war products all critical to the war effort.[45] By June, 1943, the company was on 100% war production footing.[46]

Following peace in 1945, International Silver under the leadership of Evarts Stevens began the process of returning to their core flatware industry. This presented an entirely new set of problems ranging from the Federal government's control of silver stockpiles to how to reintegrate returning veterans into the work force thus displacing women and minorities that had filled their positions during their absence.[47] There was also the issue of rebuilding consumer demand for company flatware products which by the early 1950's were facing increasing foreign competition. By 1955, that competition, especially from low cost stainless steel Japanese flatware, was cutting deeply into the company's market share and those in charge decided to begin the process of diversifying.[48] The irony here was that those who had suffered the impact of the company's incendiary bombs were now burning into the company's profits. This started International Silver on its move out of the flatware industry and into electronics, communications, automotive components, office products, and specialty publishing. By 1965, flatware products made up less than 50% of the company's sales. In 1969 the company was officially renamed Insilco and International Silver became a small subsidiary with an ever shrinking contribution to company profits.[49]

Beginning in 1970, local flatware plants began to close and the workforce shrank accordingly. Like many other Connecticut and Northeastern manufacturing cities at the time, Meriden started to spiral downward into a slow but steady decline as factory after factory closed. The reasons were complex and varied, but the high costs of labor and shipping, outdated facilities dating back to the late 19th and early 20th Centuries, the decline of the American railroad system, and fierce competition from low wage, low tax competitors in other sections of the United States and foreign countries sounded the death knell for factory after factory and job after job. In 1982 Insilco moved its headquarters to Ohio, sold International Silver to a foreign competitor, and the last factory closed in 1984.[50] 130 years of not just an industry, but all the hopes, dreams and promises of a better tomorrow inherent to it disappeared leaving behind only hulking brick monuments to the past, their cavernous and empty spaces housing dust and memories. They too would soon be gone as the once proud edifices began to crumble, burned, or were torn down in a desperate attempt to revitalize a dying city now plagued with poverty and despair as those who could fled and those who couldn't remained often the victims of joblessness and dependent on government assistance.

Like many American cities faced with decline due to the desertion of their manufacturing base, Meriden enthusiastically embraced the bewitching scheme launched in the 1960's by architectural planners and the Federal Government of revitalization through urban renewal.

According to a study done by Yale University a number of years ago, government officials, city planners, architects and sociologists touted the idea that by removing the aging infrastructure that made up the core of these declining cities and replacing it with modern yet distinctly separate residential, retail, and commercial/industrial areas serviced by accommodating highways, it was possible to rejuvenate the economic and cultural lives of these communities. The plan was simple: to solve the problems of the present the past had to be erased.[51] In the process, not only did they tear out the historic infrastructure of these once vibrant small cities, in most cases they tore the very heart out of the neighborhoods and community they had come to save. Somehow new buildings and highways would make new people and solve all the problems of economic and social decay.[52] Meriden bought in wholeheartedly in 1970.

The result was the whole-sale destruction of large sections of the city's central core including industrial, commercial, retail, and residential buildings that formed the heart and soul of the community. The plan was to locate a modern retail mall there that would miraculously save the city and bring businesses, people, and consumers back. Although the mall was built, it was doomed from the start.[53] Instead of revitalization, Meriden faced only accelerated decline. This well-intentioned plan, together with the building of Interstate 691 that tore through the northern half of the city only made it easier for motorists to avoid Meriden rather than stop and shop or do business. The final blow came with the building of a larger enclosed retail mall just off the Interstate on the city's western outskirts that siphoned what was left of downtown retail customers away from the center to join regional shoppers who now could avoid what was increasingly seen as a decrepit and possibly dangerous central core.

Visionary plans had failed. The good, well-paying jobs were gone. The Meriden that allowed residents to walk to church, shop, or jobs was gone. The factories stood vacant, neighborhoods crumbled, and there seemed to be no solution, no fix. Yet city leaders kept trying; new plans were imagined, proposed, and sometimes enacted throughout the 1980's and 90's but the scale of what had to be done was beyond the capacity of even the best of intentions.

But the people of Meriden have never given up. The middle class, those who did not flee, are still present though perched on the city's periphery in the more suburban-like sections. Together with inner city activists they continue to push for a new vision, one that will merge the best of the old with the best of the future and the focus of this vision is once again the central core. The site of the now forgotten center mall is being transformed into a large, multi-purpose city green complete with an uncovered Harbor Brook that once provided power to 19th century mills. Directly to the west, a plan has been submitted to turn the dilapidated and closed railroad station into a modern intermodal commuter hub with revitalized housing and retail utilizing still existing historic structures. The center will once again be the livable, people friendly heart of the city.[54] From there it is envisioned, revitalization will spread to the old Victorian neighborhoods that surround the center bringing back the tidy streetscapes the proud workers of Meriden Britannia and International Silver once walked. But can this vision work without the good paying jobs those workers once had?

The quest for success and wealth unleashed in places like Northford, Wallingford, and Meriden in the 19th century epitomized what was then the American Dream; be creative, take risks, and work hard and you can make your fortune and change the world. Men like the Maltbys', Fowlers' and the Stevens' all believed it to be true and lived it. As a result, they helped to transform their communities, state, and nation in the process. Could they ever have imagined in little more than a century so much would change? Although there were certainly manifold negative economic, social, cultural aspects to their time, it was still a world of progress and possibilities, not regression and anxiety. What would they think if today they visited the places where their soaring dreams had become a reality for themselves and so many others?

Once again, what about Milo Todd?

CHAPTER 9
Utopias on the Quinnipiac

Milo Todd knew he had finally made it to the place where his scheme to build a life of achievement and success might finally take hold and earn for him a place in that utopian paradise of innovation and creation that was transforming society along the Quinnipiac. He was confident his place would be assured as he moved his machines and dreams the six miles west to their new home in the factory buildings just vacated by David Stevens. Here he knew was the one thing that had always kept him frustrated and had blocked his success. Like the life giving blood that flowed through his veins, his machines needed water and here there was plenty. It was here in Quinnie, straddling the North Haven-Wallingford line, that he would make his mark. Connecticut, he was confident, needed his paper.

Like a man possessed, Todd dove frantically into a web of financing and property purchases to secure for himself a position as a player in the exploding industrial age before he had even begun to produce a single sheet of paper for that eager market waiting within his imagination. Land records show, in rapid succession beginning in the fall of 1868, that he was a man impatient to arrange all that he needed to become the entrepreneur his ambition was pushing him to be. I can't help but picture Milo impatiently pacing the floor of his factory building, inspecting the dam, checking the water wheels, tinkering with his equipment, and making the deals he just knew would soon get his machines mixing, drying, rolling, and cutting his straw and rag paper. He could feel his future.

In the September, 1868 transaction that brought Stevens to Northford, Milo had been paid $3000.00.[1] This then set off a series of six transactions recorded in the North Haven Land Records between October 29th to November 10th that show Milo buying two tracts of land along the Quinnipiac, one from Stevens for $9,500 where he would open his factory and move his family, and the other from Henry Rogers just to the north for $3,500.00.[2] The reason for this purchase, which included six acres, a manufacturing house, other buildings, and water privileges is not really clear but I surmise that Todd did not want any interference with his supply of water which this property might potentially have threatened. Obviously his anxiety over water problems along the Paug still haunted him. Recorded on the same day is another transaction, this time between Milo and his uncle Ambrose Todd of New Haven. Apparently Milo had borrowed $2,000.00 from his uncle to help purchase the Rogers land and in this transaction he promised to pay the above sum to his uncle as part of the purchase.[3] Later, in November 1870, Milo paid a quit claim to Ambrose of $1.00 for the property and thus owned it outright, his debt to his uncle erased.[4]

On November 6, 1868, Todd's purchase of the Stevens property was entered into the North Haven Land Records. In return for the payment of $9,500.00 Milo received nine acres with factory buildings and dwelling houses except for that of Stephen Morse. How many factory buildings and dwelling houses there were is not mentioned. More important for Todd however was the "… fixtures and machinery, gristmill, and all water privileges on the Quinnipiac River". Also included in the record is a notation that the purchase was subject to David Stevens paying a mortgage claim of $2,500.00 to the heirs of Henry Elliot which he apparently did.[5] But this was not the end of Milo's transactions. The next day, November 7th, it is recorded that he made an additional purchase of two acres and a building bordering the Stevens tract from Erastus Pierce for $1,000.00.[6] This brought him to a total of seventeen acres on or along the river at a cost of $14,000.00. This was a substantial sum in

Stories on the Trail of a Yankee Millwright

1868 for an individual whose assets, based upon his success or lack of it back in Northford, may have been limited. Even when the $3,000.00 from Stevens is deducted, Milo had spent $11,000.00. Where did the money come from?

One source was listed in the Land Records two days later, on November 9th. It detailed a rather complex agreement with Samuel Morse who owned not only the dwelling of Stephen, but also operated a Bolt Shop on the parcel bought from Stevens. Milo sold to him ¼ acre of land on the river that included the shop and house. This parcel was part of what had once been the Doolittle Mill and had water rights which Todd needed to acquire in order to forgo any future water disputes. The language of the agreement gives us a snap shot look into the intricate world of 19th century water rights and an interesting view of the property as well. It states that Morse is "…allowed to draw three square feet of water ten hours per day as long as they choose so long as water shall keep running over the dam except in severe drouth. Said Todd reserves the first use of the water sufficient to run two wheels. Morse & Co. to own and maintain 1/3rd part of the dam twenty feet from the headrace being included as part of dam. Grantees also have the right to pass to shop in front of the gristmill".[7] Here we can clearly see Milo's concern for sufficient water to run his paper machines and his need to specifically come to an equitable agreement with Morse.

In return for his arrangement with Morse & Company, Todd received $3000.00. This along with the $3000.00 from David Stevens gave him a total $6,000.00 leaving a negative balance of $8,000.00. On November 10, the last of his flurry of transactions was recorded when Milo again turned to the Townsend Bank in New Haven for a mortgage of $5,000.00.[7] This left him with a deficit of $3,000.00 plus the $2,000.00 he owed his uncle Ambrose for a total of $5,000.00. Adding the mortgage from Townsend Bank, Milo went into production with a $10,000.00 debt. How this debt was dealt with is a mystery; did Todd have savings from his paper operation in Northford that he used? Did he rely on the support of family members besides his uncle Ambrose? A clue is found in the Land Records entered on January 5, 1869 which states that Milo granted his father one acre at his new factory site and in return, Thelus paid $1.00 and "valuable consideration".[9] Did his steadily conservative father decide to help his ambitious and maybe in his eyes, impetuous son and in return receive a piece of Milo's future? Did other family members, including those of Cornelia, the Cooks of Wallingford, also help out? We'll never know, but my guess is yes. Who could resist what must have been the enthusiastic appeal, promise, and salesmanship of a man determined to go beyond the steady and secure role of a millwright grinding the grain of his neighbors and kin?

Whatever the circumstances were, as 1869 began, Todd's new venture was off and running and though it had come to life after a frenetic and shaky financial birth, he was ready for the next step in his scheme to take his place in the pantheon of modern manufacturing. In order to do so, and strapped for cash and in substantial debt, Milo continued to work that spring and summer to maneuver himself and his newly named the Quinnipiac Paper Company into the modern era by creating a joint stock company and selling shares. Investors he hoped would help settle his debt and give him the capital he needed to begin the production of paper on a sufficient scale to make a profit. Just up the river for example, the Wallingford Community was running a profitable and well respected printing operation and to connect with them and other high volume printing operations would be much more likely if the Quinnipiac Paper Company carried the legitimacy of a stock company instead of an individual owner.[10] Then there were all those Britannia manufacturers. Milo Todd was thinking big.

Who his investors were and how many actually signed on is unfortunately unknown but my suspicion is that they were once again local family and maybe a few residents of Wallingford and North Haven willing to take a risk with the ambitious go-getter. By mid-summer, Todd had made the prudent financial step of turning over the ownership of his dream on the river to the Quinnipiac Paper Company for "$1.00 and valuable considerations". In the North Haven Land Records it is stated that Milo sold to the new company "...all my right, title, and interest in and to a certain piece or tract of land situated in North Haven... together with buildings thereon and water power upon said land appurtenant to the paper mill thereon said water being conveyed in a raceway from the dam of said Todd a short distance above said mill".[11] The boundaries of the tract are defined by its borders but not in terms of the size of the lot. The boundaries were the eastern bank of the river, land Milo owned on two sides, and that of the neighbors. Todd had carefully turned over to the paper company only the buildings and the lot they were on and not the rest of his acreage, buildings, and dam.

In the *History of Wallingford* by Charles Davis, published in 1870, along with a prideful telling of the town's history from its founding in 1670 until its bicentennial year in 1870, there is a detailed account of its many distinguished citizens followed by a listing and brief description of all the businesses and manufactories located there. Notable among them are the flatware giants such as Wallace Brothers Silversmiths and the other manufacturers that had been transforming the once sleepy agricultural village into a growing industrial center over the past decades. Listed on page 494 is: "The Quinnipiac Paper Company established at Quinnipiac two miles south of Wallingford Village for the manufacture of paper".[11] It is fun to imagine how Milo must have felt when he opened his copy of the book explaining the illustrious history of 200 years of Wallingford's growth and progress and there listed along with all the other successful industries—his. At last, he must have felt, he had finally become part of that elite and magical world he had dreamed of all those years ago in his grandfather's gristmill. There it was for all to see; The Quinnipiac Paper Company.

But all was not as it seemed. During March of that year, Milo had turned to his uncle Ambrose once again and borrowed $5,500.00 against "...one acre together with paper mill building and waterpower".[12] Listed as well was his agreement to repay the promissory note in six months. How he could have turned over the paper mill and water power to both his uncle and the stock company is a rather interesting question but maybe, by the time the stock company had been formed in July Milo had somehow come up with the cash to pay his uncle back. Regardless, the constant maneuvering and scheming inherent to the creation of the

Quinnipiac Paper Company does not suggest Milo's dream had yet to find sound financial footing and presents an image of a man desperately trying to still make it all a reality.

In November, 1870, Milo registered one more real estate transaction ending two years of a continuous quest to secure his factory operation in Quinnie and one that may have resolved what could be viewed as a series of manipulative decisions. On the 15th of that month the record shows that Todd paid the Quinnipiac Paper Company $1.00 and valuable considerations to regain control of significant portions of his property. The deal stated that he would regain ownership of "…the gristmill, spoon shop, and other buildings known as the office and packing room, hay scales, and all the shafting and machines in said mills and shops and also all the water power afforded by the Quinnipiac River and the dam there situated excepting that portion previously sold to Morse & Company and the Quinnipiac Paper Company".[14] As a result, Milo controlled all the property, factory buildings, dwelling houses, dam, and water power except for that deeded to Morse & Company, the one acre lots sold to his father and uncle, and the paper company mill and its water power. The questionable element of all this was having turned the paper mill over to Ambrose Todd in March and then to the Quinnipiac Paper Company in July, where did actual ownership lie? The land records are silent. But in regard to the property where the paper mill sat, things settled down and I would like to think that Milo was finally able to put his attention to doing what he had intended to do when he first purchased the site from David Stevens—make paper and hopefully some money.

Whether Todd ran the gristmill, which he may very well have due to his experience of operating the family mill back in Northford, and how the spoon shop might have been used is not known. My guess is that the grist mill provided a steady seasonal income and that he may have rented out the spoon shop. Once on Milo's trail, I had hoped to be able to visit the site of the paper mill, other buildings, and the dam he owned and operated along the Quinnipiac River in order to gain a better understanding of the property from any structures or their remains that still were visible and might tell of past activities. Unfortunately, the property, sandwiched between the river and the old colonial Hartford Turnpike had the four lane Wilbur Cross Parkway (Connecticut Rt. 15) running right down the middle of it and any possible remnants from the site were long gone. It is an unfortunate fact of history that so many places that had once housed vibrant and significant chapters in the lives of those who had come before us such as Milo's have been erased forever. For the many thousands of people who drive over the place of his dreams each day as they speed their way north towards Hartford or south towards New Haven, Milo Todd is not even a memory and why would he be? But the world he had lived in, the hopes he had put into his schemes along the Quinnipiac, and the industrial growth he sought so hard to be part of are significant parts of our collective past and helped to shape the places and world we live in today. Perhaps Milo Todd would find comfort in that.

Less than two miles up the Quinnipiac from Milo's paper factory something different was happening. It was also a place where dreams of a different life were taking root, a place where God's Heaven on Earth was being created called the Wallingford Community of Perfectionists. They had come to Wallingford in 1851 when the Allen family, long time and distinguished residents of the town, donated their farm on the western bank of the Quinnipiac River as a second home for the utopian Oneida Community that had grown around the leadership of John Humphrey Noyes.

Noyes (1811-1886), originally from Brattleboro Vermont, was the son of a prominent banker and Congressman, and cousin of President Rutherford B. Hayes. Educated at Dartmouth College, he was a child of wealth and privilege who entered the Yale School of Theology intent on becoming a foreign missionary like so many of his fellow New Englanders during the first half of the 19th century. I would like to think that while there he likely knew a few of the young men from Northford whose religious fervor had brought them to Yale as well. While in New Haven however Noyes fell under the influence of a local revivalist preacher whose passionate zeal revealed to him the vision of a new way of obtaining salvation known as Perfectionism.[15] Enthusiastically embracing Perfectionism, his study of the Bible intensified leading Noyes to search for the date of the Second Coming of Jesus, which he determined through a revelation, to have had already taken place in 70 A.D. Noyes thus concluded that mankind was now living in a new age in which God's Kingdom on Earth was possible for those who could truly see and embrace it. Noyes also concluded that only those who were truly free from sin were true Christians and that the beliefs and teachings of established churches were false. He declared that because only those who were free of sin were true Christians, he in fact due to this revelation, was. His radical pronouncements set off a firestorm within the school and Noyes was expelled.

Upon his return to Vermont in 1834, Noyes settled in the town of Putney and began to preach and write about his vision of salvation. Slowly he began to attract around him a following including the daughter of the local Congressman named Harriet Holton, who was an early convert and became his wife in 1838. By 1847 John Noyes had gathered together a small but devoted congregation of forty followers and through correspondence and publications had become the de-facto leader of various bands of Perfectionist around the country.[16]

Perfectionists believed that it was possible for individuals to perfect an immediate and complete cessation of sin and by coming together to form a church on Earth, they would presage the approaching and imminent Kingdom of Heaven. This church would make it possible for members to enter into a direct communion with God which would lead them to perfect holiness, and salvation.[17] Perfectionism, born out of the country-wide religious revival known as the Second Great Awakening that began in the 1790's and reached its peak in the 1830's, was one of many religious movements that Americans turned to in the face of the enormous economic, social, and political changes that were reshaping the country during the first decades of the 19th century. Like some of the other religious movements at the time, among them the Millerites, Harmonists, and Shakers, Perfectionists hoped to create a utopian community on Earth that would allow them to worship and practice their beliefs removed from a world they saw as corrupt and increasingly depraved and sinful. But unlike more mainstream denominations such as the Methodists, Baptists, and Pentecostals whose numbers swelled during this time, the utopian movements were seen as an extreme and radical answer to the quest for redemption and salvation and thus outside the norm of acceptable religious revivalism.

As Noyes' Putney congregation slowly grew in the early 1840's, he continued to refine his views on what God's Kingdom on Earth would entail and moved steadily towards a number of social positions for which his Perfectionists would be noted; Communalism (communal property and possessions), Complex Marriage, Ascending Fellowship, and Mutual Criticism.[18] By 1845 he had begun the process of preparing his followers for communal life which he preached would duplicate life in the Kingdom of Heaven. All property would be shared in a true communist fashion, all members would be equal, and the efforts of each would contribute to the well-being of the whole.[19] The result, Noyes believed, would be a completely different culture in which the pressures of a competitive economic society would be removed allowing members to emulate the conditions he believed existed in Heaven. Without property, distinctions between individuals ceased to exist and harmony within the community would be possible.[20]

In his 1870 *History of Wallingford*, Charles Davis interviewed members of the Wallingford Community about the benefits of communal living. The members explained to Davis many of the aspects of their form of communism that they believed had a positive effect on both the community as a whole and the individuals within it. The Perfectionists claimed that by eliminating the distinctions between rich and poor, they had eliminated all forms of social oppression inherent to that distinction and had consequently elevated the idea that all labor, no matter how menial, was of equal value as that it benefited the entire community. Under their system, the Wallingford Community members felt each individual was better able to pursue and develop their particular talents and interests while experiencing a greater variety of occupational opportunities. As a result, each individual felt that they were contributing to the betterment of the entire group while advancing their own growth as a person. This equality of opportunity extended to both sexes, something that raised eyebrows to outside observers as on occasion women performed roles traditionally those of men.[21] Women, for example were found in the Printing Office in Wallingford working as writers, editors, and printers.[22] Tirzah Miller, who lived and worked in Wallingford for a period of time, wrote in her journal how she had been promoted to editor of *The Circular*, the Onieda Community's main monthly publication. What might have been Milo's reaction the first time he called at the Printing Office and found Tirzah in charge?

The Perfectionists further explained to Mr. Davis that their communal life-style had led to substantial relief among their members from the economic and social anxieties routinely experienced by those living in the greater society. Removed from those economic and social pressures found within the established culture, they claimed to have experienced a remarkable improvement in their physical health and psychological well-being.[23] With this freedom came a blossoming of personal growth in all aspects of life, including education, which was encouraged for both sexes while allowing all to concentrate on furthering their spiritual growth. This in turn led to what the members described as improved conditions of intellectual and religious life.[24]

Probably no other aspect of life within the Wallingford and parent Onieda Communities was seen as more controversial than their practice of Complex Marriage. Since the Perfectionists were recreating Heaven on Earth, Noyes preached that, according to the teachings of Jesus, there was no marriage in Heaven and therefore all men were married to all women and thus all should be sexually intimate with a variety of partners. This practice of complex marriage was seen as essential to the well-being of the community in that it eliminated traditionally divisive commitments to one partner and raised the level of loyalty and love inherent in those relationships to the entire family as the community was called.[25] This practice of what the outside world called "free sex" was believed by Noyes to have deeper social and spiritual functions beyond just being a biological act and thus was another path leading to perfection.[26] He often determined what partnerships were formed and very often encouraged relations between the more and less devout with the goal being that those more advanced spiritually would influence the attitude and behavior of their lessors. This practice, called Ascending Fellowship, was understood to elevate the less developed individual to greater moral and spiritual heights through association with one who had achieved a more advanced state. These sessions, called interviews, were also encouraged to be with a variety of partners in the hopes that exclusive or romantic attachments would not develop. Liaisons were always arranged through a third party in order to make sure that both parties were in agreement.[27]

Post-menopausal women were encouraged to have relationships with teenaged males in order to allow both to experience partners without the fear of pregnancy and for the older women to act as spiritual role models while teaching the young men the important practice of "male continence", the primary form of family birth control.[28] At the same time, younger women were often introduced to sex by older men. Married couples entering the community were not asked to dissolve their marriage but rather to expand the circle of those they entered into relationships with. As the Perfectionists explained to Charles Nordhoff in his interviews with them for his study of 19th century utopian societies titled *American Utopias*, these expanded sexual/spiritual relationships resulted in a degree of social harmony not found in the outside society.[29]

Because the practices of the Perfectionists discouraged any form of what they termed "sinful selfishness" and "exclusive and idolatrous attachments", this belief also extended to the decision to have children. The supervision over relationships thus included who would produce children with the idea that a child was to be conceived only after suitable partners were chosen and arrangements made by Noyes and other members of the leadership based on the spiritual growth and moral qualities of the perspective parents. This program of social engineering was called stirpiculture and was introduced in 1869 first in the main Oneida Community and consequently in Wallingford as well. The goal of this selective breeding was to create increasingly perfect children who would populate God's Kingdom on Earth as spiritually advanced individuals.[30]

In order to discourage a sense of selfishness and special attachment between parent and child, children were raised in a communal nursery under the supervision of women and men specially chosen for that position. It was felt however, that it was best that newborns and infants be left in the care of their mothers until weaned in order to assure the health of the child until he or she was moved to the general nursery. From that point on parents were allowed to visit their children on a regular basis but discouraged from developing too exclusive a relationship. This was not done out of cruelty to hurt the child or parent, but rather as part of a desire to raise more perfect people who would as an adult embrace all members of the community with caring and love.

Charles Nordhoff, in his visit to the Oneida Community in the 1870's visited the two nurseries there, one for children under the age of three or four, and the other for those older. He reflected on what he saw by stating: "The children I saw were plump, and looked sound; but they seemed to me a little subdued and desolate, as though they missed the exclusive love and care of a father and mother. This, however, may have been only fancy; though I should grieve to see in the eyes of my own little ones an expression which I thought I saw in the Oneida children, difficult to describe—perhaps I might say a lack of buoyancy, or confidence and gladness".[31] How much Nordhoff allowed his personal bias, as he states, to influence his view of the nursery is unknown but the communal raising of children was viewed by the general public as a substantial departure from societal norms. As for the Wallingford Community with its much smaller population, the same practice would have been put into practice there though a photograph taken in 1868 does not show any infants and only two or three older children.[31] Since the movement of members between the two communities was quite fluid, expectant women more than likely went to live at Oneida where proper numbers made communal child raising more functional.

William Alfred Hinds, who became a member of the Oneida

Community as a sixteen year old boy in 1849, reflected on the child rearing practices which he witnessed as a community member in his study of American communistic societies, *American Communities* published in 1878. In his interviews with community members they stated that through the entire period of childhood, no mother is ever separated from their child for any length of time. One interviewee explained: "We aim to deal with our children according to the dictates of the most enlightened common sense combined with a tender regard for human weakness; but how to bring them up under the best moral, spiritual, intellectual, physical and social conditions has been a problem requiring the deepest study on the part of the community for many years".[32] Their system the Perfectionists believed, freed parents to pursue activities which best benefited the community as a whole as well as their own continued spiritual growth.

Communal childrearing was seen as still allowing parents the liberty to freely associate with their children whenever they wanted while the practice was believed to be in the best interest of both and thus a significant improvement over the more common way of raising children.[34] Without selfish attachment, all would contribute to the creation of God's Heaven on Earth.

In a society such as that of the Perfectionists built upon the bedrock of common interest and selflessness, a system of reflection and criticism was seen as critical to the ability of the community to survive. Somehow the human tendency towards self-interest had to be eliminated and replaced with collective interest or else personal desire would in the end destroy God's Kingdom. Since selfish attachments and desires did not exist in Heaven they had no place at Oneida or Wallingford. In order for this to happen, Noyes early on instituted a practice called Mutual Criticism. According to Hinds, this was a practice John Humphrey Noyes first encountered as a member of a secret society while studying at the Andover Seminary to become a missionary.[35] Each member of that society would routinely submit themselves to "sincere comment" and criticism from the other members as a form of self-improvement and growth which Noyes claimed benefited him greatly in his personal and spiritual development. This practice he understood if instituted on a regular basis would root out self-interest and help each individual member experience the benefits as he had in the past and continued to benefit from as a member of the Perfectionist Community.

At Oneida and Wallingford this practice of Mutual Criticism formed the basis of how each community was run. The practice took place during the evening meetings that were held each day following dinner during which all matters pertaining to community life were openly discussed. Usually an hour in length, these evening meeting were conducted in an informal manner while information about the business interests of the community, its government, and general news of the day were shared. Meetings often included scientific and literary lectures and talks, religious testimony and discussion, and music.[36] No topics were forbidden and the input of all was encouraged as discussion was looked to as the lifeblood of the community and the foundation of communal harmony. All family members were expected to attend since the meetings and Mutual Criticism were believed to be critical to their notion of how the community was to function.

According to Noyes, "the system of mutual criticism takes the place of backbiting in ordinary society, and is regarded as one of the greatest means of improvement and fellowship".[37] Family members were accustomed to voluntarily submit themselves to the process from time to time with the belief that the experience would benefit not only themselves but the other members of the community. The person to be criticized had the option of inviting the entire family to take part and contribute or might chose a group of six to twelve who they felt knew their character best. During the entire process, the person to be criticized was expected to accept what was said without replying with the understanding that any comments given were meant as a means to help them better themselves spiritually and as a member of the group. Noyes further explained in his description of the process that "…it is an ordeal which reveals insincerity and selfishness; but it also takes the form of commendation and reveals hidden virtues as well as secret faults. It is always acceptable for those who wish to see themselves as others see them".[38] Besides strengthening the bonds between the Perfectionists, the experience of Mutual Criticism also had the added benefit of exposing members or potential members not fully committed to the ideals of the community since those who could not willing endure the process almost always found it best to leave God's Heaven on Earth.

In 1848, Noyes made the decision to move his community of forty followers from Putney to the town of Lenox in Western New York to begin the process of building the organization he believed would begin the transformation of the world. Named the Oneida Community, this new home in Madison County would give them the space to grow and practice their beliefs away from what they called the "world" that was increasingly encroaching upon them in Vermont. Their views on communal living, Nordorf wrote, had never been concealed from their Putney neighbors who gradually began to regard their presence with growing hostility. In the spring of 1848 they openly attacked the Perfectionist with the intent of driving them from the town. The decision to move to the Oneida section of Lenox was hastily made and they joined another small group of fellow Perfectionist living there.[39]

From the outset of their arrival at Oneida, Noyes and his followers began to practice their vision of communal living in earnest and created a diversified set of businesses that took advantage of the physical and human resources available to them. In order to support themselves, the community experimented with a variety of ventures that included farming, blacksmithing, sawmilling, and the production of silk. They found their economic salvation however in the production of steel traps that quickly became the gold standard for the fur trapping industry. Their biggest customer was the Hudson Bay Company which had all but cornered the market for beaver pelts in North America.[40] While finding success through the production of traps, the Perfectionists diversified their manufacturing to include traveling bags, satchels and mop holders.[41] Their landholdings at Oneida expanded as well and by 1874 they owned 654 acres of farmland, meadows, orchards, vineyards, pasture, and woods. With this economic growth came a growing membership as well and in 1874 Nordhoff recorded a membership of

283 with 45 living at the time in Wallingford.[42]

When the Allen family gave their farm on the west bank of the Quinnipiac River to the Perfectionists in 1851, it soon became evident that the new community would, while being a satellite of Oneida, play an important role in the diversified business activities that had been launched in New York. Though initially the 240 acres in Wallingford were used primarily for grazing and the production of small fruits such as strawberries, raspberries, and grapes it would prove to be the location on the river that would make the community viable. Taking advantage of the river valley that lay below their farm, the Perfectionists built a dam just north of the bridge that crossed the Quinnipiac that connected the western section of Wallingford and Yalesville with the town's center and east. Just to the south of the bridge and dam they built a factory that would during the coming decades house a number of different manufacturing enterprises. The large pond created by the dam became known as Community Lake.

The factory initially housed the main printing office for the Perfectionists where most of their publications, including their main pamphlet *The Circular* was published throughout the second half of the 1860's. It is here that Milo Todd would have called, eager to secure a customer for his paper manufacturing. According to Charles Davis in his *History of Wallingford*, the Community's Printing Office was noted for "its excellent work that attracts business from surrounding towns and cities as well as local citizens".[43] In 1869 the Community began the production of silk in the factory and by 1870 employed thirty local residents. There is a wonderful photograph showing the employees of the factory in the collection of Syracuse University showing them all proudly gathered outside the building in 1872.[44]

According to Davis the silk made in Wallingford was sent to Oneida for dyeing and spooling to be shipped to outside markets.[45] Eventually all silk production was moved to Oneida in 1873 and the factory on the Quinnipiac, for a short time manufactured the steal traps the Oneida's had become famous for before moving on to what the Oneida Community and later their Company would become most noted for, high quality silver plated cutlery.[46]

The Perfectionists, sitting in the heart of the Britannia and Silver Plating industry that was exploding around them, had succumbed to the temptation that drew so many to the Quinnipiac including Milo Todd; the lure of the wealth being generated by the dynamic growth of the cutlery industry that had become an industrial colossus of capitalism and free enterprise. There was money to be made and the Perfectionists had never been adverse to it. God's Heaven on Earth could be bought it turned out.

Milo was curious as well as eager. He had heard many stories about the Communists on the hill; some told of how warm, generous, and kind they were while others spoke of the scandalous life they lived in the big old Allen house overlooking the mill pond they had built. No, he thought, it's more a lake and that's what all in the area had come to call it. If nothing else these people are great builders when it comes to water power and they know how important it is to all of us downstream from them and that we are all beholding to them for what they have done except for those at Wallace who never seem to be happy.

He was on his way to the Community's printing office hoping to work out an opportunity to provide them with some of the high quality paper he was carrying a sample of with the intention of helping them see how it would be perfect for their bulletin, The Circular, that they sent out on a monthly basis. After all he thought as he rode along the roadway northward along the west bank of the Quinnipiac, "I have big plans, not to just make straw wrapping paper, but to eventually produce paper suitable for the printing industry and am happy with this combination of rags and straw I have experimented with. I am confident they and others will be interested" he reassured himself as his horse climbed to the top of a rise and he could gaze down at the sparkling Community Lake with its dam and the bridge just below it that linked the western part of Wallingford to the rest of the town. Just below the bridge along the western bank of the river he could see the Printing Office and as his horse plodded along he told himself, partly to buoy his confidence, "After all, I do have a fine reputation that I have brought with me from Northford and know that here in Quinnie that will carry some weight".

As Milo descended the road leading towards the Printing Office, he looked up at the Mansion House as the members called it, to his left perched on the hill overlooking the lake below. As he did so he began to wonder what would motivate a person, especially a man, to give up all his possessions, even his wife and family to become part of a group where the basic drive to succeed is supplanted by an eager willingness to sacrifice his own self-interest for that of others. "It's not" he thought, "the same as when a man sacrifices for his wife and children. These people are not kin and yet they give everything up". Since settling in at his mill downstream, Milo had encountered members of the group on numerous occasions and had found them to always be pleasant and seemingly happy. That only added to the mystery for how was it he often thought to himself, could they be so content? Even the women were different for they always held their heads high and moved and talked confidently within the world of men and he had often been told by others in town, sometimes in a tone of disapproval, that they viewed themselves as equals to men in every way. "This could lead to all types of problems in our world if that idea spread" he chuckled to himself. But Cornelia thought them courageous for that and he did not wish to dispute her belief for the sake of peace in his household.

As Milo arrived at the printing office, he could not help but continue a bit further to the bridge and stop to look upon the large stone dam with its spillway on top that allowed the river to flow down towards his place and the other factories below. "This structure is magnificent" he said to himself as he viewed the large stonewalled raceway that brought water to the printing house and could be fully opened to increase the flow of water to him and the rest further down the river. "These Perfectionists sure know how to build; this all is so well built it will easily last 100 years" he speculated. The thundering sound of the water as it dropped from the top of the dam to the river bed below was music to his ears and he thought to himself how he had finally arrived at the place of his destiny. "No more struggles like on the Paug" he said to Nell, his old mare as he patted her neck. "Yes, this is where we belong".

Just as he began to turn Nell to cross back across the bridge Milo could see that Robert Wallace was exiting the front door of the Printing Office.

Stories on the Trail of a Yankee Millwright

"I assumed they do all the printing for the Wallace Britannia works and here's my proof. That can be another angle I can use in my talk with those in charge about how I can supply them paper and at a fair price while emphasizing how working together locally will be a benefit to them" he said to himself with a growing feeling of confidence. As Milo crossed towards the edge of the span Wallace, on foot entered it. "Good day Mr. Wallace" said Milo quickly wanting to acknowledge such an important member of the manufacturing community. "A fine one, don't you think?" he said knowing a question would elicit a response and Milo was always eager to connect on a person to person level.

"Mr. Todd" Wallace replied with a quick nod and touch of his hat. "How are things with the Quinnipiac Paper Company?"

Milo was pleased to be recognized and quickly responded "Oh very well Mr. Wallace. I am excited about the growth in business already having just recently begun production".

"These are fortunate and glorious times Mr. Todd and I wish you the greatest success in your enterprise".

"Thank you Mr. Wallace" replied Milo gratefully. "I wish the same to you sir". With that, the two parted and Milo found himself before the entrance to the printing house where he could hear the clanging rhythm of their presses. He tied Nell to a post and with a deep breath entered the shop. A counter stretched across the front room with a number of desks behind it then a wall with shelves and a large double door that was open revealing the presses with men busy working them.

The front room was empty accept for a young woman who rose from her desk to greet him and Milo immediately felt the disappointment of thinking the editor or man in charge was absent. "Hello" said the woman pleasantly, "May I be of assistance?"

"Yes miss, I am Milo Todd, owner and operator of the newly established Quinnipiac Paper Company just down the river here in Quinnie" Milo said with an air of confidence he knew was important in the art of salesmanship. "I would like to speak with the man in charge, is he available?"

"I am indeed" the woman replied much to Milo's surprise. "My name is Tirzah Miller Mr. Todd, I am pleased to meet you. I am the editor of The

Circular and the other publications we Perfectionists here and in Oneida produce. How might I help you Mr. Todd?"

It took a moment for Milo to recover from his surprise but he responded. "Miss Miller, I am also pleased to meet you and would like the opportunity to speak with you about supplying your printing operation with a high quality printing paper I will soon begin the production of. I have a sample here in my bag". He then went on to say, for he could not hold back his curiosity, "Miss Miller, if you do not mind me asking, I find it most interesting that a woman, especially one as young as you are, would be in the position you hold. How did this come to be?"

Tirzah looked squarely at Milo and smilingly said "Not a problem at all Mr. Todd for we in our family believe each person, regardless of gender or age should contribute towards the welfare of the community to their utmost ability and mine is here. There is no mystery in that for we encourage all members of our family to develop their talents according to their interests which is simply a reflection of God's Plan and His Kingdom on Earth".

"It is certainly a new world of opportunity for us all Miss Miller and I am happy to have made your acquaintance" Milo stated while trying to suppress the tone of wonder in his voice. "Now if I might show you a sample of my high quality printing paper made according to my own formula of straw and rags Miss Miller, I know you will find it suitable to your needs".

"Oh Mr. Todd, you have not heard. The family has decided this year to close this office and move our printing operation to Oneida. We are to convert over to silk manufacturing as the primary business of this community starting next month". She could see the disappointment in Milo's face so she quickly added "I too am disappointed Mr. Todd and would like to think that your paper might have worked well for us".

Milo, in an effort to recover his professional demeanor reached out his hand as he would towards a man as a parting gesture and then suddenly began to pull it back when Tirzah grabbed it and shook it warmly. "I am quite sorry for this missed opportunity for us all" she said as Milo gently withdrew his hand.

"I am too Miss Miller, for the Quinnipiac Paper Company aims to be one of the finest producers of paper in the state" he said as the depth of this

disappointment began to sink in. "I wish you the best Miss Miller".
"And you and the Quinnipiac Paper Company Mr. Todd".

CHAPTER 10
The Realities of Circumstance

Despite our best efforts, the twists and turns that make up our journey through life can often bring on unexpected and often disastrous consequences through no fault of our own. The realities of uncertainty can wreak havoc with even the most well made plans and so it was for Milo Todd and the Perfectionists of Wallingford. Life along the Quinnipiac for both suddenly became not the dreamy utopia they had envisioned, but the start of a sad retreat brought on by the forces of chance and circumstance beyond their control. By 1880, Milo and his neighbors to the north had left the river valley in their respective quests to find what they knew was their rightful place in a better world.

After the Wallingford Community closed their silk operation in 1873, the factory sat empty for a period of time while they considered its next use. It turns out that the 1870's had become a time of transition for the Perfectionists family along the Quinnipiac. Discussions both there and at the parent Oneida Community centered around what would be the focus of the smaller community's economic efforts. They had once planned on founding a college of religious and educational publishing on the land behind the Mansion House, tucked under the slope they called Mt. Tom. The plan was abandoned.[1] In 1872 they had spent an astonishing $100,000.00 on a state of the art water power delivery system along with reconstruction of the dam to provide more power to the factory that had once been home to the Printing Office and then Silk Manufactory.[2] But now the factory stood idle.

According to Wallingford Community member George Cragin, it was his brother Charles who came up with the idea of manufacturing spoons and forks in 1877. As the story was told during an interview in 1913, Cragin recalled that his brother had been sitting one early summer morning on the abutment built to supply the factory with water from the dam and his job was to open a gate so as to provide a greater flow downstream to the Wallace Britannia and Silver Plating factory. As he contemplated their machines coming to life as he watched the water flow he suddenly had a revelation: "Why couldn't we make spoons as well as Wallace? Here was the power and the empty factory only waiting for someone to start a busy hum of our own".[3] Charles brought the idea to Dr. T.R. Noyes who had been sent from Oneida by his father John Humphry to oversee what was transpiring in Wallingford at the time and Noyes quickly embraced the idea. By the end of July, the first spoons had been produced after hiring craftsmen from surrounding businesses and securing the necessary machines and equipment.[4]

The first spoons that came off production were tin coated and made of iron for the Meriden Britannia Company. The Wallingford Community remained a subcontractor for only a short time before they also began producing their own line of quality silver plated spoons, forks and knives which were well received and the market turned promising despite all the competition from the established producers that surrounded them. By autumn's end the leaders of the parent Oneida Community realized that this more than any of their other enterprises was potentially more profitable and the decision was made in 1878 to expand the operation.[5]

Unfortunately for the Wallingford Community, just as the production of their cutlery manufacturing was really taking off, the year 1879 proved pivotal and fateful. As far back as 1870 and continuing each summer since, malaria had become a scourge for them and over time took a terrible toll. Unaware of the causes of malaria which would occasionally flare up in Connecticut during the summer months since the days of early settlement, for an unknown reason beginning in 1870 the disease became a recurring and yearly visitor to the Community. In his 1913 telling of the history of the start of Oneida's cutlery business in Wallingford, George Cragin called malaria the "Dweller of the Threshold".[6] Since malaria is carried by mosquitoes, I can only speculate on why the disease became increasingly prevalent for the Perfectionists but having spent many boyhood hours in the river and swamps behind Community Lake where the river water was often backed up by the dam, the swamps there were likely the breeding ground for the mosquitoes.

We now know that malaria is not a virus or bacteria that can be spread by common infectious methods, but is a parasite that can exist in the red blood cells of infected individuals or in the gut of the Anopheles Mosquito. It therefore can only be spread from an infected person via a mosquito who carries the parasite to a new human host. The mosquitoes in themselves are not the cause, it is the infected people who in the end infect others. Without a human host, malaria cannot exist. The Wallingford family members were in essence, infecting each other. By rebuilding their dam, the Community had inadvertently laid the seeds of their own demise.

Cragin went on to describe the impact of the disease on the Community over time. He said: "One after another of our strongest workers had felt the blight of this pitiless invader and had left this beautiful home for a clime that knew no malaria. Our brilliant editor and father of the Wallingford family, George W. Noyes (brother of John Humphrey), had fallen before this disease. His sister, Charlotte A. Miller—Mother Miller of both Wallingford and Oneida had also left us, a victim of this insidious foe; and finally J.H. Noyes himself was attacked".[7] In all during the decade, over 60 members would fall ill from the disease and many of them did not survive it.[8]

To combat this hidden enemy, John Humphrey Noyes had sent his son, Dr. T. R. Noyes to Wallingford in 1875 to try and somehow end the onslaught and prevent further cases. To help those suffering from the endless chills and fevers, a Turkish Bath was built that apparently brought some relief to the afflicted but certainly was not a cure and did not stem the steady progression of new victims. Desperate to somehow help those suffering, Noyes announced, according to Cragin, that "We have tried both faith and the Turkish Bath and they do not win the fight, we will now try Quinine". It appears that taking quinine, according to Cragin, did help some of those suffering from malaria but brought with it a full range of side effects from severe nausea and vomiting to bleeding and heart problems. Cragin said the effects of the quinine were "little better off" than the disease itself.[10]

The malaria outbreaks continued during 1876 and 1877, resulting in a general reluctance on the part of family members to leave Oneida in the warmer months to take positions in Wallingford. Increasingly, Community members considered the place a death trap.[11] Charles Cragin, the young man responsible for guiding the increasingly prosperous flatware operation fell ill with the disease in early 1877 and as his brother George explained, refused to give in to the disease and continued to push himself to improve the quality and quantity of production at the factory. He died shortly after that Christmas.[12] Serious discussion began among the leadership at Oneida as to whether or not the production of the utensils should be moved to another location, well aware that malaria had already forced the earlier abandonment of silk manufacturing there.[13]

Production continued in Wallingford through 1878 and into 1879 as did the debate as to whether to sell the entire Wallingford Community property or simply move the flatware operation. Large quantities of spoons continued to be made, especially iron "blanks" that were sent to Meriden Britannia for finishing. Describing that year in his account, George Cragin explained that "fever and ague continued to cripple them".[14] The term ague, commonly used from the 17th century until the end of the 19th, denoted any condition under which a person experienced fever and chills. With our much more sophisticated medical technology and knowledge, a catch-all term such as ague seems quaint and is certainly no longer needed as each sickness that would result in symptoms is most often quickly diagnosed and treatment prescribed. Those of the past were not so lucky.

Stories on the Trail of a Yankee Millwright

But there were deeper problems in 1879 for the Oneida Perfectionists than what to do about Wallingford and their successful flatware operation. Internal disputes within the parent family at Oneida rose to a breaking point that year and could be traced back to the appointment in 1876 of Dr. T. R. Noyes, John Humphrey Noyes' son, to become head of both Communities.[15] This set off a power struggle between John Humphrey Noyes and his supporters on one hand and those who opposed the appointment of Theodore, as the family called him, on the grounds that he was an atheist and did not have the leadership qualities of his father. At the same time, a generational debate began to rage over the practice of Complex Marriage with the younger members arguing for the establishment of monogamous and exclusive unions.[16] It appears God's Heaven on Earth was beginning to unravel in the face of exclusive self-interest.

While these disputes were disruptive enough, what really pushed the Community into crisis were the relentless pressure put on them by attacks from a group of more mainstream Christians who saw the Oneida practices as an insidious sacrilege and threat to what they considered the Christian moral fabric of American society. These attacks had become persistent and grew in intensity as the Perfectionists appeared to become more established and successful over time. Led by a Professor Mears of nearby Hamilton College, they were determined to end this threat to Christian civilization once and for all.[17] In June, 1879, Noyes was tipped off by one of his trusted advisors, Myron Kinsley that a warrant had been issued for his arrest on the charge of statutory rape. The truth of the allegation will never be known but it certainly was associated with the increased condemnation of Complex Marriage by the outside public. Noyes fled Oneida in the middle of the night and crossed into Canada beyond the reach of New York authorities. From Niagara Falls, he contacted his followers and advised them to end the practice of Complex Marriage.[18]

Following Noyes' self-imposed exile and upon his urging the Oneida Community did end Complex Marriage and over seventy members entered into traditional unions by the end of that year.[19] By that time the family had begun to break apart and some of the members reorganized the Community as a joint stock company in order to continue their various ventures and protect their common assets. From Canada, Noyes convinced the business council of the new stock company to close the factory in Wallingford and move it to Niagara Falls despite offers from two Connecticut silverware manufacturers. Buildings, land, and power were secured from the Niagara Falls Hydraulic Company in September 1880 and by early 1881 the Wallingford factory was closed and production had begun in the new home of what was now called the Oneida Community, Ltd.[20] In the end, it had been decided that because of the ongoing health conditions moving the business was the best option and it became the cornerstone of the new company.

With the move, the Wallingford land and buildings were put up for sale and all but a few members joined those at Oneida or left to make their way alone. The grand experiment on the Quinnipiac had ended, defeated by disease and the increasing hostility of outside forces. There is no record however of any growing public outcry against the Community in Wallingford. From the start it appears that the Perfectionists on the western bank of the river had been accepted for who they were, thought of as a bit odd certainly, but also recognized as good, decent, and hard-working members of the greater community. They had employed many from outside their family in their businesses, on their farm, and even in the Mansion House. They had also paid their employees from the outside higher wages than most local businesses did. For the Perfectionists, it was a moral duty to treat others the way God would envision. It turned out the Connecticut Yankee neighbors of God's Heaven on Earth were much more tolerant and appreciative than their fellow members of the larger society elsewhere.

John Humphrey Noyes never returned to the United States but took over management of the Oneida Community, Ltd. after the move to Niagara Falls. Following his death in 1886, former members of the Community who were now stock holders broke into factions and fought a protracted battle over control of the company that all but destroyed it by 1895. Eventually a group under the leadership of another son of Noyes,

Pierrepont, gained control and stabilized the company.[21] The structures and beliefs in communal living; selfless obligation to the common good, and Mutual Criticism that had sustained the Community for more than four decades had been vanquished by the temptations of profit, capitalism, and individual gain.

By the turn of the 20th century, the Oneida Community, Ltd. had shed all its businesses other than flatware to focus on the manufacture of silverware which they continued to produce through the rest of the century. Their high quality products were recognized worldwide as an industry standard. However, like their major competitor, International Silver, by the second half of the 20th century the writing was on the wall and in the end changing tastes and stainless steel competition would doom the business that Charles Cragin had realized was the Perfectionists salvation as he sat on the dam along the Quinnipiac. In 2005 the Oneida Company ceased their manufacturing operations thus ending a 124 year tradition that had first begun on the banks of the river in Wallingford. They had outlasted all their former competitors it turned out but in the end succumbed to the same market forces that had laid them all low. The company still exists and markets products manufactured outside the United States and Canada.[22]

The Mansion House and some of the original property at Oneida still remain in the hands of the company and thus the descendants of the Community. The enormous Mansion House along with the remaining complex and property, which was declared a National Historic Landmark in 1965, contains thirty five apartments, nine dorm rooms, nine guest rooms, meeting and dining facilities, and a museum open to the public.[23] Many of the apartments are still lived in by family descendents. Through the Mansion House if nothing else, the legacy of the Perfectionists and their dream of creating God's Heaven on Earth live on as a quaint anomaly to the American story.

Theirs is an interesting study of the contradictions within individuals and society that can spawn both a promise of a utopia and all things inherent to it and the destructive temptations and forces that can work so hard to destroy it. In the end was it the human frailties of individuals or the relentless desire of those from the outside who feared something different that doomed the Perfectionist's experiment? Or was it simply circumstance and bad luck that brought about their end? I guess we will never know.

The saga of the Wallingford Perfectionists, so closely linked to the fate of the parent community, ended quietly in 1880 as members dispersed, either back to Oneida or went off on their own. Unlike Oneida, where the memory of the Perfectionists has been kept alive through the preservation of the Mansion House, in Wallingford one must look hard to see even a fragment of their legacy. But it is there, unbeknownst to most residents.

When the decision was made to close the silverware factory, the Community's fate was sealed. In June 1880, prior to selling the factory, a lawsuit was filed against Wallace Silversmiths alleging the theft of the Community's secret recipe for making their silver coatings.[24] The buzzards were beginning to circle. But in an interesting twist to the story, when the Oneida's did sell the factory in 1881, it was to the Maltby, Stevens, & Curtis Company which, though eventually absorbed by Meriden Britannia and the International Silver Company, continued to operate the factory well into the 20th century.[25] David Steven's boy had come back to the Quinnipiac. One of Insilco's subsidiaries, Times Wire and Cable, is still located there along with another corporation, Amphenol.[26]

With the sale of the factory, the sole activities at the once bustling farm and Mansion House overlooking Community Lake were those of hired local caretakers and farm hands. For all intents and purposes the 240 acres and buildings had been abandoned and though buyers were sought by the Oneida Company for many years, it sat dormant in testimony to their lost utopia. Eventually, in 1895, The Fraternal Order of Freemasons stepped forward and purchased the property in order to create a retirement home and later a hospital for their national membership. The old Perfectionist Mansion House became the heart of the home, housing members of the order either too ill or old to care for their selves. The farm continued to be worked throughout most of the 20th century with a dairy operation that provided a bucolic and relaxed environment for residents of the home. The Masons embarked on an ambitious building plan from the outset however and the old Mansion House was quickly replaced with a large brick residence that continued to grow with additions during the first fifty years of the new century.

During the 1980's, the Freemasons began in earnest to transform their home into a multi-faceted health care facility for their membership with an explosion of development that completely obliterated the farm by building complex after complex of housing and care facilities that range from retirement homes to assisted living units and critical care residencies. Their building spread out over the entire 240 acres, creeping up the hill the Perfectionists called Mt. Tom and across the pastures where cows once grazed. It is a world class medical facility under the name of Masonic Care and they provide the high quality care their members have come to expect at the start of the 21st century. Sadly though there is no trace of what had once been on the grounds before the Freemasons arrived, no marker recognizing the Perfectionists or any token indication that they had once existed. Their memory has been erased in the name of progress and quality health care.

If one looks closely though, there are still a few hidden reminders of the Perfectionist's presence elsewhere. Their stout brick factory building still stands, tucked between the Quinnipiac River and the bridge that spans it. The original building is now dwarfed by many 20th century additions that have all but swallowed it, but it's there, painted white so as to better blend with all the newer parts. I'd like to think that the Cragin brothers and the rest of those inventive Perfectionists would recognize it still. Then of course there is Community Lake, or should I say, what once was Community Lake. It had been formed when the Perfectionists constructed their first dam across the Quinnipiac to power their silk operation and was enlarged when they rebuilt the dam in the 1870's. From that point on, the lake was considered one of the real jewels of the town as it created a scenic and tranquil vista along the road out of the center village towards the western part of town and the old Hartford Turnpike that wound its way north through Yalesville to Meriden and beyond. The prestigious boy's boarding school in Wallingford, Choate, had its boat house on the lake and hosted crew races on it and on many a warm summer afternoon small boats and fishermen could be seen drifting laconically on its waters. It was truly a special gift to the entire community that the Perfectionists had given the town and one that was greatly appreciated and loved. For me, my brother, and friends it was always our destination as we played Tom Sawyer and Huck Finn as boys navigating our rickety rafts on the river that was our Mississippi on those hot August days that seemed to last forever, our destination, the lake.

At some point in the early 20th century, while building a new bridge to span the river which ran directly in front of the dam, the stone structure of the Community was replaced with an earthen one that would hold the lake in place without the need to provide energy to the factory it once powered. But earthen dams in particular need frequent maintenance and over time that was not the case. A series of torrential downpours over a number of days in 1979 caused the time-weakened dam to give way and in a matter of hours the idyllic lake was gone and the river returned to the bed the Perfectionists had first laid their dam across. What was left was a muddy and sandy savannah that over the years, while the town talked about their great loss, became quickly reclaimed by nature. Within years, any trace of the lake was pretty much gone. The town did excavate a few small ponds in a feeble attempt to make something out of what once was but their efforts only added to the sense of loss.

A group of concerned citizens was formed shortly after the dam breach to investigate its rebuilding and this restoration committee presented the town with a plan to rebuild the 36 foot tall dam at a cost of $500,000.00 in 1982.[27] The cost was deemed beyond the reach of the town that in the early part of that decade was still reeling from the disappearance of its once thriving industrial base, most notably International Silver and Wallace Silversmiths. In 1989, the cost was estimated at $2,000,000.00. According to a more recent report (2004), the estimated cost to restore the dam and lake is now $25,000,000.00.[28]

Sadly, Community Lake seems destined to go the way of the Perfectionists who built it; erased over time and generations from the memory of the community.

Stories on the Trail of a Yankee Millwright

There is one more part to the story of the Wallingford Perfectionists however that needs to be mentioned and it occurred during the summer of 1878. On a warm August afternoon Wallingford was hit by one of New England's worse weather disasters, the Great Tornado of 1878. Although the Perfectionists compared to the rest of the town suffered little, it was in their minds an omen of what was to come and it undoubtedly had a profound effect on the family psychologically.

During the last week of July and the first of August that summer severe and unsettled weather plagued Southern New England most days. Lightning storms and torrents of rain seemed the norm.[29] August 9th had been a sultry but fair day until late in the afternoon when clouds began to thicken and billow in an ominous fashion. The sky became so threatening that the work day at the Community's silverware factory was ended early to allow the workers time to get home before another great deluge of rain struck.[30] By 6:00 pm witnesses later recalled, two great, black, towering clouds seemed to rise above Mt. Tom behind the Perfectionist's Mansion House; one from the northwest and the other from the southwest, and with them came a sudden blast of wind accompanied by vicious sheets of lightning.[31] To those who witnessed the storm's birth, it must have been an awful and terrifying site.

Suddenly, the Perfectionist's windmill, located twenty five rods (400 feet) up the hill to the north of the Mansion House was torn from its base and thrown to the ground and a huge and ancient tree near their house uprooted and tossed to the side narrowly missing the building.[32] A funnel cloud instantly formed over Community Lake and according to witness accounts later given to the Boston Globe became a water spout that literally emptied the lake of its water. One lucky survivor told the story of being in a small boat on the lake when the twister hit. He dove overboard and clung terrified to a large tree root near the shore as his boat was sucked up into the vortex and the water vanished instantly from the lake bottom around him.[33] As the tornado hit the eastern shore of the now waterless lakebed it smashed into a one story brick shop owned by the Community and leased to a Mr. Grasser who operated a small Britannia operation in it. The shop was pulverized but somehow Mr. Grasser escaped serious injury.[34]

The tornado swiftly proceeded on to an area known as the Sand Plains on the east shore of the lake on a northeast heading towards the center of Wallingford. The Sand Plains was the home of mostly Irish working families who it would later be known suffered the greatest number of casualties from the onslaught of the whirlwind. As the twister moved through their neighborhood families had just sat down to their evening meals when their homes exploded around them. Roofs were blown off and houses were tossed off their foundations as the wind battered and destroyed the homes and barns in its path. Uprooted trees were thrown about as if mere sticks as the storm swept everything before it as it crossed the railroad tracks of the New York, New Haven, and Hartford Railroad and then frenetically spun itself across Colony Street heading north-northeast up the gradual slope towards Main Street. John Kendrick in his telling of the disaster later that year in *The History of the Wallingford Disaster* noted from the time the tornado formed to its final blows crushing a stretch of Main, Christian, and Elm Streets in Wallingford Center was exactly one and a half minutes.[35] The town had no idea what hit it. Modern meteorologists now estimate that the cyclone probably measured an F4 on the Fujita Scale of F1 to F5 that charts the intensity of tornadoes. In that one and a half minute period of time the winds swirled at a lethal 207 to 250 miles per hour.[36] During those brief, destructive moments the storm laid waste to a track that measured two miles long and a quarter mile wide.[37]

To the survivors, numb with shock, the destruction was beyond comprehension. Rain continued to torment the town in an unrelenting downpour for an hour after the tornado had carved its swath of mayhem and destruction through the community. Fires broke out from overturned lamps and cooking stoves adding to the already desperate situation as church bells began to peel and those lucky enough to have not been directly impacted by the tornado began to respond to the needs of their fellow townsmen.[38] By 8:00 that evening the sky was clear and the air fresh, except for the smoldering smoke left from fires that the rain

Stories on the Trail of a Yankee Millwright

had extinguished and the acrid smell of dust and debris. It must have been a surreal and eerie scene.

According John Kendrick, one of the very first groups to respond to the needs of those in the path of the tornado were the Perfectionists.[39] Upon witnessing the disaster from their perch on the hill, family members immediately rushed to the town to help as many of the injured as they could and help to search for survivors. The first wounded person they came across was a young girl named Mary O'Rourke who was one of their employees and had been caught in the storm on her way home from work. Kendrick recorded that if not for their efforts, Miss O'Rourke would surely have died.[40] Members of the community nursed and stayed with many of the injured during the first twenty four hours following the storm and were credited with making them at least comfortable and in a number of cases saving their lives as in the case of Mary. Other members helped search for the injured amidst the rubble and later helped sort the debris. In the words of Mr. Kendrick "The quiet and noble action of the Wallingford Community must not escape notice."[41]

In the days following the disaster as the scope of the tragedy became apparent, the Community did what they could to assist the victims across the lake. They encouraged their employees at the silverware factory to assist in first the search and then later the clean-up and paid them their wages while they did. They immediately donated $100.00 to the relief fund established and the factory workers voted to donate one day of their wages to the effort as well.[42] Remarkably, none of the Perfectionists or their workers were among the casualties other than young Mary O'Rourke but a number of the employees no doubt suffered damage to or loss of their homes. The Community itself besides the windmill, lost some trees including the ancient one by the Mansion House, a section of the factory roof, and the building rented out to Mr. Grasser.

The town of Wallingford was not as lucky and property damage along the two mile path of the tornado was horrific. In all, 160 buildings were destroyed including the Catholic Church and a newly built high school.[43] Forty houses were completely destroyed or so damaged they proved uninhabitable and fifty barns simply disappeared. The total value of property damaged or destroyed by the one and a half minute storm was put at $2,000,000.00.[44] Although the loss of life was terrible as well, with 34 people killed by the storm and 28 severely injured[45] under the circumstances it is a wonder more people were not killed or injured when the scope of the storm is looked at from even today's perspective. Yet the impact of the tornado, for the survivors and those who worked hard in the following weeks and months to help rebuild their broken lives, the shock of what they lived through and witnessed must have left an indomitable impression. In the words of Mr. Kendrick: "This destruction, so sudden, so complete, so fearful in every respect, coming truly like a "thief in the night" seemed to them as it would have seemed to us—the agony and passion of the world's last hour".[46] I cannot help but think that the horror of what happened that hot August evening must have had a profound effect on the Wallingford Perfectionists. After all, the storm had formed above and leapt off their hill, the home of God's Heaven on Earth. They had been spared while so many had suffered. Could this be God's judgment? Was it an omen that maybe they should leave the shadow of Mt Tom? Taking into consideration the persistent torment of the malaria outbreaks and the discussion that had been raised from them about closing the community, perhaps this was a significant sign. Was it a verdict on the factional divisions developing both at Oneida and Wallingford over the future of both communities? Was it their sudden success in the silverware industry by which the family was becoming a wealth generating organization that seemed to be turning away from their communal roots? I would have loved to have been present at the evening meetings as the family discussed and processed what had happened and its meaning. One thing for sure, if an omen was meant to be read; in retrospect it clearly was foreshadowing the events of 1879 that would force John Humphry Noyes to flee to Canada and the Community break-up that followed.

By the time the tornado had struck Wallingford, Milo Todd had left the Quinnipiac Valley never to return. His dreams too had been destroyed by circumstance, not natural or social ones like those of the Perfectionists, but economic and personal ones which, to a certain extent, were not of his doing. For Milo timing was everything and unfortunately for his Quinnipiac Paper Company, his timing proved too late. You might even say it all came down to just plain bad luck.

To begin with, even though he had spent the good part of three years maneuvering his Quinnipiac Paper Company into a position where it might become financially viable, in the end by 1871 that viability proved tenuous. Milo had worked hard to create a web of land deals and financial transactions that left him holding what he considered to be valuable and vital properties along the river as well as control of the water rights he knew he needed, but the final result was substantial debt. Without a long term market for his straw and rag paper there was no way that he might work his way out of his obligations. Unfortunately for Todd, the paper making industry by 1870 was experiencing a technological revolution that was completely transforming the materials used and the methods of production that made it. These rapid changes would prove devastating for those who were unable to adopt them.

The biggest problem paper makers always faced was a consistent supply of the raw materials needed to produce their product—most often cloth rags. Chronic shortages of cloth scraps constantly forced manufacturers to look for alternatives and each found either had its shortcomings as a substitute for rags or were often in short supply as well. Milo Todd had moved into the business using straw, a readily available material in rural Northford and had become relatively successful using it to produce wrapping paper. Its coarse quality always limited its use and it was inferior as a paper for printing compared to rag paper. Thus Todd always had a limited and specific market and the lack water power in Northford had always limited his production ability. In 1870, just as he had become fully established in Wallingford and ready to begin production, Todd found the industry had made a major shift in its constant search for a better source of raw material and had finally found it in wood pulp. Wood pulp was more abundant and much less expensive than rags or even straw, which meant the cost of manufacturing paper dropped dramatically. The only down side to the use of wood pulp was that its production required new and more technologically advanced and sophisticated equipment to produce it.

The use of wood pulp to make paper was first pioneered in Europe during the early 1800's but proved too expensive to have much of a market. The problem centered around the issue of how to break down the wood fibers in order to create a usable pulp that could then be transformed into sheets of paper. The first discovery of an industrial process to do so is credited to Matthias Koops in England as early as 1801 but it wasn't until a German inventor and machinist, Friedrich Gottlob Keller, came up with a process of cooking and reducing the wood fibers into pulp in a machine called a grinder that paper from wood pulp became a viable option in 1844.[47] The process was also simultaneously discovered by a Canadian poet and inventor by the name of Charles Fenerty the same year but both men never pushed their discovery beyond practical demonstrations. However, two German industrialists, Johann Matthaus Voith and Heinrich Voelter saw the potential in Keller's invention.[48]

In 1845 Voelter received a patent for a wood grinder based on Keller's model that would grind the fibers into a usable pulp and with capital from the industrialist Voith began to produce wood pulp paper in 1852.[49] Voelter and Voith also began to sell the wood grinding machines and it was only a matter of time before they began to make their appearance in the United States. Shortly after the Civil War ended a German immigrant by the name of Alberto Pagenstecher and his brother Rudolf imported two of the Voelter pulp grinders and set up a mill outside of Stockbridge, Massachusetts.[50] The result was the first commercially successful wood pulp to be used in the mass production of paper that the nearby Smith Paper Company made into newsprint and sold to New York newspapers. By the early 1870's ground wood pulp had become the industry norm and its use became widespread.[51]

But this was not the only process that was transforming wood pulp into the raw material of choice when it came to the production of paper. During the late 1850's Henry Lowe in Maryland began to experiment with another process from Europe that literally cooked wood fibers in a highly caustic alkali solution. This method employed a double boiler in which the wood pulp and the alkali solution were placed inside an inner boiler and heated by an outer boiler holding water and steam. The double boiler was called a digester and it produced a wood pulp that could be made into usable paper. Following the Civil War, a paper mill in Herkimer New York utilizing a pulp grinder and Lowe's digester put it all together and began to make wood pulp based paper at an affordable price.[52] This process took the paper industry by storm by 1870, the year Milo was finally ready for production, and there was no turning back.

Other chemical combinations to break down the wood fibers were also experimented with, most notably that of Benjamin Tilghman of Philadelphia, who used sulphuric acid to cook the wood pulp in 1866. His process led to the establishment of paper mills throughout the Northeast by the early 1870's, most notably in Maine with its abundant supply of wood, especially soft woods which were easier for these chemical digesters to digests.[53] The scale of the factories of these paper manufacturers were enormous compared to the relatively small operations that predated the wood pulp revolution of the late 1860's and early 1870's and small manufacturers utilizing the earlier technologies of rag and straw paper such as Milo Todd were suddenly left without markets. For Milo, the shock of all this, after all his maneuvering and hustling to establish his dream, must have been devastating.

For Todd the dilemma was clear—he needed to invest in this new wood pulp process and all the new equipment and technology it required or somehow stick with his straw paper production as an industry niche that was still in demand for wrapping paper. It was still a pre-plastic age and items whether it be meat from the butcher or a gift for a loved one still needed to be wrapped with paper.[54] Maybe Milo could make it still. Besides, the types of soft woods necessary to produce wood pulp did not exist in the Quinnipiac Valley let alone the region which had been clear cut except for an occasional farmer's woodlot generations ago. For Todd the dream of being an important and highly successful manufacturer on the scale of the Maltby's, Steven's, and others was suddenly gone.

The 1870 United States Census gives a bit of insight into Milo Todd's life at that moment in time. He is age 36 and is listed as living on the property along the Quinnipiac in North Haven with his wife Cornelia and two daughters Lillie age 5 and Cora, age 3. His real estate wealth, the property he owns after all his frantic wheeling and dealing, is listed at $2500.00 and his personal property at $1500.00. He is identified as a paper manufacturer.[55] How much business if any he is doing in the paper business is unknown but based upon his overall wealth it must have been marginal at best. Milo, it appears, was faced with some tough choices. The realities of circumstance had caught up with him.

Milo paced the room in a constant pattern from the door to his office to the work area and the press on which he had pinned so many of his paper making plans. Sure he thought to himself, I can still make straw wrapping paper but that too is being eclipsed by the new light wood pulp wrapping. Seemingly overnight the market had changed and he could not get over the fact that all his efforts to create the Quinnipiac Paper Company suddenly appeared fruitless. As he looked around the floor of his production area, with its piles of straw and rags ready to begin the pulping process, his frustration became almost unbearable. "Everything has changed and I am just too late" he said out loud as he stopped his pacing and put his hands on his hips. "There has to be a way to move forward".

　"But I have been in this position before and have always been able to think my way forward" he said with a tinge of panic to the silent and still machines that had been his future just a short time ago. I just need to find a market for my wrapping and with Uncle Ambrose making inquiries in New Haven and even New York there is still time, but how much is the question he wondered as his mind began to race with growing frustration. "Even if I could raise the money to purchase one of those wood digesters I saw up in Windsor Locks, I would not have an adequate supply of the soft wood needed here in this valley. At the Locks they bring it down from up north but here that is not an option. And to ship it here by rail is too cost prohibitive" he said aloud as Cornelia called from just outside the door.

　"Milo you must stop dwelling on your plight for a moment as it is time for us all to visit St. Paul's for the service. Perhaps it is there through prayer you will find your answer she said as she came through the open door to touch his

shoulder. "You have always been able in your cleverness and ambition to find a way. Just ask the Lord for some help in this matter".

Milo turned to his wife and thought what a wonder she was, always supportive of his schemes and it now appeared she might be his only crutch on which to rely. Cornelia had a confidence in him which he often found to be almost miraculous and his thought immediately focused on the fact that indeed he did need a miracle. "Cornelia, you are and have always been a beacon of hope and I am so grateful. Perhaps the Lord will be of a mind to listen this morning to the petition of one of his sinners" he said in an almost whisper to her as he took his wife's hand. As they both turned to walk through the door Milo's thoughts drifted to how his mother, a good and faithful Anglican, had always said to him that the true test of the quality of the character in a man was his ability to humble himself before God. Perhaps now I should put that advice to the test he told himself as he saw that Cornelia had already hitched Nell to their buggy knowing of his preoccupation with his plight.

Cornelia often scolded him that he should spend less time with his business affairs and more time in prayer and at this point perhaps he could see her point. He certainly was not a religious man but he both feared and trusted in God and had always felt he was on the Lord's good side. Perhaps not, he thought to himself as he turned Nell towards the old Hartford Turnpike and the way north towards Wallingford Center, along the river and eventually across the bridge past the Perfectionist Printing House, the scene where his current dilemma first came to light. He thought of the composure and peaceful nature he saw in the members he met including Miss Miller and for an instant thought perhaps that is where his fate lies—with that crowd in the old Allen place. As he did he laughed and Cornelia turned to him and asked what would possibly draw out a laugh from her up to that point quiet and somber husband.

"You are a puzzle Mr. Todd" she said as she smiled at him and added "you will scare the girls who will think their father mad!"

"Yes you are mad father" added Lillie as she enhanced her faint with a display of condemnation highlighted by a pretended shriek of fright that was quickly mimicked by little Clara.

"Do not torment your father in his time of need" scolded Cornelia mockingly and they all laughed together.

"I was thinking of the Communists when I laughed" said Milo "for how simple it would be to abandon everything for the security of their community".

"Now I am convinced you are truly mad Mr. Todd" she quickly replied. "For the scandal that would create for the Todd's and Cook's would be apocalyptic. Plus you would share your wife" she winked as she blushed and nudged him in the ribs. "No" Cornelia continued, "I believe it best we remain Episcopal and give our fate over to the Lord". With that they crossed the bridge in front of the Perfectionist's dam remaining silent as they began to travel the last bit of distance to the town center where St. Paul's sat prominently on the rise to the left of the crossroad of Main and Center Streets.

As they crossed the tracks and passed the fine new railroad station they all sat silently, each in their own thoughts. Milo brought the buggy to a stop in front of the church and climbed out to help Cornelia down and as he did he heard a voice call out. "Milo Todd, just the person I was hoping to see". It was Frank Whittlesey of Harford, in Wallingford no doubt to visit relations. Milo had known him when they were both children since on occasion he had stayed with his kin on the farm near that of Thelus. "Milo, I would like to speak with you at your convenience about paper".

CHAPTER 11
Insuring a Place

Milo and his wife Cornelia had to make some decisions. Things had not worked out as they had planned and now their perch on the Quinnipiac was becoming a prison of broken dreams. But Milo was anything but a pessimist when it came to his future and he began to cast his efforts to find his place in bustling world of the 1870's in a different direction. 1873, found him in Windsor Locks, Connecticut, a small but blossoming industrial center on the Connecticut River north of Hartford and just south of Enfield the most northerly Connecticut town. The sights and sounds of the river town must have reminded Milo of the halcyon days of Northford forty years before when the world seemed full of possibilities and invention and manufacturing were the hallmarks of that transformation.

The little village of Pine Meadow, the northern most section of the ancient river town of Windsor, had been just a quiet back water for most of its history since first settled in the 17th century. But starting in the 1820's that had all begun to change. Pine Meadow began a rapid transformation into the town that would become Windsor Locks which today is the home of Bradley International, Southern New England's busy regional airport. The irony is that most of the thousands of passengers who travel through the terminals at Bradley each day have no idea why the town has the odd name of Windsor Locks or may not even know its name at all and there is no real reason they should. To most they are simply at Bradley or their airline's location designation of Hartford/Springfield. In an interesting coincidence, Connecticut's most important transportation center just happens to be located where once there was the state's greatest hindrance to travel; the rapids on the Connecticut River known as the Enfield Falls. Until the advent of the railroads in the 1840's, the most efficient and reliable way to travel in the state was by water and the Connecticut River was the state's main highway. The rapids however were a major obstacle to trade and transportation.

When Adrien Block voyaged up the Connecticut in 1614, fighting its strong current and the dangerous and shifting sand bars, he made it as far north as Windsor Locks and the rapids. The Enfield Falls, are really a series of rapids formed by glacial deposits, boulders and an outcrop of granite that cover an area five miles long and the width of the river. Over that distance the river also drops 32 feet halting any hope of navigation of vessels large enough to be ocean going.[1] The rapids stopped Block and later many Europeans hoping to exploit the unlimited natural resources of the upper Connecticut. The Falls formed the terminus of navigation.

In 1633 the English established their first permanent settlement in Connecticut placing it at the confluence of the Farmington and Connecticut Rivers just south of the rapids.[2] It was an intentional move to try and dominate the growing trade in furs coming down both rivers and being north of the Dutch House of Hope the English hoped to syphon the trade away from them. Located on the western bank of the Connecticut, the settlement was named Windsor and because it was accessible for ocean going ships, quickly took on a growing significance in the race to gain an advantage in trade with the native population. But not for long. William Pynchon of Salem, Massachusetts had other ideas. Having arrived in Massachusetts in 1630, Pynchon was a well to do country gentleman who within a short time established himself as one of the most successful fur traders in New England securing for himself a network along the entire coast of the region.[3] By the mid 1630's the competition had heated up and traders had increasingly turned their attention to the Connecticut River Valley and its abundant supply of animal pelts and native groups eager to trade.

With his English competitors settled in Windsor and the Dutch still holding out in their House of Hope, Pynchon literally leapt over them and set up a trading house north of the Enfield Falls in a native village called Agawam on the east bank of the river in 1636.[4] He also wisely built a warehouse on the edge of the falls at a spot on the eastern river bank where goods and people moving up and down the river had to either portage around the rapids or transship on small flat bottomed scows that could navigate them. The site of his warehouse became known as Warehouse Point and that section of the town of East Windsor still bears that name.[5] By claiming both locations, Pynchon quickly came to control a large percentage of the trade in furs making their way down the Connecticut from points north in what are now Vermont, New Hampshire, and even Quebec. Pynchon quickly learned the local native dialect while at Agawam and became the intermediary between the English and the natives along the river while becoming the dominant trader and supplier of goods for both.[6]

Initially, Pynchon allied himself with the new Connecticut Colony that had been established in 1635 under the leadership of the Rev. Thomas Hooker that was comprised of the three river towns of Windsor, Hartford, and Wethersfield. But ongoing disputes over Pynchon's trade practices with the native population and his domination of trade wore the alliance thin and by 1640 he and the fellow members of his growing community at Agawam voted to sever their relationship and look to Massachusetts Bay and Boston for affiliation. Coincidently at the same time, the Bay Colony had decided to reassert its authority over land bordering the Connecticut River and they named William Pynchon the chief magistrate of the region. In his honor, Agawam was renamed Springfield after Pynchon's home in England.[7] The relationship with Pynchon and now Massachusetts continued to deteriorate when Connecticut Colony decided to force Springfield to contribute to the maintenance of Fort Saybrook at the river's mouth which was really a not so veiled attempt to collect a toll to be paid for shipping furs and supplies up and down the river. Massachusetts Bay retaliated by announcing that Connecticut would hence forth have to pay a fee for use of Boston Harbor and the entire matter was quickly dropped.[8]

Initially furs and supplies to and from Springfield were off loaded at Warehouse Point and carted by oxen the remaining distance along the eastern bank of the river. But enterprising individuals both at Windsor and Springfield solved the problem of the falls by developing a flat-bottomed, shallow draft craft called a scow that could safely navigate the rapids. These flat boats, as they came to be called became the standard means of transport on the falls and north up into Vermont and New Hampshire for the next 200 years. These versatile and sturdy boats drew very little water and were designed to carry between twelve and fifteen tons of cargo. Any shipment heavier than that had to be carted around the five miles of rapids by oxen. The flat boats also had a square sail to aid in movement when the wind was up but most often were propelled by men on board with long poles whether going with or against the current as they moved along the river above or below the falls. When in the rapids, extra men and poles were needed and these "falls-men" over the years made a steady living.[9] The standard allotment of falls-men per scow when coursing through the falls was said to be twelve; six to a side to keep the flat boat steady and on course.[10]

By 1800, Pine Meadow was still a sleepy little village making its living by manning the flat boats that took on the falls and supporting the usual gristmill and saw mill found in communities where most residents farmed. Change came suddenly however with a decision by Hartford to construct a bridge across the Connecticut and in 1809 ocean-going sloops that had been present in Windsor, Pine Meadow, and Warehouse point for 170 years were suddenly a thing of the past, the bridge cutting off their ability to move further north.[11] With the bridge in place, Hartford quickly came to dominate trade on the river as it was now the furthest point ships could reach and all trade coming down or up the Connecticut north of the city had to be transferred there. Almost overnight, the city became a boom town at the expense of their northern neighbors including their old nemesis, Springfield. But the flat boats were still needed and with their destination now Hartford instead of Windsor or Warehouse Point it seemed those two communities might begin the slow drift into quiet obscurity. But the leaders in Hartford had another idea.

Following the end of the War of 1812 with Great Britain in 1814, the United States started to turn its attention to the development of its economy as the entire nation began to focus inward. Under the "American System" trumpeted by Kentucky senator Henry Clay and others, the national government began to promote policies that encouraged that over-arching vision. Among the many policies that encouraged the development of industry was a concurrent push to improve the national infrastructure. The goal was to unite the nation through a system of roads and canals and by 1817 a number of ambitious projects to do so were in the works. By far the biggest began in that year when the state of New York started building the Erie Canal that when finished in 1825 linked the city of New York to the Great Lakes capturing the commerce of that quickly developing region of the country and making the city the economic heart of the nation.

Not to be outdone or left out of the growing bonanza that the canal craze might bring, the merchants and leaders of New Haven in 1821 began to explore the building of a canal that could divert much of the commerce then flowing through Hartford and the Connecticut River towns. The plan was to excavate an eighty seven mile long canal that would connect Northampton, Massachusetts on the Connecticut River north of Springfield via the Farmington River with New Haven. It was the largest transportation project in Connecticut history and the group promoting it was granted a charter in 1822 by the state legislature.[12] In the end politics would play a serious role in the fate of the Farmington Canal as the Connecticut River towns led by Hartford vehemently opposed it even though the project was strongly supported by New Haven and the communities along its route. Ironically, since the days of the 1662 Connecticut Charter and Governor John Winthrop Jr. in the 17th century, the state had two capitals, a legacy of the joining of New Haven Colony with their larger neighbor. The seat of government literally shifted yearly between Hartford and New Haven.[13] The canal proposal and charter only accentuated the economic and political competition between the two cities and the leadership in Hartford was determined not to lose their economic and thus political advantages the Connecticut River had always brought them. Ultimately they would prevail when the capital was permanently moved to Hartford in 1876.

With the state charter secured however, the leaders of the new Farmington Canal Company began to sell shares necessary to raise the capital needed to begin the survey of the route and then the excavation of the canal. Three years later a ground breaking ceremony was held in Granby, Connecticut to initiate construction, but according to historian Ellsworth Grant, from the start the project was cursed when the spade Governor Oliver Wolcott Jr. used in the ceremony broke.[14] Apparently, though Wolcott was a great promoter of economic development in the state, especially when it came to the building of textile mills, he made no effort to aid in the construction of the canal either personally or by offering aid from the state government.[15] The reason was obvious to all that the governor was strongly supported by the Hartford merchants who by 1825 had their own canal project in place. As a result, the Farmington Canal project struggled financially throughout the ten years it took to construct its entire route and in the end would ultimately fail for lack of funding and bad timing.

The scope of the project however was enormous as the eighty seven mile canal came to contain twenty eight locks to account for the rise in elevation between New Haven and Northampton and three aqueducts.[16] By far the most spectacular was the 280 foot long, 40 foot tall stone and wooden aqueduct that spanned the Farmington River itself in Farmington, Connecticut The aqueduct held a twelve foot wide, six foot deep wooden trough that allowed the canal boats to float above the very river that gave the canal life. The trough was held above the river by six tremendous stone peers the remnants of which can still be seen in the river today. The horses that towed the boats across the aqueduct walked along a wooden tow path alongside the water filled trough.[17] Though the project was always strapped for cash because the sale of shares never lived up to expectations and the continued opposition of the Hartford faction, somehow the longest leg of the canal, from New Haven north to Simsbury on the Farmington River, was completed and in the summer of 1828 it opened for business. *The Hartford Courant*, the Hartford region's leading newspaper was not impressed, calling it "the little ditch".[18] By our modern standards, we might have to agree; the canal trench was twenty feet wide at the bottom and thirty six at the top and held only four feet of water.[19] Yet it was more than sufficient to carry the flat bottomed tow boats that easily floated on its surface. The distance from Simsbury to New Haven could be covered in less than four days and the canal promised to live up to all expectations. By November, despite some maintenance setbacks, shipments of goods began to flow north from New Haven and south to the city on a regular basis. In 1835, the last leg of the canal was opened from Simsbury to Northampton and the dream of the citizens and merchants of New Haven, despite their persistent financial struggles and passive opposition from their own state government, had become a reality.

Unfortunately for New Haven and those along the canal route who hoped to gain from it, the lack of capital, the company's constant nemesis, would bring about its doom. Repeated breaks in the embankments along the entire route caused the canal to be often shut down and costly repairs consumed whatever income the company brought in. Storms flooded the canal causing extensive damage as well and spells of dry weather and drought at times made the canal impassable. In 1836 alone the original investors lost $1 million dollars and by 1840 the company was spending four times its revenue.[20] Yet the Farmington Canal struggled on through the early 1840's and in 1844 it finally made a profit hauling a record amount of tonnage with few maintenance problems. Perhaps the fortunes of company might turn around after all or so hoped its investors. But nature and new technologies would step in over the next two years to end it all. Beginning in July, 1845, a severe drought shut the canal for two months and the investors of the company, seeing its inevitable demise, decided to petition the state to replace their canal with the tracks of a new form of transportation that was sweeping the nation and spelling the end of the canal era in America; the railroad. By 1848, locomotives were hauling the goods that tow boats once carried.[21]

Meanwhile on the Connecticut River, at Hartford, and even little Pine Meadow, things were radically different and business was better than ever by 1840. Back in early 1824, a group of prominent Hartford area businessmen and politicians began to meet to discuss the possibility of improving navigation on the Connecticut River north of Hartford. The greatest impediment to doing so was still the Enfield Falls and they quickly developed a plan to build a canal to bypass them. They formed a company that was chartered by the state and the Connecticut River Company immediately went to work creating plans to build a canal on the western bank of the river in Pine Meadow that would go around the rapids and deal as well with the persistent problem of shifting sand bars all along the river. The original plan was to also secure charters from Massachusetts, Vermont, and New Hampshire to improve navigation along the river's entire reach but only Vermont granted one and the plan was scaled back to just focus on the Enfield Falls.[22] Construction started in 1827 and the entire 5.25 mile length that included four locks was completed in 1829. The locks, one at the north end and three at the south, were designed to raise or lower shipping the 32 feet that formed the height of the falls over the 5 miles.[23] Each of the four locks were 80 feet long, 18 feet wide, and 4 and 1/2 feet deep when the water level was not being raised or lowered.[24]

The toll to use the canal was set at $0.75 per ton of cargo and $0.17 per tonnage of the boat or barge which set up an interesting dynamic with the falls-men who traditionally worked the rapids guiding the flat-boats through them. During times of high water, shipping would skirt the canal in order to avoid paying the toll and the falls-men were only too happy to assist. Because of this possibility, the Connecticut River Company charter allowed them to charge a lesser toll downstream for those that ran the rapids of $0.50 per ton of cargo and $0.17 per tonnage of the flat-boat.[25] Either way, the investors made their money. Unlike the Farmington Canal where the company owned the canal boats and thus only charged for cargo, the locks and canal at Pine Meadow allowed all matter of privately owned craft to pass through as long as they paid the toll. With the opening of the canal, the size of boats increased in terms of tonnage, up to 35 tons, and as long as 75 feet.[26] The Enfield Falls Canal could also accommodate the new steam powered craft increasingly used on the river as the 1830's began.[27] As traffic on the river increased over the next two decades, that variety of privately owned craft that utilized the canal was an increasing advantage for the Connecticut River Company over their competition to the west.

When the Enfield Falls Canal was first envisioned, the investors had another idea in mind that would in the end prove more lucrative than any amount of tolls they might collect. Since the water from the river falling 32 feet over the span of the canal represented the potential for water powered energy, the organizers of the canal project hoped that they would be able to supplement the profits from the tolls with the leasing of water power rights to manufacturers willing to locate their factories along the canal.[28] The canal structure as a result included a system that allowed the lock keeper to monitor the water level in the canal to keep it constant by opening and lowering a gate adjacent to the most northern lock. Gates built into the side wall opened into a sluiceway that ran along the western side of the canal that allowed water to flow through raceways to each mill to power water wheels along the entire length of the structure. The amount of rent each mill owner paid was directly related to how much water they could draw through their individual gate; the larger the gate the more power they could generate and thus higher the rent. The result was a steady and reliable source of energy for manufacturers who decided to locate their mills along the canal.[29]

In essence, the organizers of the Connecticut River Company created Connecticut's first industrial park providing both a source of energy for mills located there and a reliable system of transportation for raw materials and finished products.[30] In the process they also revolutionized transportation on the river for the first time allowing an efficient and safe flow of commerce from the northern reaches of the Connecticut to Long Island Sound. Even the old rivals Springfield and Hartford benefited when a daily steam powered passenger packet was established to run between them.[31] The boon to regional commerce was immediate once the canal opened in 1829 and its use continued to grow for the next fifteen years until it was eclipsed by the opening in 1844 of the Hartford & New Haven Railroad.[32] Like the Farmington Canal, innovation in transportation technology brought an end to that aspect of the canal's use but unlike its New Haven based competitor, what came to be known as the Windsor Locks Canal continued to be used through the rest of the century but in a constantly diminishing capacity.

During the halcyon days of the canal as a major transportation asset on the river, industrial development along its right of way proved much slower than the investors of the Connecticut River Company might have liked. Altogether, the canal saw only five mills established along it during those first fifteen years and of those two failed. Yet the foundation for future growth had been created and by the outbreak of the Civil War in 1861 Pine Meadow had been transformed into the industrial center the Connecticut River Company had first imagined. As the little community snug against the rapids continued to grow it petitioned the state and became the separate town of Windsor Locks in 1854 in honor of their canal that was bringing them such good fortune.[33] Their canal became known as the Windsor Locks Canal.

In 1831 the first mill to locate along the canal was built by Jonathan Danforth of New York to manufacture door hinges or in the 19th century usage, "door butts". His mill failed. Danforth was followed in 1833 by Samuel Williams of Hartford who built a paper mill along the canal and even though his business failed in the Panic of 1837, he established Windsor Locks as a paper making center.[34] Over time the canal attracted more and more businesses and by the 1870's was home to a growing and diverse industrial base all brought there by the reliable flow of water for power. When Milo Todd arrived some time before 1873, he must have felt he had died and gone to heaven. Here before him was everything he had always imagined he would be part of. Although many of the factories came and went, the number and size of the enterprises grew over the last four decades of the 19th century. At one point the canal hosted cotton and silk mills, foundries, machine shops, a sewing

Stories on the Trail of a Yankee Millwright

machine manufacturer, and a rifle factory among others.[35] But by far the biggest industry to blossom along the Windsor Locks Canal was paper.

Even though the Williams paper mill failed as so many did in the Panic of 1837, it was bought by Dudley Persse and Horace Brooks and by the early 1840's their operation had successfully expanded to the point where they had a contract to supply one of New York's leading newspapers, *The New York Herald* with paper. This was still the rag paper era and though profitable, Persse & Brooks must have always been in a constant search for materials from which to produce their paper. Meanwhile, in 1836, Charles H. Dexter began producing paper in the basement of a gristmill he operated not on the canal, but on a stream called Kettle Brook. He reportedly made little profit at first but his efforts eventually led to the creation of the Dexter Corporation, an important and innovative manufacturer of specialty paper.[36] Dexter's first efforts at making paper were by hand using fibers from manila rope which made a sturdy and reliable wrapping paper.[37] Rather than having to face the problem of rag supply, Dexter must have had a steady source of used rope from the shipping along the river and in time was able to increase his production with the introduction of machinery. By 1840 he had moved his operation to the canal. Over the next few decades Dexter would be joined by other paper manufacturers including the Anchor Mills Paper Company and the Seymour Paper Company.[38] There were smaller operations as well including one operated by Frank H. Whittlesey who for a time had a partner by the name of Milo Todd.

By far and away the biggest of these paper manufacturers, the Dexter Company throughout the last three decades of the 19th century continued to experiment and innovate with materials and new paper making processes. They remained well established in the fine manila wrapping paper market but as wood pulp began to change the industry Dexter added wood pulp paper in 1875 from timbers floated down the river from the upper Connecticut and Northern New England.[39] In 1873 however, the company faced disaster when their factory burned to the ground. Rather than close down while rebuilding they leased and produced their paper in a mill then operated by Frank H. Whittlesey of Hartford and Milo Todd.[40] According to the *History of the Dexter Company*, Milo and Whittlesey were leasing the Albro and Bennett paper factory on the canal at the time and decided to sub-lease the factory to the Dexter Company which quickly restarted production in their temporary home. The size of the Whittlesey and Todd mill and the amount of equipment in it however could not keep up with the demand for their manila wrapping paper thus Dexter leased another factory in neighboring Suffield just north of Windsor Locks to meet demand.[41] In 1875 they were back in business in a new and larger factory on the canal.

So how was it that Milo found himself in Windsor Locks?

During the first few years of the 1870's Todd must have realized that for a variety of reasons, his factory on the Quinnipiac would not be able to compete with the growing paper industry in Windsor Locks. How he ended up in Windsor Locks I can only speculate but his connection appears to have been Frank H. Whittlesey. As previously noted, Milo and Whittlesey were in a partnership operating a leased paper making factory in 1873 when they turned it over to the Dexter Company. Whittlesey lived in Hartford for the majority of his adult life and did continue in the paper industry along the canal later when he purchased a factory in 1878 and produced tissue paper until the time of his death in 1908 according to his obituary in the *Hartford Courant*.[42] He was born in Clinton, Connecticut and as a young man moved to Hartford where he worked in a number of different businesses. There also seems to be no clear reason as to why Whittlesey ended up in Windsor Locks either but my guess is he was drawn there by Charles H. Dexter who in 1855 had become the president of the Connecticut River Company and in that capacity may have come to know Whittlesey in Hartford.[43]

Although Milo Todd had no clear previous connection with Frank Whittlesey, sometime between 1870 and 1873 their relationship had developed; perhaps Todd had traveled to Windsor Locks to observe his competitors and met Whittlesey and possibly Dexter. Because it does not appear that Whittlesey had a previous background or experience in the paper industry that I could identify, perhaps a partnership between the two men had come about through Dexter. After all,

Stories on the Trail of a Yankee Millwright

Milo had experience in paper making while Whittlesey apparently had managerial skills that might have led to financial backing from Dexter and others, maybe even the Connecticut River Company itself. There is also another possible connection between the two men—the Whittlesey's were an old and established family in Wallingford and although Frank was from the Shoreline branch, mutual acquaintances might have brought them together.

When the Dexter mill burned in 1873 and the company turned to Whittlesey and Todd to use their mill, it seems they quickly turned over their operation to them. Were they beholding to Dexter or did they simply get an offer they couldn't refuse? I guess we will never know the circumstances but whatever they were, immediately following their deal with Dexter their partnership ended and while Whittlesey remained in paper making for the rest of his life, Milo did not. From what I have been able to discover, Milo Todd, after twenty years of planning and scheming to become a success in the industrial age, had given up on his dream. I can only speculate as to why but the pattern of his life over the next five years reveals a man whose life was in disarray; disillusioned and struggling to grasp his place in a new reality.

As early as 1870, Milo began to sell off pieces of property he owned in Wallingford and North Haven and as I went through the history of these transactions it became clear that he had progressively begun to give up on his Quinnipiac Paper Company. His residence is still listed as Wallingford as late as January and February of 1873 the same year he is identified as a partner with Frank Whittlesey so that year appears to be the year of transition for him.[14] Having worked so hard to set up his factory by 1870, it is clear that by the following year he knew he could not either compete with others in the industry or may have been lured north to Windsor Locks and a better opportunity. One question that will never be answered is whether or not Todd was approached by Whittlesey and felt a move was in the best interest of his family or he had somehow ingratiated himself into a position of partnership. One thing for sure, Milo did not bring financial assets to the partnership but only his expertise in paper making. That apparently was enough. Meanwhile, in 1871 he is hit with a judgment against him which probably triggered the start of his disengagement from his hopes and dreams along the Quinnipiac. How absolutely devastated Milo must have felt as he watched all his life's ambition begin to dissolve.

In June, 1871 Todd's property along the Quinnipiac was attached in a law suit filed by North Haven resident Lewis Hills when apparently damage had been done to his property and Milo was judged to be at fault.[45] The suit attached all title, rights, and interests to Todd's property against a sum of $500.00. Had the Quinnipiac Paper Company been operating successfully in 1871, the judgment might have been paid quickly and he might have been able to move on since the monetary penalty was a relatively high sum for a small businessman at the time but certainly not insurmountable if the factory was producing a profit. It is not clear what impact this had on Todd's business but my hunch is it might have been significant. The *1870 United States Census* lists Milo Todd as living in North Haven and thus on the property along the Quinnipiac River but the value of his real estate was reduced to only $2500.00. His personal property is listed at $1,500.00.[46] When considering the amount of money Milo spent over the past two years to purchase property along the river and assuming that he should have begun producing paper by then, the value of his real estate and personal property should have been much higher. Obviously things were not working out as Milo had planned.

The judgment against him may have in fact been the major development that caused Milo to search for other options for his future. For the rest of the year he appears to be in a holding pattern and there is no record of any financial or property transactions on Milo's part in 1872 either. This is interesting only from the point of view that up to the start of 1871, he had been relentless trying to get his factory up and running. Was 1872 the year his straw paper actually began to be produced and he was able to make a name for himself in the industry or was he simply sitting tight? We will never know. Life along the Quinnipiac for Milo did begin to unravel for sure in 1873 however. He signed a quit claim in January to Emery Morse for the six acres bordering the Quinnipiac

Paper Company that surrounded Morse's shop. In doing so he turned over to Morse the property he had so carefully set up around the Morse mill back in 1868.[47] More important, this is the last mention of the paper factory and whether or not Todd is producing paper by then is unknown. In February of that year the tax collector of Wallingford put a lien on "two tracts and buildings" for $300.00 a further sign that he was financially in trouble.

In the autumn of 1873, Milo continued to disengage himself from his holdings in Wallingford and North Haven. On September 6th land records in Wallingford reveal that he sold some land he held in the Sand Plains section of town in return for the buyer assuming the tax lien on the property giving further credence to the fact he was in financial distress.[48] On that same date, Milo, identified as living in Wallingford, sold to George Blodgett "a certain piece of land with a two story framed dwelling house in North Haven, the property subject to a mortgage with Townshend Savings Bank for $5,000.00 in connection with the gristmill property".[49] No mention of the paper factory. Todd must have been in Windsor Locks and in partnership with Whittlesey by then having moved away from the scene of his failure and desperate to simply shed his liabilities.

There is no record of the Todd's in terms of land transactions for all of 1874 and my guess he must have taken on a position in Windsor Locks, possibly with the Dexter Company after they began to use the mill he had been operating with Whittlesey. I cannot help but hope he was finally involved in the industry he knew and understood though it is clear he would no longer have been the entrepreneur he had always hoped to be but rather an employee. In 1875 Milo and Cornelia are identified as living in Windsor Locks when in June of that year they sold a 100 acre farm in Wallingford to Cornelia's father George W. Cook.[50] Milo must have inherited the farm from his father Thelus and the sale of it really marks what must have been a psychological and emotional break with his past. What must it have been like for Todd to let the family connection to Wallingford and Northford go?

Todd's sell off of his Wallingford assets continued in 1876 when he again sold to his father-in-law a large lot in the center of the town for "$1.00 and valuable consideration".[51] In all these transactions Todd is turning over the properties and not making any money, arrangements must have been made to take them in lieu of debt Milo owed each party or to satisfy tax liens. In September, while still identified as residing in Windsor Locks, Milo and Cornelia's third daughter Alice was born.[52] In December that happy event was terribly overshadowed by the death of their nine year old daughter Clara. Such family tragedies were still too common during the latter half of the 19th century and it must have been a terrible blow to her parents and one that may in fact have pushed Milo to further seek to turn his life and the future welfare of his family in a new direction. As 1877 began, Milo and Cornelia appear to have decided to make a complete break with their past and Milo made what was probably the most significant and quite possibly emotional sale of what was left of his property. The record shows that in June, 1877 he sold his mill on the Quinnipiac. The land records state that Milo and Cornelia Todd of Windsor Locks sold to John Bishop of New Haven for $1600.00 two pieces of land with buildings, machinery, and water privileges there-on in North Haven. Both properties were identified as bordering land already sold off or included in what was left of Milo's original purchase from David Stevens.[53]

What must it have been like for Milo to see everything he had dreamed of and worked so hard for since his days as a young man disappear with his signature? Was he bitter or was he sadly content that he had done his best against the market forces of the industrial age that had in essence been stacked against him? Did he comprehend why he had failed? What was it like for him to be in Windsor Locks and witness the Dexter family building a colossus of the paper industry, the very thing he had begun to plan and scheme to create so long ago on the Paug in Northford? In the end Milo Todd, despite his drive and ambition, in 1877 was simply one of thousands of casualties in the grinding and often ruthless competition that typified late 19th century American capitalism. The reality was Todd never stood a chance even when he first made his move to the

Quinnipiac River. Already paper making and all industry for that matter had moved beyond him and out of his reach. He could see it in the giant factories of the Britannia makers up and down the Quinnipiac; he could see it when he first visited Windsor Locks. The little company that he had put his heart and soul into was obsolete before he ever made a sheet of paper; it was a relic in size and financing from the earlier era of small scale industrial development that had characterized the Northford of his youth. That realization, coupled with the death of his daughter, must have broken his heart. But Milo Todd was nothing if not resilient.

"Perhaps Cornelia is right" Milo reflected as he sat in the small office the Dexter's let him share along with the other foreman in their new factory on the canal. They have been good to me and have encouraged me to learn more about their operation and appreciate my skill and ability to work with others and manage the men. But it will always be their business and should I be content to stay with them, I know I can provide a comfortable life for her and the girls. Yet my heart is not here and I cannot see myself working for another man's profit forever.

I know I should not dwell on what has transpired and should accept my lot in life, but the lure and call of something else is too strong and if only I knew where it was my future lay. Every day I see and hear of men who through their own initiative and hard work become a success and yet for me, these last years have held nothing but frustration and disappointment. To make matters worse, I see the spirit of my father in my dreams telling me of my mistake and now I have even let his farm in Wallingford go. Maybe father was right after all. Was the life of a farmer so bad?

The noise of the paper making machinery, which was once a source of excitement and anticipation for him in Northford and Quinnie, had, on the floor outside the office door, come to a halt as a bell rang for the half hour lunch break and he rose from his chair to remind the men of their need to return to their work by half past 12:00. As he shouted out the reminder, some half sullenly replied "yes Mr. Todd" while others just shuffled by. He walked over to the young Polish boy who spoke no English but was eager to work and learn and gave him his pocket watch, a gift from the Dexters. Milo pointed to the 6 on the bottom of the dial and the boy eagerly shook his head in agreement. He knew that the lad would ring the bell at 12:30 as he had been taught and promptly return the watch to him as the men filtered back to their tasks. Milo liked the boy, he reminded him of himself so many years ago sitting on his stool as the Fowler brothers talked and he dreamed of his future in industry. "This definitely is not where I thought I would be, running another man's shop when I think back to those days in Northford".

Milo walked out into the sun and sat on an old and rotting wooden bench next to the canal as he looked out beyond it to the rapids in the river. "Water" he murmured to himself, "water and all it promised me. What a cruel mistress she has been. To chase her, and finally catch her and her power only to have her trick me and abandon me for others such as the Dexter's who take her for granted here on the Connecticut. If only…" he grumbled as he found himself begin to sulk and as he turned away from the river, he looked up to watch a flock of birds flying south towards Hartford using the river as their ancient highway. Yes, Cornelia is right he thought. I will speak to Mr. Dexter this evening.

What Cornelia had been urging her husband to do was leave Windsor Locks and the paper industry behind and take their savings, as meager as they were, and go to Hartford or even Middletown further down the river and start a new life. What that life might be she said she did not know but she had looked him keenly in the eyes and told him how she had always trusted in his cleverness, his ambition, and his willingness to work hard and that she knew would carry them forward. "Yes, it is time to leave paper and its manufacture behind, and follow those birds to a fresh start in a new place" he whispered quietly as the birds slowly passed from his view. After all he thought with growing sense of confidence, I know I may yet succeed in a new endeavor and maybe Mr. Dexter and Whittlesey may know of some potential opportunities. They certainly both have the pulse of the area's business running through their veins and I have never been one to be shy when it comes to exploring possibilities.

Resilient he was. Apparently Milo never lost the drive and tenacity that had always characterized his determination to find his place in the frantically transforming industrial economy of the last decades of the 19th century. In the process he did eventually find his place and when he died in 1907, he must have felt content that he had become a relatively successful man. But the process of obtaining success would be often difficult for him and the record shows he at times made calculated choices and even took risks in his quest to rebuild his life and future following his failure on the Quinnipiac.

After what must have been the shattering events starting in 1875 that upended their lives, Milo and Cornelia sought a new direction and Todd turned his back on the paper industry for good as well as his new home in Windsor Locks and moved to the nearby bustling and vibrant capitol of Connecticut. Hartford had been experiencing a period of tremendous economic growth since the end of the Civil War and by the late 70's had become an important industrial and financial center. It was there that Milo pursued his future and according to *Geer's Hartford Business Directory* for the year 1878 was living at 100 Seymour Street in the city and was listed as a "marketman" for his occupation.[53] Apparently he was starting from scratch and exactly what a marketman was is a bit innocuous as the definition, even for Merriam-Webster, is unclear. Their definition is that a marketman is a dealer in markets. Was Milo a stock trader? It is possible knowing his connections with the Dexter family. A marketman might also be a simple employee in a grocery. If that was the case, he had fallen from would be entrepreneur to a simple grocery clerk. But Milo still had the kind of ambition that within a few years would move him up the economic ladder that typified the capitalism of the era. Between 1878 and 1880 there is no record of Todd, even in the U.S. Census for that year so exactly what he was up to in Hartford is impossible to know. By 1880 however he had moved to Heron Street and was listed as one of the wardens for St. James Church, Episcopal on the corner of Washington and Park Streets in the center of the city.[54] He seemed to have established himself in the community and was intending to stay. There is no record of his occupation however.

In 1881 Milo and his family moved again, this time to 75 Main Street in the heart of the city. He also opened a grocery store next door at 77 Main and is listed in *Geers* as owning a shop selling groceries and meat. The listing is the same for 1882 and 1883.[55] He had settled into an occupation and the choice indicates that his earlier identification as a marketman was probably in the grocery trade. Main Street was the center of commerce in Hartford and Todd's store was in a prime location for him to gage and keep track of the ebb and flow of economic possibilities in the city. Though not the industrial magnate he had hoped to be, Milo had established himself and become part of the fabric of business that swirled around him. He must have loved it. In 1884 he moved his shop to 73 Main Street and home to 1 Congress Street.[56] It appears Milo was moving up, possibly to a bigger store and a better home but based on the evidence of what he did next, he was not content with staying a respected grocer. As always Milo Todd wanted more and he saw in the explosive growth of the insurance industry that was turning Hartford into "the insurance capitol of the world" his opportunity. In 1885, he jumped in.

During the 18th century, Hartford merchants, like their counterparts in other Connecticut towns, had developed a prosperous trade with European colonies in the Caribbean providing them with a variety of agricultural products and timber gathered from the surrounding countryside. In order to protect themselves against possible losses inherent to the voyages, they began to pool their resources in order to insure their vessels against potential risks. As the 19th century dawned, they continued the practice and as Hartford began to capture more and more of the commerce on the Connecticut River these private practices of the merchants and businessmen coalesced into the formation of the first insurance company in the nation, The Hartford Insurance Group.[57] The Hartford insured against a variety of possible calamities that ranged from the loss of a ship, attacks by pirates, fires, storms, and accidents.

As industry began to develop and grow in Hartford and surrounding towns during the first four decades of the century, the need for a variety of other types of protection against damages and loss evolved resulting in an ever growing list of insurers ready to offer clients for payment of a premium financial protection against those potential losses. It was a great scheme; you pay us now and in a continuous and ongoing manner and we will protect you against any future loss you might suffer. The system provided piece of mind for the insured and a steady income and profit for the insurer provided they carried enough capital to cover any potential payouts that would cover losses. To ensure the viability of the insurance companies, each was required to apply for a charter or license from the state that showed they had on reserve enough capital to cover any potential losses.

The Hartford group was followed by other insurers that covered a number of different risks including fire, damages and accidents, life, and even steam boiler explosions. Some of these new companies were The Connecticut Mutual Life Insurance Company (1846), Aetna Insurance Company (1850), American Temperance Life Insurance Company (1851) which became The Phoenix, National Union Life and Limb Insurance Company (1863) which became Metlife, Travelers (1864), Connecticut General Life Insurance Company (1865), and Hartford Steam Boiler and Inspection (1866).[58] By 1900 dozens of others came and went based on their capitalization, market share, and in some cases ultimately losses. For individuals eager to make their mark and money too, this new industry was the perfect mechanism. For an ambitious and eager man like Milo, working his way not only back but up, insurance offered the opportunity of a lifetime and he took it.

1885 was the year that started Milo's life on a path he had always wanted to follow; one towards wealth and success. But this time he knew it would take time and he seems to have been willing to accept that. Gone was the impetuous young man from Northford, impatient to make his mark. He was fifty one years old, still eager, but obviously chastened by his life's experiences and willing to work his way forward in a more patient manner. Thus in 1885, Milo started off in his new career selling insurance policies and is listed as an insurance agent in *Geers Hartford Business Directory* with a business address at 236 High Street.[59] Unfortunately which company he was affiliated with is not stated but in the following two years he is identified as working as an agent at 274 Main Street, the home of the National Life Association. He had also moved his residence to 554 Main.[60] The switch to selling insurance at his age reveals some interesting insights into Milo's personality in that he was willing to give up what was by then a stable grocery business for the risks of starting a new occupation in a very competitive industry. To this day it is a job that requires tenacity, organization, and a personality that allows an individual to make connections with others in a comfortable and trusting manner. Traits it seems Todd must have always possessed.

Milo must have been a successful agent for he stayed with the occupation for the rest of his life and in 1888 moved to a company building at 278 & 1/2 Main Street where he remained until 1901.[61] Meanwhile he and Cornelia stayed at their home at 554 Main Street until 1895 when they moved to 110 High Street.[62] The fact that for the first time since leaving Northford in 1868 he and Cornelia remained in a home for ten years is a good sign that their life through his new occupation had become much more stable. The move back to Main Street had been their fifth since moving to Hartford in 1878. His ticket to this new stability was working for the Charter Oak Life Insurance Company, which had resurrected itself after a series of financial and legal problems that at times typified the tenuous and often shady side of the insurance industry during the late 19th century.

Organized in 1856 as the Charter Oak Fire and Marine Insurance Company, the company had capital assets listed at $300,000.00. The company however ran into continuous financial problems during the Civil War as its liabilities often outstripped its resources and in 1866 the State of New York revoked its license to do business there and the company was forced out of the nation's most lucrative market. Charter Oak was then re-organized with a reduced capitalization of $150,000.00 until the disastrous 1871 Chicago Fire destroyed what was left of its solvency.[63] Somehow the company hung on but again ran into serious financial difficulty in 1875, came close to bankruptcy in 1877, and its officers were indicted by New York for financial maleficence in 1878. They were found not guilty at their trial.[64] Charter Oak was again re-organized in 1886 following a long series of court proceedings associated with legal actions taken against them in New York by policy holders and this time it emerged as a joint stock company with a capitalization of $400,000.00.[65] This is the company Todd joined in 1888 and it is interesting to note that like Milo, it had so often lived on the edge yet constantly resurrected itself. In Charter Oak's trials and tribulations he must have seen a reflection of his own life's struggles; they were a perfect match.

After ten years in their home on Main Street, the Todd's move to 110 High Street in 1895 demonstrated that for Milo the location of his residence became a mark of his success. As he was moving up in the insurance world his new home in a residential section of the city was a statement that after all his struggles he had established himself as a member of the solid and growing middle class that was transforming Hartford and the nation. Main Street by that time must have been bursting with increased commercial activity and no longer a proper location for a family with more genteel aspirations. High Street would remain the Todd home until Milo's death in 1907.

To add credence to Milo's ascending position in the community, he applied for and became a member of the *Sons of the American Revolution* in 1896 through the service of his grandfather Thelus.[66] As earlier noted, this was a time of nostalgic patriotism when descendants of families that had been present in Connecticut during the Colonial period and Revolution worked hard to distinguish themselves from the increasing flood of European ethnicities providing an unlimited source of cheap labor for the Yankee owned factories. Membership in the Sons brought with it a degree of recognition and a pedigree that surely opened many doors for Milo and proved a balm for his desire to elevate himself to the status as one of the Yankee elite. Milo's social and economic climb was given an additional boost when he was registered with the State as a Notary Public in 1898.[67] For a man like Todd, it was a badge of legitimacy that undoubtedly wiped away all those painful years of humiliation he must have felt. He now carried the recognition from the State that he was a trusted, honest, and successful member of the community.

An interesting chapter in Milo's story next developed in 1900 when though retaining his residence in Hartford, he is found in the U.S.

Census to be living along with his family in Newtown, Connecticut. He was identified as an insurance agent by occupation, and the document states that Todd owned his Newtown home outright without a mortgage. Besides Cornelia, their daughter Ally (Alice), age 23 was living with them along with a servant with the curious name of General Perry.[68] In retrospect, this was an incredible turn of events, Milo Todd with a servant. How distant those hard days of losing everything on the Quinnipiac must have seemed from the perspective of his country home in Southwestern Connecticut. Exactly why Milo was in Newtown is not known, perhaps he was there to expand the company's policy base into Fairfield County or maybe they were there due to an illness in the family and the country air was seen as beneficial. The Todd's remained there in 1901 as well according to Geer's Directory but the company he worked for had changed as he had become an agent for The John Hancock Mutual Life Insurance Company of Boston with an office address in Hartford of 756 Main Street. The family still retained their Hartford home.[69]

In 1902, Milo really came into his own in the commercial world when, he and his family moved back to Hartford and while still working for John Hancock, established his own agency with Benjamin Jewett. Their agency, called Jewett & Todd was listed in the *Geers Directory* in the Hancock offices on Main Street along with another business he and Jewett formed by the strange name of Ken-a-Wakut Med. Company.[70] What exactly this firm did is far from clear as the "Med" is not spelled out in the directory. They may have been selling unregulated patent medicines which were very popular at the time or perhaps they were offering medical insurance. Either possibility would have been potentially lucrative. As to why the odd name that appears to be a take-off on a Native American word or even Connecticut we can only speculate.

Milo spent his last years in Hartford and died in 1907 at the age of 73. After years of struggle and unfulfilled dreams, he had become a success in an industry that seemed to suit him and one he would never have even imagined existed years earlier as he stood in his grandfather's gristmill dreaming of his future. If he did contemplate his life's journey, I'm sure he would have looked back with pride at what he had overcome and accomplished in the end. But my sense was he was not a man who wasted his time looking back. His life had always been one looking forward, like the nation and time he had been born in. Certainly he must have identified with and revered his and his family's past. Milo always knew where he was from and where he was going and I believe that gave him the strength and confidence to stay focused on the future. He had become what he had always wanted, a self-made success in the dynamic new age he had witnessed the birth of when the Maltbys and Fowlers were tinkering with the future. It was the world he had watched the Stevens family and the Dexter's make, and one he had desperately wanted to be part of. Yes, Milo Todd had made it. Did he die a content and happy man? I'd like to think so.

As he watched the doctor and Cornelia leave the room his eyes wandered to the open window and its fluttering curtain, the gentle breeze moving it in a lively yet soothing manner while the sounds of the street thirty yards distant brought a certain sense of satisfaction to him. "Yes, all is in motion in this world" he thought, "constantly moving forward towards their inevitable destiny whether nature or man. There is no denying destiny".

Milo knew he was dying and his doctor merely confirmed what he already knew. It was his heart that was failing him, after all these years it had grown tired, tired of the emotional struggles and drive he had put it through he mused to himself as he began to reflect on his life's journey and how it had brought him to a place where he had become finally content in these later years, knowing that despite the setbacks that so often plagued him, he had become a success but in a way he had never imagined so many years ago. "Yes", he continued his reflection, I would never have imagined that my path would lie in providing people with security against risk and even death, especially the idea that they might provide for their loved ones after they have met their maker. A far cry from what I had ever dreamed of so many years ago in Northford and even Quinnie. Yes, destiny and fate can take one to unexpected places".

Cornelia returned to their bedroom just as his thoughts were collected on the breeze and drifted gently through the window and the world beyond. "Milo you should rest now but from the look on your face you must be fussing over the work you have been told to let go for a while by Dr. Cole. You know others can manage in your absence" she said with a scolding look that ended with a smile. "You have never been one to sit back and rest while others work. Now it is time".

"For once I was not thinking of affairs in my office for they, it may shock you for me to say, are the worries of others now".

"It does surprise me dear husband as I know how you are, a man of ambition and pride in your work and have always been" Cornelia said as she came around the foot of the bed to sit in the chair she had placed earlier by its head for the doctor. "So what brings such a look of concern?"

"I was watching the breeze as it gently lifted the curtains and was thinking of fate and its workings and how all one's efforts in the end are like the wind, ever moving towards an inevitable destiny".

"So philosophical for a man so practical" she replied with a smile.

"Cornelia, I know my time is limited as do you and that I want you to make sure I return to Northford after I die. As we had discussed when we ordered the monument for our family plot, it would give me great pleasure to know I will be with my ancestors and that together we can await Judgment Day" Milo reminded her with an earnest expression.

"Milo, as always you are planning ahead and thinking of the future. You know your wishes will be taken care of for they have always been mine as well no matter where our life together has taken us" she said with a look of compassion and care. "We have discussed this countless times this past year and you must trust Ally and I to ensure it is done".

"I know" he replied, taking his hand and placing it on hers. "It is just that my pride, which has always been my sin to carry, so desires those where I began my life to know that I, Milo Todd, had become more than a millwright grinding the grain of others, that I had become a man of wealth and stature in this dynamic world where anything and everything is possible. That it was possible for a man from my humble beginnings to rise, despite obstacles, to become part of all this land blessed by God can offer. In the end, I, Milo Apollos Todd, had built on my past and embraced the future. That is what

Stories on the Trail of a Yankee Millwright

I want the good people of Northford to know when they view my eternal resting place".

"Yes Milo, and so they will" she said softly as she raised his hand to gently kiss it, tears in her eyes.

Milo did in the end return home to Northford, but this time to its Old Cemetery. His monument, an Egyptian obelisk, is an expensive type erected by prominent and affluent members of many communities throughout Connecticut during the late 19th and early 20th Centuries. Made of solid grey granite and not local sandstone, the choice of design and material was his final statement that he had come back home a success. Milo Apollos Todd had ultimately and triumphantly made it in the industrial age and he wanted everyone to know it. His monument, dominating a family plot enclosed with metal fencing, was his final signature. How different it was from that little boy's name scratched long ago on the window glass of his grandfather's gristmill.

The story of Milo's life and time as well as that of his family is in many ways America's story. It was for them as well as for us a journey to find a way through an often confusing and ever changing present that has been shaped and determined by what and who came before. Like the forgotten history of the Quinnipiac, an earth covered fort on an ancient sand dune, or the tragic events of one fateful day on Groton Heights, so much of what has shaped who we are as a society and culture has been buried by time, both literally or figuratively, and is threatened to be lost forever. Does it really matter that the Fowler and Maltby factories have disappeared, that the silver industry along the Quinnipiac and in Meriden is a fading memory, or that a utopia once thrived in Wallingford? Do their stories have anything to do with who we are today? Is it really necessary to know that canals were once the engine of economic development for our region and the nation? And does it really matter that the son of a country gristmill owner and farmer could rise to success in the competitive and unregulated world of the 19th century finance and capitalism? Is there a lesson to be learned in the life of a man who was determined to persevere despite setbacks that might have broken others?

In the end we are who we are because of our collective past; as a society and as people. To deny that is to turn our back on our present and future. In the context of time, we are in many ways merely the reflection of all that came before us with an opportunity to build on that legacy and hand off to those in the future something better. I think Milo Todd would agree; it was the secret to his time and ultimate success. Progress after all, and a better tomorrow depend on retaining a memory of what came before, of seeing the past and understanding that as participants in a journey across time and place, we walk in the shadows of yesterday.

END NOTES

Chapter One

1. (Branford, p. 675)
2. (Miller H., p. 1)
3. (Miller H., p. 2)
4. (Miller H., p. 2)
5. (Algonquian Confederacy of the Quinnipiac Tribal Council, 2013)
6. (Algonquian Confederacy of the Quinnipiac Tribal Council, 2013)
7. (Algonquian Confederacy of the Quinnipiac Tribal Council, 2013)

Chapter Two

1. (Miller J. W., 1976, p. 21)
2. (Higginson, 1630 (1908 Reprint), p. 6) (Wood, 1634 (1865 Reprint), p. 18)
3. (Varekamp, p. 1)
4. (Varekamp, p. 1)
5. (Jacobs, Early Dutch Explorations in North America, 2013, p. 62)
6. (Van Dusen, 1961, p. 19)
7. (Wilcoxen, 1974, p. 235)
8. (Jacobs, *New Netherlands: A Dutch Colony in Seventeenth Century America*, 2005, p. 32)
9. (Jacobs, *New Netherlands: A Dutch Colony in Seventeenth Century America*, 2005, p. 32)
10. (Varekamp, p. 2)
11. (Bailyn, 2012, p. 191)
12. (Blaeu, 1635)
13. (Bailyn, 2012, p. 209)
14. (White, 2014)

15. (Fowler's Follies, 1992, p. 69)
16. (Pfeiffer J. P., 1999, p. 4)
17. (Pfeiffer J. P., 1999, p. 4)
18. (Pfeiffer J. , 2000)
19. (Pfeiffer J. P., 1998, p. 4)
20. (arno665, 2015)
21. (Bailyn, 2012, p. 199)
22. (Bailyn, 2012, p. 199)
23. (Bailyn, 2012, p. 208)

Chapter Three

1. (Calder, 1934 (1970 reprint), p. 149)
2. (Gregan, 2014, p. 2)
3. (Calder, 1934 (1970 reprint), p. 54)
4. (Calder, 1934 (1970 reprint), p. 54)
5. (Bailyn, 2012, p. 191)
6. (Calder, 1934 (1970 reprint), p. 79)
7. (Gregan, 2014, p. 1)
8. (Van Dusen, 1961, p. 55)
9. (Gregan, 2014, p. 3)
10. (Bailyn, 2012, p. 512)
11. (Calder, 1934 (1970 reprint), p. 157)
12. (Van Dusen, 1961, p. 70)
13. (Van Dusen, 1961, p. 73)
14. (Van Dusen, 1961, p. 73)
15. (Van Dusen, 1961, p. 74)
16. (Gregan, 2014, p. 3)
17. (Gregan, 2014, p. 4)
18. (Gregan, 2014, p. 4)
19. (Branford, 1747, p. 675)

Chapter Four

1. (Caulkins, 1895, p. 43)

2. (Van Dusen, 1961, p. 157)
3. (Meals, 2005, p. 1)
4. (Caulkins, 1895, p. 545)
5. (Allyn, 1882 (1999 Reprint), p. 13)
6. (Andriopoulos, *The Burning of New London*, 2014, p. 1)
7. (Allyn, 1882 (1999 Reprint), p. 13)
8. (Andriopoulos, *The Burning of New London*, 2014, p. 1)
9. (Van Dusen, 1961, p. 154)
10. (Caulkins, 1895, p. 545)
11. (Allyn, 1882 (1999 Reprint), p. 14)
12. (Andriopoulos, *The Burning of New London*, 2014, p. 2)
13. (Caulkins, 1895, p. 545)
14. (Caulkins, 1895, p. 545)
15. (Andriopoulos, *The Burning of New London*, 2014, p. 2)
16. (Caulkins, 1895, p. 545)
17. (Andriopoulos, *Battle of Groton Heights*, 2014, p. 1)
18. (Caulkins, 1895, p. 546)
19. (Andriopoulos, *Battle of Groton Heights*, 2014, p. 4)
20. (Caulkins, 1895, p. 546)
21. (Andriopoulos, *The Burning of New London*, 2014, p. 6)
22. (Allyn, 1882 (1999 Reprint), p. 62)
23. (Andriopoulos, *The Burning of New London*, 2014, p. 8)
24. (Andriopoulos, *The Burning of New London*, 2014, p. 9)
25. (Van Dusen, 1961, p. 169)
26. (Andriopoulos, *The Burning of New London*, 2014, p. 10)
27. (Bill Memorial Library, 2003, p. 3)
28. (Andriopoulos, *Battle of Groton Heights*, 2014, p. 5)
29. (Andriopoulos, *Battle of Groton Heights*, 2014, p. 5)
30. (Andriopoulos, *Battle of Groton Heights*, 2014, p. 6)
31. (Andriopoulos, *Battle of Groton Heights*, 2014, p. 6)
32. (Allyn, 1882 (1999 Reprint), p. 49)
33. (Andriopoulos, *Battle of Groton Heights*, 2014, p. 8)
34. (Allyn, 1882 (1999 Reprint), p. 49)
35. (Allyn, 1882 (1999 Reprint), p. 52)
36. (Allyn, 1882 (1999 Reprint), p. 52)
37. (Allyn, 1882 (1999 Reprint), p. 52)

38. (Allyn, 1882 (1999 Reprint), p. 72)
39. (Allyn, 1882 (1999 Reprint), p. 37)
40. (Allyn, 1882 (1999 Reprint), p. 53)
41. (Allyn, 1882 (1999 Reprint), p. 93)
42. (Allyn, 1882 (1999 Reprint), p. 53)
43. (Andriopoulos, *Battle of Groton Heights*, 2014, p. 13)
44. (Allyn, 1882 (1999 Reprint), p. 53)
45. (Allyn, 1882 (1999 Reprint), p. 38)
46. (Van Dusen, 1961, p. 169)
47. (Allyn, 1882 (1999 Reprint), p. 53)
48. (Allyn, 1882 (1999 Reprint), p. 40)
49. (Allyn, 1882 (1999 Reprint), p. 41)
50. (Allyn, 1882 (1999 Reprint), p. 54)
51. (Allyn, 1882 (1999 Reprint), p. 43)
52. (Andriopoulos, *Battle of Groton Heights*, 2014, p. 13)
53. (Andriopoulos, *Battle of Groton Heights*, 2014, p. 15)
54. (Caulkins, 1895, p. 548)
55. (Allyn, 1882 (1999 Reprint), p. 22)
56. (Department of Energy and Environmental Protection, 2014)

Chapter Five

1. (Daughters of the American Revolution 2014)
2. (Root 1904, 2)
3. (Root 1904, 235)
4. (Root 1904, 235)
5. (Root 1904, 235)
6. (H. Miller n.d.)
7. (*Sons of the American Revolution.* Connecticut Society 1896, 517)
8. (*Sons of the American Revolution.* Connecticut Society 1896)
9. (Allyn 1882 (1999 Reprint), 22)
10. (Lincoln 2014)
11. (Bill Memorial Library 2003, 3)
12. (Farrow, Complicity 2002)
13. (Green 2002, 21)
14. (Farrow, Connecticut Slave Owners in 1790 2002, 19)

15. (Farrow, Connecticut Slave Owners in 1790 2002, 17)
16. (Farrow, Connecticut Slave Owners in 1790 2002, 17)
17. (Lang 2002, 8)
18. (Lang 2002, 8)
19. (Lang 2002, 6)
20. (Farrow, From Settlement to Reconstruction 2002, 38)
21. (Farrow, From Settlement to Reconstruction 2002, 39)
22. (Petry 2002, 33)
23. (Bailey 2014, 1)
24. (Bailey 2014, 1)
25. (Allyn 1882 (1999 Reprint), 285)
26. (Allyn 1882 (1999 Reprint), 242)
27. (Allyn 1882 (1999 Reprint), 242)
28. (Allyn 1882 (1999 Reprint), 286)
29. (Allyn 1882 (1999 Reprint), 49)
30. (Allyn 1882 (1999 Reprint), 91)
31. (Allyn 1882 (1999 Reprint), 102)
32. (Allyn 1882 (1999 Reprint), 91)
33. (Weslley, Dorothy Porter and Uzelac, Constance Porter 2002, 188)
34. (Lincoln 2014)
35. (Lincoln 2014)
36. (Lincoln 2014)

Chapter Six

1. (G. S. Miller, Study of Northford-North Branford Industrial Sites 1973)
2. (G. S. Miller, Northford, The Athens of Connecticut 1768-1826 1997)
3. (G. S. Miller, Northford, The Athens of Connecticut 1768-1826 1997, 8)
4. (G. S. Miller, Northford, The Athens of Connecticut 1768-1826 1997, 1)
5. (G. S. Miller, Northford, The Athens of Connecticut 1768-1826 1997, 6)

6. (G. S. Miller, Northford, The Athens of Connecticut 1768-1826 1997, 8)
7. (G. S. Miller, Northford, The Athens of Connecticut 1768-1826 1997, 16)
8. (G. S. Miller, Northford, The Athens of Connecticut 1768-1826 1997, 17)
9. (Branford Land Records 1786)
10. (Connecticut Todd Family 2014)
11. (H. Miller n.d., 42)
12. (H. Miller n.d., 43)
13. (Lewis 1986, 84)
14. (E. Grant 1992, vi)
15. (E. Grant 1992, vii)
16. (E. Grant 1992, 223)
17. (Family Ties Bring Together North Branford Industry 2013, 2)
18. (H. Miller n.d., 44)
19. (H. Miller n.d., 44)
20. (G. S. Miller, Study of Northford-North Branford Industrial Sites 1973, 5)
21. (May 1947, 125)
22. (H. Miller n.d., 44)
23. (May 1947, 127)
24. (G. S. Miller, Study of Northford-North Branford Industrial Sites 1973, 5)
25. (H. Miller n.d., 45)
26. (G. S. Miller, Study of Northford-North Branford Industrial Sites 1973, 6)
27. (H. Miller n.d., 45)
28. (H. Miller n.d., 45)
29. (G. S. Miller, Study of Northford-North Branford Industrial Sites 1973, 4)
30. (G. S. Miller, Study of Northford-North Branford Industrial Sites 1973, 4)
31. (H. Miller n.d., 47)
32. (May 1947, 120)
32. (May 1947, 120)

33. (May 1947, 131)
34. (H. Miller n.d., 44)

Chapter Seven

1. (Todd Family 2014)
2. (May 1947, 121)
3. (*The Political Graveyard: Connecticut State House of Representatives, 1830's* 2014)
4. (Connecticut State Agricultural Society 1855, 44)
5. (Connecticut State Agricultural Society 1855, 56)
6. (Connecticut State Agricultural Society 1855, 84)
7. (May 1947, 122)
8. (Powers 1992-1994)
9. (Powers 1992-1994)
10. (May 1947, 127)
11. (North Branford 1857, 258)
12. (History of Paper Making 2014)
13. (Valente 2014, 209)
14. (Valente 2014, 209)
15. (Valente 2014, 210)
16. (*History of Paper Making*, 2014)
17. (Hutchinson 2014, 4)
18. (Valente 2014, 211)
19. (Valente 2014, 211)
20. (Hutchinson 2014, 4)
21. (Valente 2014, 211)
22. (G. S. Miller, Study of Northford-North Branford Industrial Sites 1973, 1)
23. (Hunter 1979, 298)
24. (Hunter 1979, 302)
25. (Hunter 1979, 302)
26. (Powers 1992-1994)
27. (May 1947, 127)
28. (Todd Family 2014)
29. (Larkin 1988, 193)

30. (Larkin 1988, 194)
31. (Schlereth 1991, 280)
32. (Todd Family 2014)
33. (Town of Wallingford, 1868, pp. Vol. 61, Page 122)
34. (North Haven, Ct 1868, Vol.14, p537)

Chapter Eight

1. (May 1947, 130)
2. (May 1947, 20)
3. (Britannia Metal 2014)
4. (Davis 1870, 476)
5. (*The Columbia Electronic Encyclopedia* 2014)
6. (May 1947, 20)
7. (May 1947, 18)
8. (May 1947, 21)
9. (Meriden Britannia Company History and Marks 2014)
10. (Meriden Britannia Company History and Marks 2014)
11. (Hasluk 1907, 697-699)
12. (Davis 1870, 481)
13. (Meriden Britannia Company History and Marks 2014)
14. (Family Treemaker.Org 2009)
15. (United States Census 1870, 447)
16. (Powers 1992-1994)
17. (Powers 1992-1994)
18. (Powers 1992-1994)
19. (Powers 1992-1994)
20. (Wight 1879)
21. (Wight 1879)
22. (Wight 1879)
23. (Wight 1879)
24. (Wight 1879)
25. (Wight 1879)
26. (Hasluk 1907, 697)
27. (White 2014)
28. (Wight 1879)

29. (Wight 1879)
30. (Wight 1879)
31. (Wight 1879)
32. (Family Treemaker.Org 2009)
33. (G. S. Miller, Study of Northford-North Branford Industrial Sites 1973, 6)
34. (H. Miller n.d., 49)
35. (DePauw 2014, 1)
36. (North Branford Land Records 1880, Vol.Viii, 41)
37. (DePauw 2014, 2)
38. (G. S. Miller, Study of Northford-North Branford Industrial Sites 1973, 6)
39. (May 1947, 130)
40. (DePauw 2014, 2)
41. (May 1947, 130)
42. (Family Treemaker.Org 2009)
43. (May 1947, 172)
44. (May 1947, 179)
45. (May 1947, 181)
46. (May 1947, 210)
47. (May 1947, 211)
48. (Raber 2011, 4)
49. (Raber 2011, 4)
50. (Raber 2011, 4)
51. (urbanreviewstl.com 2014, 1)
52. (urbanreviewstl.com 2014, 1)
53. (BL Companies 2014, 1)
54. (BL Companies 2014)

Chapter Nine

1. (Wallingford, Connecticut 1868, V.61, p.122)
2. (North Haven, Connecticut 1868, V. 16, p. 53)
3. (North Haven, Connecticut 1868, V. 16, p. 54)
4. (North Haven, Connecticut 1868, V. 16, p. 54)
5. (North Haven, Ct 1868, V. 14, p.537)

6. (North Haven, Connecticut 1868, V. 14, p. 540)
7. (North Haven Land Records 1868, V. 14, p. 542)
8. (North Haven Land Records 1868, V. 14, p. 539)
9. (North Haven Land Records 1869, V.14, p.614)
10. (Davis 1870, 496)
11. (North Haven Land Records 1869, V. 14, p. 614)
12. (Davis 1870, 494)
13. (North Haven Land Records 1869, V.14, p. 567)
14. (North Haven Land Records 1870, V.16, p.70)
15. (Nordhoff 1993 (reprint of 1875 Edition), 259)
16. (Nordhoff 1993 (reprint of 1875 Edition), 259)
17. (Oxford Dictionary 2014)
18. (Onieda Community 2014)
19. (Hogan 2014, 2)
20. (Hinds 1878 (1973 Reprint), 127)
21. (Davis 1870, 500)
22.(Tirzah's Posts–1868 2014)
23. (Davis 1870, 500)
24. (Davis 1870, 500)
25. (Hogan 2014, 2)
26. (Hogan 2014, 2)
27. (Nordhoff 1993 (reprint of 1875 Edition), 276)
28. (Nordhoff 1993 (reprint of 1875 Edition), 276)
29. (Nordhoff 1993 (reprint of 1875 Edition), 276)
30. (Hogan 2014, 3)
31. (Nordhoff 1993 (reprint of 1875 Edition), 281)
32. (Syracuse University Library, Department of Special Collections 2014)
33. (Hinds 1878 (1973 Reprint), 130)
34. (Hinds 1878 (1973 Reprint), 130)
35. (Hinds 1878 (1973 Reprint), 134)
36. (Hinds 1878 (1973 Reprint), 137)
37. (Nordhoff 1993 (reprint of 1875 Edition), 289)
38. (Nordhoff 1993 (reprint of 1875 Edition), 289)
39. (Nordhoff 1993 (reprint of 1875 Edition), 260)
40. (Hogan 2014, 2)

41. (Nordhoff 1993 (reprint of 1875 Edition), 262)
42. (Nordhoff 1993 (reprint of 1875 Edition), 262)
43. (Davis 1870, 496)
44. (Syracuse University Library, Department of Special Collections 2014)
45. (Davis 1870, 497)
46. (Hughes, Wallingford's Commune on the Quinnipiac 2004)

Chapter Ten

1. (Cragin 2014 (reprint of 1913 article), 5)
2. (Wonderley 2014, 1)
3. (Cragin 2014 (reprint of 1913 article), 6)
4. (Cragin 2014 (reprint of 1913 article), 6)
5. (Wonderley 2014, 2)
6. (Klekowski 2015, 2)
7. (Cragin 2014 (reprint of 1913 article), 5)
8. (Cragin 2014 (reprint of 1913 article), 5)
9. (Wonderley 2014, 2)
10. (Cragin 2014 (reprint of 1913 article), 5)
11. (Cragin 2014 (reprint of 1913 article), 5)
12. (Wonderley 2014, 3)
13. (Cragin 2014 (reprint of 1913 article), 6)
14. (Wonderley 2014, 2)
15. (Cragin 2014 (reprint of 1913 article), 7)
16. (Cragin 2014 (reprint of 1913 article), 5)
17. (Onieda Community 2014, 4)
18. (Onieda Community 2014, 4)
19. (Wonderley 2014, 2)
20. (Onieda Community 2014, 4)
21. (Wonderley 2014, 2)
22. (Wonderley 2014, 3)
23. (Onieda Community 2014, 4)
24. (Onieda Community 2014, 5)
25. (Hughes, Wallingford's Commune on the Quinnipiac 2004, 2)
26. (Silver Threads 2014, 2)

27. (Hughes, Wallingford's Commune on the Quinnipiac 2004, 3)
28. (Hughes, Wallingford's Commune on the Quinnipiac 2004, 3)
29. (Hughes, Wallingford's Commune on the Quinnipiac 2004, 3)
30. (Horton 2014, 1)
31. (Kendrick 1878, 21)
32. (Wallingford Tornado, 1878 2014, 1)
33. (Kendrick 1878, 25)
34. (Wallingford Tornado, 1878 2014, 2)
35. (Kendrick 1878, 25)
36. (Kendrick 1878, 8)
37. (Wallingford Tornado, 1878 2014, 1)
38. (Horton 2014, 1)
39. (Horton 2014, 2)
40. (Kendrick 1878, 21)
41. (Kendrick 1878, 21)
42. (Kendrick 1878, 21)
43. (Kendrick 1878, 61)
44. (Kendrick 1878, 10)
45. (Horton 2014, 2)
46. (Horton 2014, 2)
47. (Kendrick 1878, 29)
48. (Norman 2015, 1)
49. (Norman 2015, 1)
50. (Norman 2015, 2)
51. (Hutchinson 2014, 6)
52. (Hutchinson 2014, 7)
53. (Valente 2014, 214)
54. (Valente 2014, 214)
55. (Valente 2014, 214)
56. (Milo Todd in the 1870 United States Federal Census 2015)

Chapter Eleven

1. (U.S Army Engineers 1891, 606)
2. (Windsor 2015)
3. (Klekowski 2015, 1)

4. (Klekowski 2015, 2)
5. (Osgood 2015, 6)
6. (Klekowski 2015, 2)
7. (Klekowski 2015, 2)
8. (Klekowski 2015, 3)
9. (Love 1903, 403)
10. (Osgood 2015, 6)
11. (Love 1903, 405)
12. (E. S. Grant 2015, 1)
13. (E. S. Grant 2015, 1)
14. (E. S. Grant 2015, 1)
15. (E. S. Grant 2015, 2)
16. (Farmington Canal Heritage Trail 2015)
17. (E. S. Grant 2015, 2)
18. (E. S. Grant 2015, 3)
19. (E. S. Grant 2015, 2)
20. (E. S. Grant 2015, 4)
21. (E. S. Grant 2015, 4)
22. (Osgood 2015, 6)
23. (Enfield Falls Canal 2015, 1)
24. (U.S Army Engineers 1891, 606)
25. (State of Connecticut 1914, 31)
26. (Love 1903, 403)
27. (Kervick 2015, 1)
28. (Kervick 2015, 1)
29. (Kervick 2015, 1)
30. (Kervick 2015, 1)
31. (Osgood 2015, 7)
32. (Kervick 2015, 1)
33. (Osgood 2015, 1)
34. (Osgood 2015, 7)
35. (Kervick 2015, 2)
36. (Osgood 2015, 7)
37. (Coffin 1967, 10)
38. (Kervick 2015, 2)
39. (Coffin 1967, 12)

40. (Coffin 1967, 11)
41. (Coffin 1967, 11)
42. (Courant 2015)
43. (Coffin 1967, 10)
44. (North Haven Land Records 1873, Vol. 16, 428)
45. (North Haven Land Records 1871, Vol. 2, 30)
46. (United States Census 1870, 47)
47. (North Haven Land Records 1873, 428)
48. (Wallingford Land Records, Volume 62, page 194 1873)
49. (North Haven Land Records, Volume 16, page 503 1873)
50. (Wallingford Land Records, Volume 65, page 175 1875)
51. (Wallingford Land Records, Volume 63, page 353 1876)
52. (Todd Family 2014)
53. (North Haven Land Records, Volume 17, page 362 1877)
54. (Geers Hartford Business Directory, 1878 2015, 148)
55. (Geers Hartford Business Directory, 1880 2015, 272)
56. (Geers Hartford City Directory, 1881 2015, 153)
57. (Geers Hartford Business Directory, 1884 2015, 354)
58. (*History of Insurance in Hartford*, Connecticut 2015, 1)
59. (*History of Insurance in Hartford*, Connecticut 2015, 1)
60. (*Geers Hartford Business Directory*, 1885 2015, 179)
61. (*Geers Hartford Business Directory*, 1886, 1887 2015, 353)
62. (*Geers Hartford Business Directory*, 1888-1901 2015, 217)
63. (*Geers Hartford Business Directory*, 2015, 303)
64. (Woodward 1897, 52)
65. (Charter Oak Insurance 2015)
66. (State of Connecticut 1886, 165)
67. (*The Sons of the American Revolution*. Connecticut Society 1896)
68. (Office of the Connecticut Secretary of State 1898, 171)
69. (United States Census 1900, 2)
70. (*Geers Hartford Business Directory*, 1901 2015, 792)
71. (*Geers Hartford Business Directory*, 1902 2015, 400)

BIBLIOGRAPHY

Algonquian Confederacy of the Quinnipiac Tribal Council. *Connectedness*. December 13, 2013. www.acqtc.org.

—. *Quinnipiac Tribal History*. 2013. www.acqtc.org (accessed December 13, 2013).

Allyn, Charles. *Battle of Groton Heights*. New London, Connecticut: Charles Allyn, 1882 (1999 Reprint).

Andriopoulos, Evan. "Battle of Groton Heights." BattleofGrotonHeights.com . March 21, 2014. www.battleofgrotonheights.com.

—. The Burning of New London. March 21, 2014. www.battleofgrotonheights.com.

arno665. "Dutch Clay Pipes." Dutch Pipe Smoker. January 14, 2015. https://dutchpipesmoker.worldpress.com.

Bailey, William. "The Battle of Fort Griswold: Jordan Freeman and Lambert Latham Distinguish Themselves 230 Years Ago." The Founder's Blog: The History of the Founding Fathers You Did Not Learn In School . May 10, 2014. http://williambailey.wordpress.com/2011/09/06/the-battle-of-fort-griswold.

Bailyn, Bernard. *The Barbarous Years; The Peopling of British North America: The Conflict of Civilizations*, 1600-1675. New York: Vintage Books, 2012.

Bill Memorial Library. "Bill Memorial Library, Fort Griswold." *Bill Memorial Library*. November 20, 2003. www.billmemorial.org/griswold.

BL Companies. "Meriden Industrial Development." *citycenterinitiative.com/phase1/asitwas.asp*. August 10, 2014. www.citycenterinitiative.com.

Blaeu, Janzoon Willem. "Nova Belgica et Anglia Nova." *Norman B. Levanthal Map Center, Boston Public Library*. 1635. http://maps.bpl.org.

Branford. "Branford Land Records." Branford, Connecticut, August 20, 1747. 675.

"Branford Land Records." *Branford Land Records* Volume VII, Page 122. Branford, Connecticut: Town of Branford, November 6, 1786.

"Britannia Metal." *PewterSociety.org*. July 30, 2014. www.pewtersociety.org/pewter/britannia-metal.

Calder, Isabel MacBeath. *The New Haven Colony*. New Haven: Yale University Press, 1934 (1970 reprint).

Caulkins, Frances Manwaring. *History of New London, Connecticut*. New London: H.D. Utley, 1895.

"Charter Oak Insurance." *Public.coe.edu*. March 6, 2015. www.public.coe.edu/theller/soj/unc/tame.

Coffin, David Linwood. *The History of the Dexter Corporation, 1767-1967*. New York: The Newcomen Society in North America, 1967.

Colonial Homes Magazine. "Fowler's Follies." August 1992: 68-71.

Connecticut State Agricultural Society. *The Connecticut State Agricultural Society*. Hartford: The Connecticut State Agricultural Society, 1855.

Connecticut Todd Family. May 15, 2014. www.accessgenealogy.com/genalogy/Ct-Todd.

Courant, Hartford. "Frank Hillard Whittlesey Obituary." *Ancestry.com*. February 3, 2015. www.ancestry.com/whittlesey-frank.

Cragin, George. "1877: The Iron Spoon." *The New Circular*, 2014 (reprint of 1913 article): 5.

Daughters of the American Revolution. April 25, 2014. www.dar.org/natsociety/history.

Davis, Charles Henry Stanley, MD. *The History of Wallingford, Connecticut From 1670 to Present*. Meriden, Ct: Charles Henry Stanley Davis, MD, 1870.

Department of Energy and Environmental Protection. April 29, 2014. http://www.ct.gov/deep.

DePauw, Karen. *Sending Season's Greetings: Christmas Cards in Connecticut*. April 22, 2014.

www.connecticuthistory.org/towns-page/north-branford.

Dudley, Sir Robert. "Dudley's *Arcano del Mare*." Maps ETC. November 10, 2013. http://etc.usf.edu/maps.

"Enfield Falls Canal." *Enfield Falls Canal*. March 1, 2015. www.wikipedia.com/enfield-falls-canal.

Family Ties Bring Together North Branford Industry. December 11, 2013. http://connecticuthistory.org/family-ties-bring-together-north-branford-industry.

Family Treemaker.Org. *Ancestors of Richard R. Wilson and Catherine G. Stevens.* Ancestry.com. 2009. www.familytreemaker.genealogy.com/users/w/i/l/Richard-Wilson (accessed May 13, 2014).

Farmington Canal Heritage Trail. "Farmington Canal Heritage Trail." *Farmington Canal Heritage Trail.* March 3, 2015. www.traillink.com/trail/farmington-canal-heritage.

Farrow, Anne & Lang, Joel. "Connecticut Slave Owners in 1790." *Complicity*, September 29, 2002: 16-19.

—. "From Settlement to Reconstruction." *Complicity*, September 29, 2002: 38-39.

—. "Complicity." *Northeast Magazine*, The Sunday Magazine of the *Hartford Courant*, September 29, 2002: 1-79.

"Geers Hartford Business Diectory, 1878." *U.S. City Directories*, 1821-1989. March 10, 2015. www.ancestry.com.

"Geers Hartford Business Directory." *U.S. City Directories*, 1821-1989. March 11, 2015. www.ancestry.com.

"Geers Hartford Business Directory, 1880." *U.S. Cities Directories*, 1821-1989. March 10, 2015. www.ancestry.com.

"Geers Hartford Business Directory, 1884." *U.S. City Directories*, 1821-1989. March 10, 2015. www.ancestry.com.

"Geers Hartford Business Directory, 1885." *U.S. City Directories*, 1821-1989. March 10, 2015. www.ancestry.com.

"Geers Hartford Business Directory, 1886, 1887." *U.S. City Directories*, 1821-1989. March 11, 2015. www.ancestry.com.

"Geers Hartford Business Directory, 1888-1901." *U.S. City Directories*, 1821-1989. March 11, 2015. www.ancestry.com.

"Geers Hartford Business Directory, 1901." *U.S. City Directories*, 1821-1989. March 11, 2015. www.ancestry.com.

"Geers Hartford Business Directory, 1902." *U.S. Cities Directories,* 1821-1989. March 12, 2015. www.ancestry.com.

"Geers Hartford City Directory, 1881." *U.S. City Directories, 1821-1989.* March 10, 2015. www.ancestry.com.

Grant, Ellsworth S. "The Ill-Fated Farmington Canal." *Ctvisit.com.* February 15, 2015. www.ctvisit.com/travelstories/details/the-ill-fated-farmington-canal.

Grant, Ellsworth. *The Miracle of Connecticut.* Hartford: The Connecticut Historical Society, 1992.

Green, Rick. "The First Slaves." *Complicity,* September 29, 2002: 20-24.

Gregan, Janet. "History of North Branford." *North Branford Public Libraries.* March 20, 2014. www.nbranford.lioninc.org/histnbr.

Hasluk, Paul N. Editor. *Metalworking Illustrated, A Book of Tools, Materials, and Processes for the Handyman.* Philadelphia: David McKay, 1907.

Higginson, Rev, Francis. *New Englands Plantation.* Salem, Ma: The Essex Book and Print Club, 1630 (1908 Reprint).

Hinds, William Alfred. *American Communities.* Secaucus, New Jersey: The Citadel Press, 1878 (1973 Reprint).

"History of Insurance in Hartford, Connecticut." *Examiner.com.* March 5, 2015. www.examiner.com/article/history-of-insurance-hartford-connecticut.

"History of Paper Making." *Paperonline.org.* July 16, 2014. www.paperonline.org/history.

Hogan, Kathleen. "John Humphrey Noyes and the Oneida Perfectionists." *University of Virginia American Studies.* October 3, 2014. www.wroads.virginia.edu/~HYPER/HNS/Cities/oneida.

Horton, Linda. "Wallingford, CT Tornado, August 1878." *gendisasters.com.* July 15, 2014. http://www3.gendisasters.com/connecticut/874/wallingford-ct-tornado-aug-1878.

Hughes, C.J. "Wallingford's Commune on the Quinnipiac." *New York Times,* August 29, 2004: 6.

—. "Wallingford's Commune on the Quinnipiac." *New York Times.* August 2004. www.newyorktimes.com/wallingfordscommune.

Hunter, Louis C. *A History of Industrial Power in the United States, 1780-1930: Volume One: Waterpower.* Charlottesville, Va: University Press of Virginia, 1979.

Hutchinson, Peter. "A Publisher's History of American Magazines." *Magazine Growth in the Nineteenth Century*. July 15, 2014. www.themagazinist.com.

Jacobs, Jaap. "Early Dutch Explorations in North America." *Journal of Early American History*, Vol.3. 2013. http://brill.com/jeah.

—. *New Netherlands: A Dutch Colony in Seventeenth Century America*. Leiden: Brill Academic Publishers, 2005.

Kendrick, John B. *History of the Wallingford Disaster*. Hartford: Case, Lockwood, & Brainard, 1878.

Kervick, Chris. "Windsor Locks History." *Windsor Locks Historical Society*. January 22, 2015. www.windsorlockshistorical.org.

Klekowski, Libby. "One Man's Search to Live Life on His Own Terms." *William Pynchon*. March 4, 2015. www.bio.umass.edu/biology/conn.river/pynchon.

Lang, Joel. "The Plantation Next Door." *Complicity*, September 29, 2002: 6-13.

Larkin, Jack. *The Reshaping of Everyday Life*, 1790-1840. Harper and Row: New York, 1988.

Lewis, Thomas & Harmon, John. *Connecticut: A Geography*. Boulder: Westview, 1986.

Lincoln, Jonathan, interview by James Powers. *Park Manager, Fort Griswold and Fort Trumbull State Parks* (May 14, 2014).

Love, W. DeLoss. *The Navigation of the Connecticut River*. Worcester, Ma: American Antiquarian Society, 1903.

May, Earl Chapin. *Century of Silver 1847-1947*, Connecticut Yankees and a Noble Metal. New York: Robert M. McBride & Company, 1947.

Meals, Michael. *Fort Griswold Home Page*. 2005. www.revwar.com/ftgriswold.

Meriden Britannia Company History and Marks. *Meriden Britannia Company*. July 25, 2014. www.silvercollection.it/MeridenBitanniaco.

Miller, Gordon S. Northford, *The Athens of Connecticut 1768-1826*. North Branford, Ct: The Totoket Historical Society, 1997.

Miller, Gordon S. *Study of Northford-North Branford Industrial Sites* North Branford, Connecticut: The Totoket Historical Society, 1973.

Miller, Herbert. *The History of North Branford and Northford*. n.d.

Miller, James W., Ed. *As We Were on the Valley Shore*. Guilford, Connecticut: Shoreline Times Company, 1976.

"Milo Todd in the 1870 United States Federal Census." *Ancestry.com*. February 22, 2015. http://search.ancestry.com/search/collections/1870usfedcen.

National Archives. "Revolutionary War Pension and Bounty-Land Warrant Application Files." Publication # M804. April 20, 2014.

Nordhoff, Charles. *American Utopias*. Stockbridge, Ma: Berkshire House Press, 1993 (reprint of 1875 Edition).

Norman, Jeremy. "Friedrich Keller Rediscovers Paper Making from Wood Pulp & Industrializes the Process." *History of Information*. January 13, 2015. www.historyofinformation.com.

North Branford Land Records. "North Branford Land Records, Vol. Viii, page 41." *Vol. Viii, page 41*. North Branford, Connecticut, Connecticut: Town of North Branford, 1880.

North Branford. North Branford Land Records, *Volume V*, page 258. North Branford: Town of North Branford, Connecticut, 1857.

North Haven Land Records. "North Haven Land Records, Vol. 14, page 539." *North Haven Land Records*. North Haven, Connecticut: North Haven, Connecticut, November 10, 1868.

—. "North Haven Land Records, Vol. 14, page 542." *North Haven Land Records*. North Haven, Connecticut: North Haven, Connecticut, November 9, 1868.

—. "North Haven Land Records, Vol. 14, page 567." *North Haven Land Records*. North Haven, Connecticut: North Haven, Connecticut, March 4, 1869.

—. "North Haven Land Records, Vol. 14, page 614." *North Haven Land Records*. North Haven, Connecticut: North Haven, Connecticut, July 30, 1869.

—. "North Haven Land Records, Vol. 16, page 70." North Haven Land Records. North Haven, Connecticut: North Haven, Connecticut, November 15, 1870.

—. "North Haven Land Records, Vol.14, page 614." *North Haven Land Records*. North Haven, Connecticut: North Haven, Connecticut, January 5, 1869.

—. "North Haven Land Records, Volume 16, page 428." *North Haven Land Records*. North Haven, Connecticut: Town of North Haven, Coneecticut, January 2, 1873.

—"North Haven Land Records, Volume 16, page 503." *North Haven Land Records*. North Haven, Connecticut: North Haven, Connecticut, September 6, 1873.

—"North Haven Land Records, Volume 17, page 362." *North Haven Land Records*. North Haven, Connecticut: North Haven, Connecticut, June 20, 1877.

—North Haven. "North Haven Land Records." *North Haven Land Records*, Volume 2, page 30. North Haven, Connecticut: Town of North Haven, Connecticut, June 17, 1871.

—North Haven, Connecticut North Haven Land Records, *Volume 14*, page 537. North Haven: Town of North Haven, Ct, 1868.

—North Haven, Connecticut . "North Haven Land Records, Volume 14, page 540." *North Haven Land Records*. North Haven, Connecticut: North Haven, Connecticut, November 7, 1868.

—North Haven, Connecticut "North Haven Land Records, Vol. 16, page 332." *North Haven Land Records*. North haven, Connecticut: North Haven, Connecticut, November 26, 1870.

—. "North Haven Land Records, Vol. 16, page 53." *North Haven Land Records*. North Haven, Connecticut: North Haven, Connecticut, October 29, 1868.

—. "North Haven Land Records, Vol. 16, page 54." *North Haven Land Records*. North Haven, Connecticut: North haven, Connecticut, October 29, 1868.

Office of the Connecticut Secretary of State. *Register and Manual of the State of Connecticut,* 1898. Hartford: Case, Lockwood, & Brainard, 1898.

"Onieda Community." *www.reference.com/browse/oneida+community.* July 13, 2014. www.reference.com/browse/oneida+community.

Osgood, Edward L. "Windsor Locks." *From the Memorial History of Hartford County, Connecticut* January 15, 2015. http://history.rays-place.com/ct/w-locks-ct.

Oxford Dictionary. "Perfectionism." *Oxford Index*. October 3, 2014. www.oxfordindex.oup.com.

Petry, Liz. "The Lash and the Loom." *Complicity*, September 29, 2002: 30-37.

Pewter Society . Britannia Metal. July 22, 2014. *www.pewtersociety. org/pewter/britannia-metal*.

Pfeiffer, John PHD, interview by James Powers. (January 23, 2000).

Pfeiffer, John PHD. "Preliminary Results: Historical and Archaeological Evidence Demonstrating an Early 17th Century Dutch Presence in Branford, Connecticut." *De Nieu Nederlanse Marcurius*, 1998: 4.

Pfeiffer, John, PHD. "Preliminary Report on Archeological Excavation of the Bentley Locus." *Bentley Locus, Branford Connecticut* September 13, 1999. www.mowhawk.net/bentleylocus.

Powers, James T. "Dig Notes, Todd/Stevens Mill Site." *1992-1994*.

Raber, Michael, Gordon, Robert, and Weinstein, Gerald. *Documentation of International Silver Company Factory H Buildings, Meriden, Connecticut Glastonbury, Connecticut: Raber Associates*, 2011.

Root, Mary Fhilotheta. *Chapter Sketches: Connecticut Daughters of the American Revolution: Patriot's Daughters*. New Haven: Edward P. Judd & Co., 1904.

Schlereth, Thomas J. Victorian America; *Transformations in Everyday Life*. New York: Harper Perennial, 1991.

"Silver Threads." *Silver Threads: Books, Silver, Slide Shows*. August 29, 2014. Http://silverseason.wordpress.com/american-silverplate/oneida/wallingford.

Sons of the American Revolution. Connecticut Society. *Year Book of the Connecticut Society of the Sons of the American Revolution*. Hartford: Sons of the American Revolution, 1896.

State of Connecticut. *Public Documents of the State of Connecticut*, Volume 4, Part 2, 1912. Hartford: State of Connecticut, 1914.

—. *Special Acts and Resolutions of the General Assembly of the State of Connecticut*, January Session 1886. Hartford: Wiley, Waterman, & Eaton, 1886.

Syracuse University Library, Department of Special Collections. "Oneida Community Collection." *Syracuse University Library, Department of Special Collections*. October 13, 2014. http://library.syr.edu/digital/images/o/OneidaCommunity.

The Columbia Electronic Encyclopedia. "German Silver." *The Columbia Electronic Encyclopedia*, 6th Ed. July 22, 2014. www.infoplease.com/encyclopedia/science/german-silver.

The Political Graveyard: Connecticut State House of Representatives, 1830's. May 22, 2014. www.politicalgraveyard.com.

Tirzah's Posts - 1868. March 15, 2014. http://tontine255.wordpress.com/tizah's-blog.

Todd Family. May 22, 2014. www.accessgeneology.com/ Todd-geneology.

Town of Wallingford. *Wallingford Land Records*, Volume 61, Page 122. Wallingford: Wallingford, Connecticut, 1868.

U.S Army Engineers. *Report of the Chief of Engineers, U.S. Army*. Washington, D.C.: Washington Printing Office, 1891.

"U.S. City Directories, 1821-1989." *Geers Hartford Business Directory*, 1895. March 11, 2015. www.ancestry.com.

United States Census. *1870 United States Census*. Washington, DC: United States Census Bureau, 1870.

United States Census. *1870 Untied States Census*, North Branford, Connecticut. Washington, DC: United States Census Bureau, 1870.

United States Census. *1900 United States Census*. Washington, D.C.: United States Census Bureau, 1900.

urbanreviewstl.com. "1960's: Model Cities Not Such a Great Model." urbanreviewstl.com/2007/05/1960s-model-cities-not-such-a-great-model. July 8, 2014. www.urbanreviewstl.com.

Valente, AJ. "Changes in Print Paper During the 19th Century." *Purdue e-Pubs, Charleston Library Conference*. June 6, 2014. www.thepress.purdue.edu/series/charleston-insights-library.

Van Dusen, Albert E. *Connecticut*. New York: Random House, 1961.

Varekamp, Johan and Daphne. "Adrian Block, the Discovery of Long Island Sound and the New Netherland Colony." *Uconn.edu/publications*. n.d. http://seagrant.uconn.edu/publications.

"Wallingford Land Records, Volume 62, page 194." *Wallingford Land Records*. Wallingford, Connecticut: Wallingford, Connecticut, September 6, 1873.

"Wallingford Land Records, Volume 63, page 353." *Wallingford Land Records*. Wallingford, Connecticut: Wallingford, Connecticut, March 24, 1876.

"Wallingford Land Records, Volume 65, page 175." *Wallingford Land Records*. Wallingford, Connecticut: Wallingford, Connecticut, June 15, 1875.

"Wallingford Tornado, 1878." *celebrateboston.com*. July 15, 2014. http://www.celebrateboston.com/disasters/wallingford-tordado-1878.

Wallingford, Connecticut "Wallingford Land Records, Vol. 61, page 122." *Walling ford Land Records*, Volume 61. Wallingford, Connecticut: Wallingford, Connecticut, September 11, 1868.

Weslley, Dorothy Porter and Uzelac, Constance Porter. *William Cooper Nell: Select Writings 1832-1874*. Baltimore: Black Classic Press, 2002.

White, John. "Fortified Encampent at Guayanilla Bay, Puerto Rico." *www.art.co.uk/products*. March 30, 2014. http://www.art.co.uk/products/p14197115-sa-i2946447.

Wight, Frank. "Exerpts From Diary of Frank Wight." *Northford, Connecticut: Totoket Historical Society*, 1879.

Wilcoxen, Charlotte. "Dutch Trade with New England." *New Netherland Institute*, 1974: 235-241.

"Windsor." *Connecticut History.Org*. January 23, 2015. http://connecticuthistory.org/towns-page/windsor.

Wonderley, Tony. "The First Silverware." *The New Circular*, 2014: 1-8.

Wood, William. *New England's Prospect*. Boston: The Prince Society, 1634 (1865 Reprint).

Woodward, Patrick Henry. *Insurance in Connecticut*. Boston: Hurd & Company, 1897.

HOMEBOUND PUBLICATIONS
Ensuring that the mainstream isn't the only stream.

At Homebound Publications, we publish books written by independent voices for independent minds. Our books focus on a return to simplicity and balance, connection to the earth and each other, and the search for meaning and authenticity. Founded in 2011, Homebound Publications is one of the rising independent publishers in the country. Collectively through our imprints, we publish between fifteen to twenty offerings each year. Our authors have received dozens of awards, including: *Foreword Reviews'* Book of the Year, Nautilus Book Award, Benjamin Franklin Book Awards, and Saltire Literary Awards. Highly-respected among bookstores, readers and authors alike, Homebound Publications has a proven devotion to quality, originality and integrity.

We are a small press with big ideas. As an independent publisher we strive to ensure that the mainstream is not the only stream. It is our intention at Homebound Publications to preserve contemplative storytelling. We publish full-length introspective works of creative non-fiction as well as essay collections, travel writing, poetry, and novels. In all our titles, our intention is to introduce new perspectives that will directly aid humankind in the trials we face at present as a global village.

WWW.HOMEBOUNDPUBLICATIONS.COM

CPSIA information can be obtained
at www.ICGtesting.com
Printed in the USA
LVOW11s0329010218
564531LV00003B/24/P